JOSHUA

AN ANCIENT BAS-RELIEF AT KARNAK
"The profile stares down the ages"

Joshua

BY
ROGERS MacVEAGH

AND
THOMAS B. COSTAIN

Introduction by
NORMAN VINCENT PEALE, D.D.

Doubleday & Company, Inc.
GARDEN CITY, NEW YORK
1948

STEPHENS COLLEGE
COLUMBIA, MO.

Contents

CONTENTS

PART VII
THE NORTH IS UP

PART VIII
SETTLING THE PROMISED LAND

PART IX
A STUDY IN LEADERSHIP

INTRODUCTION

This fascinating book re-creates with sharp, true strokes a super-lative historic figure. Also, and surely this is important, it stimulates in the reader a haunting sense, perhaps only a vague sense but persistently real, nonetheless, that there is a vein of potential greatness in all human nature, including himself. Such ought to be at least a byproduct of biographical writing.

The Athenian father, so it is related, occasionally took his son into the agora and proudly pointed out the statues of the great in Athens' history. As the ancient stories of personal and national glory were thus recounted the boy straightened himself with the incredible thought, "Perhaps I, too." No wonder little Athens produced so many mighty men.

One finds oneself wondering if the old custom, now unhappily fallen into disuse, of nurturing our young on the magnificent stories of the great men of the Bible was not in part, at least, the reason there grew so many giants in our land in other days. Moses, Joshua, Sampson, Saul, David—these were household names forty years ago. By the fireplace parental voices read of their mighty deeds. And always a moral was pointed out, namely, that they worked and battled and assumed leadership in the name of God—of God, who was always with them (when they obeyed His holy will).

Young American boys lay in their beds dreaming of far-off heroic days in the past when men did valorously as lieutenants of God. So it came about that, feeding their souls on the deeds of the colossal characters who stride across the pages of Holy Writ, many of them in their time likewise were stimulated to notable achievements, also with the feeling that they, too, were supported by God.

These thoughts swept back over me when I read MacVeagh and Costain's book, "Joshua."

The undisputed fascination which Joshua has held for men through long centuries—he at whose trumpets the walls of Jericho crashed to the dust and at whose command the sun stood still—is not weakened, but strengthened, by the admirable common sense and, I believe, factual treatment employed by these authors. MacVeagh and Costain handle the Holy Scriptures with deep respect and reverence. At the same time they forthrightly apply the highest standards of scholarship and research. The result in no way does violence to reasonable faith. On the contrary, it reveals the fact that God was then the same as now, accomplishing His wonders not through magic or the arbitrary setting aside of natural law (His law), but rather through the medium of human personality thoroughly dedicated to Divine objectives. The authors so describe their work. "Out of our study has come no atheistic or irreverent aspersions upon Divine power, but a perfectly credible and logical story of an entirely human and credible performance."

In fact, this book portrays a greater Joshua and implies even a greater God than afforded by the traditional conceptions. It is invariably a fact that sincere and truth-seeking scholarship never weakens but always strengthens faith. Indeed, faith has no lasting validity unless it is based upon all the facts or reasonable assumptions obtainable.

This volume does not dispute the Biblical record of the life and work of Joshua, or the history of the Israelites. On the contrary, an exacting scholarship is employed to determine exactly what the Bible does say. By careful reference to other documents, such as ancient folksongs and poems, drawn on by the Biblical writers, as well as archaeological research, the book reveals meanings which lay hidden for centuries under phrases which, possibly due to their sacred character, have never been thoroughly scrutinized and analyzed. This method is interestingly illustrated by the authors' analysis of the falling of the walls of Jericho and of the episode of the sun's standing still. Their treatment in both of these instances is to me not only satisfying, but stimulating.

The validity of the interpretation is evidenced by the accuracy with which we may apply it in the form of spiritual truth to the general problems of every age, including our own time. We have

walls to destroy—walls of prejudice, hatred, privilege, ignorance—
nor have we much time to disperse the enemies of man's well-being.
Today we are in a race with possible catastrophe. Would it not be
of vast help if time were again to stand still? If Almighty God
allowed ancient walls of stone to fall at a trumpet blast and arbi-
trarily stayed the march of time in those far-off days, and fails to
repeat these miracles now in a greater crisis, we have the right
to be profoundly discouraged. But considering the book of Joshua
in the light of the treatment of these scholars, we are reminded
of the solid truth that God requires of modern men the same devo-
tion to purpose, the same resourcefulness, equivalent attack, and
above all the same courage based on the assurance of God's guiding
presence which Joshua possessed. "Be ye strong and of a good
courage . . . Have I not commanded thee . . . Be not afraid,
neither be thou dismayed." The ancient words are as vital now as
when uttered by the Jordan River in the remote past.

It is this faith and courage that causes walls to fall and affords
time to complete great deeds for the common good. It is seen that
the book of Joshua teaches, as does the entire Bible, that Divine
protection and guidance are indeed afforded mankind. But, as our
authors point out, this guidance is manifested in the perfect planning of divinely appointed leaders and in the loyal support of
people who have similar faith and courage.

This volume, quite apart from any religious connotations, repre-
sents a fascinating adventure in uncovering the far-distant past.
It is a supreme reading pleasure to follow the authors as step by
step, with complete fidelity to detail, they re-create the lofty yet
human character of one of the supreme leaders of all time. Out
of the mists of antiquity is gradually yet clearly revealed a historic happening, the migration of a small group of people which
took place in a restricted area centuries ago. But this event, of
unsurpassed importance to the future of mankind, is brought to
us in a form and manner both fresh and moving. These authors
exemplify the skill and genius of master historians in re-creating
the past, breathing into men and events the breath of life so that
they live again. Upon completing the book I recalled a review of
Carl Sandburg's monumental work on Lincoln entitled *The War
Years*. The reviewer commented that when he closed Sandburg's

final book and looked out into the street it was with a shock that he saw a modern city, so completely had he been projected back into the "sixties."

These authors convey unmistakably to the reader their own pleasure in following the bewildering trail of the ancient past. We share their obvious delight in finding beneath the layers of the ages a pattern of logical fact. Both authors and readers enjoy the rare fascination of seeing these facts fit nicely into place in the restoration of events that happened beyond Jordan water in the long ago.

The authors themselves confess to this scholarly, and may it also be said spiritual, pleasure in a paragraph which seems to express the essence of their book:

"One of the keenest of human pleasures must be that vouchsafed to those persons who are able to resurrect long-forgotten beauty. The restorer who watches, inch by inch, some masterpiece of painting reveal itself under the peeling layers of later botch-work; the expert whose instruments disclose some vanished manuscript under the palimpsest: these are privileged souls whose feelings we cannot hope to share. But we can perhaps guess at them as we apply ourselves, map and Bible page in hand, to searching back through three thousand years. Under the age-old phrases, left so long undisturbed in even their probable contradictions, and between the dry monosyllables marshaled in their majesty of 'purest English undefiled,' we begin to see, or can believe that we see, emerge a flawless product of human forethought, courage, and achievement. No doubt the long weathering of time has obliterated many details that, in more recent instances of applied military art, compel us to admit the often paramount influence of chance or luck in these matters. Many times the winner clearly should have lost, and vice versa. But, as with the classic Greek buildings and statues, where the lapse of years has washed away the paint and gilding which we know their builders doted on, leaving their perfect proportions to stand out only the more clearly for being naked, so it is here. The problems of supply Joshua faced, the effects of weather and temperature, the accidents of march and bivouac, the specific orders of the day he issued—we are spared all these. What remains is the bare but utterly sufficient and convincing outline, and a deepening and solidifying impression of a man." (P. 162.)

In introducing the reader to this volume I feel that I should advise him to be on the alert for the many exquisite passages in which the work abounds. At one time the reader will be lifted and stirred by a paragraph of descriptive power. At other times he will encounter passages revealing unusual psychological insight into the operation of the human mind. The sections which describe the reasoning of Moses and Joshua, defining the play of motive on the part of these leaders and also their sharp understanding of the mental processes of others, are very choice. The remarkable powers of deduction evidenced by the authors become apparent as one follows their rethinking of Joshua's mental strategy from the meager starting point of a verse or fragment thereof. The skill with which this psychological penetration is accomplished confirms the reader's conviction that the authors have "got" the personality of Joshua to an astonishing degree.

I would feel that I had not fulfilled my obligation to the reader if I did not caution him to watch for occasional gems of worldly wisdom scattered throughout this book. For example: "It takes the truly great person to admit the ineluctable effects of time. There is something not quite ripe about the incurably young and the untiringly athletic."

It would seem that military men in particular would do well to study this volume, for, as the authors point out, the terrain over which Joshua waged his brilliantly successful campaigns is quite unchanged. His various strategies, daringly conceived and executed, are plainly revealed. I read with a fascination which kept me at it until the last page Douglas Southall Freeman's classic study of Civil War military maneuver, *Lee's Lieutenants*. The detailed study of the campaigns of Jackson and the other great generals of both North and South, Jackson in particular, has been highly evaluated by the greatest military leaders of modern times. I seem to recall that Allenby or another British general in a theater of war involving the Holy Land won a modern engagement by following to the letter a military strategy described in the Bible as having taken place at the same locale. Joshua is portrayed as a master of logistics and, as the authors point out, without even the aid of maps.

But whether for military understanding or for archaeological pleasure or for the biographical joy of rediscovering a great personality, or for the purpose of re-asserting faith in God's presence in the stream of history, this book will bring rich rewards.

When you have finished the story and continue on, as you surely will, into the Biblical "Book of Joshua," which is appended, you will find, as did I, that the familiar passages are illumined with a clearer light than ever before. It comes alive, indeed. As you read the Bible account the strong and unforgettable figure of a great man and servant of God is clearly seen across the centuries. All lovers of the Book of Books owe to Rogers MacVeagh and Thomas B. Costain a debt of gratitude for helping them to know and fully appreciate one of the notable figures of all time, the immortal Joshua, son of Nun.

NORMAN VINCENT PEALE

JOSHUA

PART ONE

Moses and Joshua

I

THE FIRST GLIMPSE OF JOSHUA, SON OF NUN

Down in the valley a desperate battle was being waged.

Dark-skinned men, wild-haired men, half naked, were shouting and struggling in the blistering heat. It was hand to hand, there in the haze of dust; jabbing with spears, swinging bronze swords, wielding heavy clubs, even hurling stones. There seemed to be little order or control, and in the milling mob men were falling, screaming with rage and pain, dying. The murderous confusion was surging slowly out of the bottom and up the barren slopes on the far side where cross gullies and hidden pockets seamed the foothills which rose to a long, grim ridge against the northern horizon.

Apart, on a small rise overlooking the scene, stood a man. Dark-skinned, hawk-nosed, with bristling black beard, head-clothed, sandaled, cloaked like the others, he looked no different from them except in his eyes. These were wide, keen, luminous with intelligence. He had borne his share of the fighting, for sweat and dust were caked on him and there were black stains on his un-sheathed sword.

The shouting had died down. The Amalekites were retreating

up the ravine slopes, but the victorious raiders from the desert had slacked pursuit. Men were stopping to strip the bodies of the fallen, turning their backs to the beaten enemy. It was all over.

The young leader of the victors was uneasy, as all good leaders are, even in the first moments of triumph. His head kept turning to the south, where a half mile or so away a tall figure in white was outlined against drab rock and sand. Immediately behind this figure—or so it seemed in that clear air—rose two gigantic mountain peaks, a lower one and behind its right shoulder one which towered in mighty majesty, carrying a brooding cap of dark cloud. Against this background the white shape had stood with arms raised to the sky all through the two desperate hours of battle.

But now as he watched with his keen eyes, the white figure seemed to collapse behind a huddle of attendants. The upraised arms, signal of victory, could no longer be seen.

The leader turned with a cry of warning. A scurry of messengers; shouts and a high, shrill squealing of curled horn trumpets. The men continued to drift back, unwilling to leave their booty; groups gathered to tend wounds, to fight for a pull at the water bottles, to boast in almost breathless exultation. To them the fight was over. But the leader was still shaking his head, gesturing frantically, his eyes turned to the appointed station where the arms of Moses could no longer be seen.

And then it happened. There was a concerted shout, the madness of confusion, a wild scrambling for weapons. The Amalekites were coming again, a charging horde, howling like madmen in a rage they could hardly understand themselves. Something had happened to put fresh courage in the beaten army. Later all Israel would know what it was. The victory which God had promised them had depended on the arms of Moses. As long as they remained stretched forth, inviting the fulfillment of Divine aims, the ranks of the children of Israel would move forward in conquest. But Moses, no longer young enough to lead them into battle and so compelled reluctantly to entrust the command to his chosen lieutenant, Joshua, the son of Nun, had wilted under the strain imposed on his aging arms. He had collapsed, and so courage had become possible again in the hearts of the Amalekites, driving them back to renew the fray. (Perhaps, however, the raising of the arm was a signal, Moses being in a position to see behind the Amalekites and judge of the strength of their reserves.)

The former victors, huddled and ungirt, each group hampering the other and each man weighed down with spoils, began to give way. For a moment perhaps the fighting heart of young Joshua knew panic. Once more he glanced back over his shoulder. He could not have hoped for what he now perceived, the white figure of his venerable chief once more upright against the wall of rock, his arms raised as before!

The signal of victory! His doubts gone, his heart exultant, Joshua plunged into the combat. The retreating Israelites heard his great cry, saw him come in with them, his sword rising and falling above the swirling tumult. They in turn took heart. They rallied, formed shoulder to shoulder. With Joshua in the lead they charged once again, their wild battle cry sounding high above the din of the enemy. The courage which had animated the Amalekites oozed away from them. Their final sortie had failed. Their ranks broke a second time. Some of them began to run. In a moment it was a rout, more complete than the first, with the eager blades of the desert men cutting down the least fleet of them.

But this time the young leader, unmindful of his wounds, did not allow himself a moment of rest. He pressed the pursuit until the fleeing Amalekites were scattered beyond all hope of a second rally. Then, with one eye always on those still-upraised arms—held aloft by Aaron and Hur, as he learned later—he posted sentinels and withdrew his forces from the field of battle; then led the weary fighting men over the sands to the south where, hidden by the eminence where their venerable leader had taken his appointed station, the tents of Israel stood.

It was a triumphant return, for the Amalekites were the most dangerous of the hostile forces which barred the desert wanderers from the goal to which they were pressing, the Promised Land. The Bible says nothing of the welcome the battle-weary men received, but it is easy to picture the outrush of happy, dancing women, clashing their timbrels above their heads and tossing garlands to the victors; the shrill clamor of the children, and the deep approval in the sunken eyes of Moses as he dropped a shaking hand on the shoulder of the young man to whom he had entrusted the command. It had been well done, and the children of Israel were happy. Later, no doubt, they would gather silently about the curtained enclosure in the center of which stood the Tabernacle, and Aaron would appear in his garments of holy office, with his miter on his head and Urim and Thummim glittering on his breastplate, to offer sacrifice to the God who had once more made good a promise to His chosen people. It is recorded only that Moses, on command of the Voice which spoke so often in his ear, built an altar which he called Jehovah-nissi and wrote certain commands in a book as a memorial for all the people, which commands later he rehearsed "in the ears of Joshua."

The battle of Rephidim is the occasion of the first mention in Holy Writ of Joshua, son of Nun, and so the story of this mighty and sagacious man who completed the task of Moses begins here. It was long ago—just how long scholars disagree. Some place it about 1450 B.C., but most authorities are now disposed to say 1150 B.C. The people of Israel had come up out of Egypt and, under the divinely inspired direction of Moses, were making their way to the north and the east where the land of Canaan awaited them, seeming sometimes to their sun-weary eyes like a mirage which receded always before them. Until this great victory over the Amalekites there had been little to distinguish Joshua from the rest of the hard-bitten, sullen wanderers fleeing from that same Egypt where, tradition says, their ancestors had sojourned for centuries and even for a time had reigned supreme. In that distant, and sometimes regretted, land, he had been called Hoshea, which means "salvation," and he was a grandson of Elishama, the prince of Ephraim. It was not his lineage, however, which prompted Moses in picking him out from the thousands of young men who toiled in that labored train across the hot desert sands. The discerning leader had kept his eyes on all of them during the Exodus from that now mythical land. The Egypt of light and color and excitement, of never-failing water, of green crops, and of vast populous cities had become almost a campfire legend to the wanderers. Contending with savage sun, savage stone, savage beasts, and still more savage men, the young Israelites began to

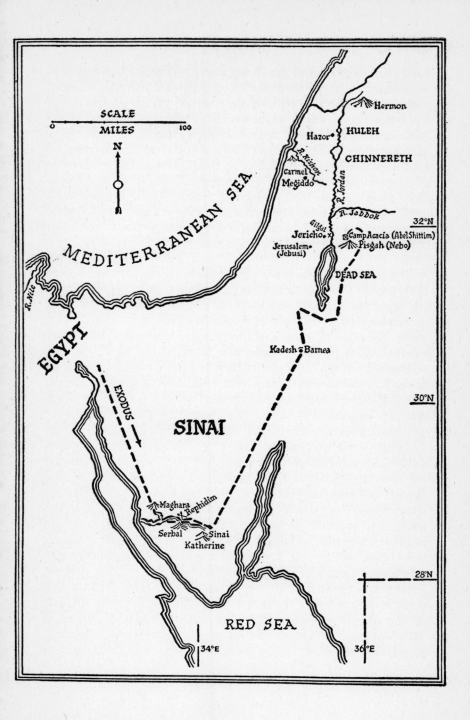

show the mettle of which they were made. Hardships forged them into a driving force of matchless vitality or flawed them with fissures which would open under certain stresses. Some it made as hard and true as the finest metal; some it turned bitter and complaining and weak; and the probing eyes of the unmatchable leader perceived that among those who became strong and true there was none to compare with Joshua.

A vast body of fable and romance has gathered about these nomads. At a time distance of almost thirty-five centuries we must peer closely into the mists of the Late Bronze Age to see anything at all. The sun-baked, shaggy men; their shrill-voiced women; their straggling encampments of low black tents propped on sticks; their milling herds of scrubby wind-straked cattle, black-haired goats, scrawny sheep, and long-suffering donkeys; all this has long since faded into the past. Fortunately, however, we can still trace their passage and find the exact spot where Joshua gave this first proof that Moses had made no mistake in selecting him from all the others.

Eastward from the Gulf of Suez runs a deep wadi, one of those dry watercourses which cut deep gashes across the terrain of the Exodus. Some fifteen miles inland a small valley branches northward to the famed copper and turquoise mines of Maghara, sacred to Astarte, the ancient moon-goddess of beauty (so feared by later Jews that they changed her name to Ashtareth and pronounced it "boshet," which means abomination). Pushing some fifty miles farther eastward, through the dry bushes and palms which speak of subterranean water, there is a wide flat plain. To the west there is a craggy and fantastic mountain called today Mount Serbal. In the south rises another rocky hump, split into three, a central peak and two supporters, sometimes called Jebel Musa but much better known as Mount Sinai. South of this again there is a still taller single peak, Mount Katherine, lifting its cloud-capped head far above them all. This was the scene of Joshua's first victory, and because of the part played in the battle by the upraised arms of Moses that narrow little wadi between the baked stone hills was called, in the tongue of the victorious nomads, Rephidim—the place of the supports.

And here at Rephidim we catch the first glimpse of two men

working in concert who were destined to form the greatest partnership perhaps in all the history of the world: Moses, the master; Joshua, the pupil.

II
THE CHILDREN OF ISRAEL

Who were the children of Israel? From what basic stock did they spring, and what corner of the world cradled them in the first stages of their existence? Of all the vexed problems of history and archaeology, these questions are the most controversial since they involve so much passionate human feeling.

One school of scholarship, largely Germanic, has ruled that sometime after 1850 B.C. a barbarian race invaded Egypt and succeeded in conquering and ruling the southern half of that country. They were called the Hyksos, or Shepherd Kings. The name seems to have been derived from Hequ-Shaasu, which means "princes of the nomads." Other authorities call them the Aat-t, which has been variously translated (in the light of Egyptian prejudice) as "rebels," "invaders," even "the plague bringers." These Hyksos, or Aat-ts, were supposed to have sprung from the wandering Semites of Arabia and Sinai, called then the Hiru-Shaitu, or Lords of the Sands, whose continuous raids into the Nile Valley are recorded in Egyptian history. Some scholars have no hesitation in declaring the children of Israel a remnant of the Hyksos, left behind in Egypt to a life of vassalage after the Theban rulers succeeded in driving the main body back into the deserts east of the Nile.

It is at best a theory or, better still, a speculation. The foundations of our knowledge of these Shepherd Kings are of the flimsiest. It is stated that one Manetho of Sebennytus, reputedly still living in 271 B.C., wrote their history, but nothing of it remains. Josephus quotes him at length to the effect that the Hyksos ruled Egypt for five hundred and eleven years, but we know that much, at least, to be impossible. It cannot be fitted into any workable schedule of the Egyptian dynasties, and the fact that Josephus endorses it should lend us caution against accepting him whole, as our forefathers did. That glib historian is an unreliable witness, as we shall find later.

The Hyksos—or so runs the speculation—were expelled by a national uprising, led by a king of the XVIIth Dynasty, and the Egyptian power was finally consolidated in 1600 B.C. by Aahmes I, the founder of the XVIIIth Dynasty. The wife of the grandson of Aahmes became the first woman Pharaoh, known in history as Queen Hatshepsut—self-willed, brilliant, cruel—who was so mortally hated by the nephew who succeeded her, Thutmose III: great Thutmose, the conquering Pharaoh who struck with his lightning chariots in the battle of Megiddo in 1429 B.C. and about whom we shall have much to say later on. This is not a digression, for a great many scholars agree that we here approach the time when the Israelites began the Exodus. Few points of history are so hopelessly mixed as the dates of the Egyptian dynasties, and there seems little likelihood now that we shall ever know who the Pharaoh was with whom Moses clashed and who by his hardness of heart brought down on himself and his people the plague of murrains and boils, the plague of locusts, and the death of the first born in all the land. The one date which seemed to be generally accepted was that the Israelites crossed Jordan water into Canaan very close to 1400 B.C., which might point to Amenhotep III, grandson of Thutmose, as the villain of the story. He had, certainly, some of the qualities ascribed to the Pharaoh of Scripture; he was cultivated, crafty, showy, cruel, and as selfish a monarch as ever built an enduring monument to his own memory, but he was more than that, a successful and diplomatic ruler who advanced the arts and came to be known after his death as Amenhotep the Magnificent. More recent research seems to point to a later crossing, three centuries later, in fact.

The long period that the Israelites had endured in Egypt seemed to have left no mark on them, which is not surprising in view of the fidelity with which the Semitic strain has preserved itself through all the long and bloody centuries since. At Karnak, dated in the fourth century B.C., is a traditional copy of the ancient bas-relief type. In vigorous and incised outline, even if stylized, the profile stares down the ages. Close cap; large but well-shaped ear; sloping forehead; heavy beard over a strong jaw; thick lips, the lower projecting and the upper shaven; wide-opened eye crinkled at the corner; unmistakable rounded nose with pinched nostril: the face cries its race aloud. Intellectual, keen-witted, humorous, sensuous, acquisitive: the unchanging Jew. It could without a doubt stand as a portrait of Moses, save that no human chisel and hammer could catch in stone the majesty and fire of the great Lawgiver; Joshua, also, with some differences perhaps, more determination and less humor in the eye, the lips more closely gripped, as befitted the warrior. Certainly it is a picture of the type of man who walked the desert in the wake of the two leaders and fought the Amalekites so successfully at Rephidim, and from it we can gain an understanding of them which cuts through the lack of all records.

A thousand years or so before Joshua the Egyptians also recorded a written thumbnail sketch of the desert rovers from whom the Israelites stemmed; call them the Hyksos if you like. They went barefoot, wore a short kilt supplemented by the universal cloak of the Middle East, used knives and axes as well as bows and lances, grazed goats and sheep, and eked out a slim diet of milk and dates with oasis-grown figs, olives, and grapes. They inclined to the immemorial occupations of the desert tribes, robbery and kidnaping: an uneasy folk, constantly alert for plunder, retiring into their tiny mountain fastnesses when pursued, no match for regular Egyptian troops of the line (or the well-trained Egyptian levies, rather), but never quite defeated, never quite extinguished—and never satisfied. It might well stand for a sketch of the close-knit brotherhood who wandered in the wilderness for forty years except that, concurring in the biblical evidence of a long sojourn among the fleshpots, we must add to this sparse outline such refinements as would inevitably have been grafted on the original type by association.

The desert could not have claimed its own completely, not with people as fiercely acquisitive and retentive as these. The nomads who were now preparing to hack a sanguinary path into Canaan still carried, we may be sure, some marks of the life they had lived along the leisured Nile. Probably they shared, even if they could not always gratify it, the Coptic preference for cool linen as a body covering; probably in their few moments of ease they laid aside the rough-woven haircloth of the sandy trail and donned long pleated skirts, tunics with full-flowing sleeves, and sandals of some elegance. They undoubtedly depended on the Egyptian calendar of 365 days and struggled with the awkward problem of unaccounted-for hours in each year, sometimes calling their three seasons Akhet, Pert, and Shemu. They must have anointed their bodies with castor oil, when they could get it, remembering the relief it provided from the heat, and when eyes were troubled by the desert winds they went back to treatments of antimony and lead which they had known in easier days. Even when subsisting on manna they could not have forgotten entirely—the older ones, at any rate—the taste of the fine bread made of millet, barley, or wheat, baked into thick cakes in hot ashes or on sun-heated stones.

Some of the patriarchs on the long trail carried bronze daggers inlaid with more precious materials which they had spirited out of Egypt. All of them, no doubt, kept their precious supply of water cool by placing it in the wind in porous vessels. Some secretive souls, perchance, concealed about their persons samples of the amulet known as the Ded which transmitted certain desirable qualities to the human frame; other backsliders—and there were so many, as both Moses and Joshua knew—retained shivery recollections of Ra, the Terrible One, and an inability to relinquish entirely a belief in the omnipotence of Osiris.

We know that the wanderers were well organized. It would have been impossible for them to fight off the aggression through which they moved if they had allowed themselves to fall into easy ways, and the blistering eyes of Moses were quick to detect any tendency toward slackness. Each man over twenty was a soldier and carried his own spear and *chereb*, a short sword most handy in the close style of combat which passed for battles in those days; or, if he were assigned to a place with the archers, he was equipped with bow and arrow, sling and dart. Each tribe had its own well-trained division, its captain, and its own flag, such as the green banner of Judah with a picture of a lion and the words, "Rise up, O Judah, and let thine enemies be scattered."

The details supplied in the Bible depict the life of the wanderers as much more highly civilized than might be assumed from all other indications. We are told that by Divine order they "borrowed of the Egyptians jewels of silver and jewels of gold," all of which came in handy, no doubt, when the command came from on high through the mouth of Moses that each man must give an offering of gold and silver and brass, "of blue and purple and scarlet and fine linen," "of oil for the light, spices for anointing oil, and for sweet incense." The ark of the covenant they built of acacia wood, two and a half cubits long, one and a half cubits wide, and they overlaid every inch of its sacred surface with solid gold. The breastplate of the high priest was covered with topaz, carbuncle, emerald, sapphire, diamond, amethyst, beryl, and jasper. The Tabernacle was a beautiful edifice of gold with hangings of fine twined linen and needlework, which the priest carried in the middle of the toiling multitude and set up each night in the heart of the encampment before flesh could be eaten or bread broken by the footsore travelers.

No suggestion here of penury and grime and a slow degeneration into the sodden, dreary, flea-bitten ways of the desert! Inevitably, of course, the leaven would begin to work, but the ark of the covenant was carried high to console them with the promise of a lofty destiny, and the bones of Joseph had been brought out of Egypt to be buried in the Promised Land, serving as a reminder that they came of noble stock. Forty years of starvation under a blazing sun would dull their memories and coarsen their ways of living. The stores of finer things with which they started would dwindle. But it is certain they never forgot, never let themselves down completely to nomadic levels.

On such conflicting indications must be based any visual conception of the people Joshua was to be called upon to lead. His assumption of authority, however, was a long way off from that day when he led the forces of Israel to victory at Rephidim. For many long years they were still to wander in the wilderness. They would progress slowly from the shadow of Sinai, the holy mountain. Their course would take them past Selah, that grim, flat-topped rock, a perfect eyrie for marauding bands, on which the curse would fall. They would struggle through Bashan, the kingdom of giant Og who slept on an iron bed nine cubits long until the Israelites planted him instead in nine cubits of earth. They would leave the pleasant high woodlands, where the grass grew lush and the anemones covered acre patches in red, crawling cautiously down the precipitous roads and gorges to the dusty plains of Moab and seeing for the first time that dazzling blue stretch on the line of the sky which on closer approach would turn into the still, rank waters of the Dead Sea, beyond which a single barrier of water, the Jordan, would bar them from the fulfillment of their quest, entry to the Promised Land.

III
FACTS AND FIGURES

Wᴴᴼ was this Joshua, the son of Nun?

Most people have no trouble at all with that question, even those with little Bible knowledge. "Joshua fit de battle ob Jericho, and de walls come a-tumblin' down." There he is, in a Negro spiritual. A select few may recall a pleasant fable (or an early miracle, if you prefer) about the sun and moon standing still, so that the Israelites, who, obviously, must have been winning, should have a longer fighting day.

In traditional Bible teaching Joshua is one of the Prophets. Besides crossing Jordan while in flood and causing the walls of Jericho to fall flat at the sound of his trumpet—no small miracle, either of these—he conquered all the land of Canaan, the Promised Land, and divided it among the Twelve Tribes.

Only careful scholars know that, by the testimony of Holy Writ itself, Joshua was unable to make good his conquest of Israel's so-called "inheritance" except in the central portion and in some particular localities, and that even after his day his followers did no better. It remained for David to conquer Jerusalem, which was to become the great capital and the center of most biblical history. Students of ethnology have striven to follow the legend of

Joshua across the mouth of the Nile into Cyrenaica and beyond, to a Mauritanian tomb near Melilla, and to various places called Nun.

Not much material for a portrait, perhaps—yet more than remains (but for Shelley) of Ozymandias, King of Kings, and many another Supreme War Lord. True, Ozymandias and his haughty company of all-highest rulers did not enjoy the benefit of the Bible toward their immortality. They did their best, no doubt, and some of the records they took such pains to perpetuate are with us still. This is particularly the case, of course, where climate, or sometimes sheer accident, has preserved cut stone or incised and baked clay, or even frail papyrus or perishable silk. Thus we can boast, today, of quite intimate acquaintance with the great leaders as well as the manners and customs of many bygone empires, mostly those which successively flourished and withered between the Tigris and the Nile (both inclusive), some interred long ago in the deserts and caves of Central Asia.

But the Bible, that mixed and still much-disputed collection of legend, folklore, and history, is another kind of record. To begin with, it was committed to writing fairly early; not all at once, of course, nor in any regular order; scholars will probably never agree exactly as to when, where, how, why, by whom, or to what degree or extent. Somehow that tough Semitic nucleus known as Israel managed to preserve, through their many vicissitudes, a set of stories which, for bald and utterly convincing detail of character, incident, and the unchanging fundamentals of human nature, are unique amid our inheritances from the past.

Another thing: the Bible (in the part we are to consider, some of Exodus, some of Numbers, most of Joshua) cannot bemuse the student with a multiplicity of parallel authority. There lies the text, as worked over by countless schools; and, with due allowance for varying interpretations and obvious corruptions, that text is not alone the best but the only evidence we have. Corroboration and contradiction, from outside textual sources, are alike impossible.

We can then proceed to examine the facts with a clear eye. As an alert jury will decide whether a witness is lying or not by little remarks, little slips of the tongue, details unconsciously furnished which could not be invented, so we can read the story of Moses and Joshua. We know the ground, the climate, the general level of civilization thirty-three hundred years ago among the wandering herders and raiders who roamed the fearful wastes of Arabian desert, the grim country east of Anti-Lebanon, the vast wet moat of Jordan and the Dead Sea. We can judge the difficulties and obstacles involved in moving even small nomad bands, with their cattle, goats, and possibly even a few camels (but we can't be sure of the camels), from oasis to oasis across those wastes. We know how far it is from Gilgal to Jericho, or to Ai, or to the immense ramparts of Hazor, so recently identified. For the first time the "waters of Merom" have now emerged from the mists of conjecture and the dust of learned dispute to make vivid and inevitable sense of the few baffling verses which preserve for us a supreme military feat. We have no longer any excuse for taking refuge in the supernatural just because the Bible text is not immediately explicable. What human records are, after thirty-three centuries?

Perhaps here is as good a place as any to emphasize that this study deliberately disregards the so-called Divine or miraculous interpretations of these early biblical events. If the walls of Jericho were knocked down by the Lord, or it was He who dammed up Jordan to let the tribes cross, or defeated the Amalekites at Rephidim while Moses held up his arms, why, then, there is no point to any historical reconstruction. Also, there is the less ground for giving either Moses or Joshua any credit. No irreverence is intended or, is it believed, involved in the explanations here given or argued for, and the sensibilities of pious persons who take their Bible as the literal Word of God need not be at all aroused.

But in the matter of numbers and in the calculation of time we cannot be bound by the text. We cannot, for instance, accept the figure of *over six hundred thousand* Israelites wandering in the wilderness of Sinai after leaving Egypt, not counting the Levites. T. E. Lawrence estimated a gross of sixty thousand tribesmen as approximately all the effective population of the Hauran, some hundred by fifty miles of fertile and populous territory. Again, *three thousand* men are said to "go up" against Ai and are routed with the loss of "about thirty and six," which, as will appear hereafter, was considered a crushing defeat. Against the Midianites we find that *one thousand* fighting men "went up" out of each of the Twelve Tribes. Even allowing ten noncombatants to each fighting man, an overestimate, usually, where most males of fighting age are in good health, the total of one hundred and twenty thousand tribespeople is far beyond the factual possibilities of subsistence and transport. Yet it is a good one hundred per cent short of the grandiose census so carefully set forth in the Book of Numbers and perpetuated by Josephus.

The rebel Arabian tribes under Feisal in 1917 were broken into chief-led groups of about one hundred men each. Nine thousand of them made a formidable force. When they moved in any numbers the problem of supply and water become acute. Yet these fighters traveled mostly by camel, whereas the Israelites, so far as the evidence goes, marched and fought on foot; and while their stomachs were susceptible of considerable training (as Lawrence's was), men cannot compete with the camel's reservoir.

No. With all respect for Holy Writ, we must dissent. The ground, the climate, the inescapable exigencies of food and water for man and beast, and the conditions of travel preclude confidence in the number of Israelites reported. The fact that the Hebraic character Alif, meaning "family group," is also used to represent the number one thousand must share the burden of incredibility. Six hundred family groups is much more acceptable than six hundred thousand. There is, it may be pointed out, a natural lust among oriental people for round numbers which add to rhetorical values.

The same for time. Scholars variously explain the Semitic predilection for "forty." It seems to have been a good, mouth-filling, comfortably impressive and conveniently noncommittal number. It crops up everywhere. Moses remains forty days and nights on the Mount (both on his first and on his second visit). The tribes wander for forty years, from Kadesh-barnea (actually some forty miles south of the Dead Sea) and back again. Caleb was forty years old when he and Joshua went out to search the land of Canaan. This journey took them, we are told, forty days.

Now Caleb and Joshua and the other ten tribal representatives "searched the land from the wilderness of Zin" (south of the

Dead Sea) "unto Rehob" (some two hundred miles northward, twenty-odd miles inland from Tyre), "as men come to Hamath" (the watershed between the Orontes River, flowing north through Homs and Hama to Antioch, and the Leontes or Litani River, the famous "River of the Dog," running south to turn into the sea between Tyre and Zarephath, the division lying about seventy miles farther north), then back by way of Hebron (west of the Dead Sea and about twenty miles south-southwest of Jericho), and the neighboring brook Eshcol, to Kadesh-barnea again, nearly six hundred miles as the crow flies, and who knows what by the paths Joshua and his companions must have trod, and did it all in forty days! Well, figure it out for yourself.

The thing is a sheer impossibility. Spies cannot emulate the forced marches of armed bodies. Forty days for such a trip through hostile country is simply incredible. The number is habitual, that is all. Indeed, it appears again in both the Old and New testaments. Christ is said to have been tempted forty days and forty nights.

We must not take the given numbers of fighting Israelites or the census of their tribes or of their herds too seriously. Similarly, we need waste no time, as many better men have done before us, in calculating the exact dates of certain events, using the given ages of the patriarchs or the duration, in "years," of their activities as a basis. Nothing in our knowledge, for instance, indicates any greater longevity in the desert Semites of thirty-three hundred years ago than in those of today. It has been calculated that half a million nomad warriors, with their families and other impedimenta, even if ranked four abreast (and without their flocks and herds), would make up *a continuous column over four hundred miles long*. It is unthinkable that Moses could have moved such a human tide, the equivalent of thirty modern army divisions, from Egypt up to the southern tip of the Dead Sea. The difficulties of march and transport must have been at least as great then as they are now: well-nigh insurmountable, even for small parties. Could a column four hundred miles long cross a narrow Jordan ford in the short space allowed for the passage under Joshua into the Promised Land? The most recent scientific estimates have placed the number of people who trod the wilderness under

Moses and later followed Joshua into the land of Canaan at six or seven thousand. Accepting that figure, it is still evident that the transit across Sinai entailed hardships and a resort to desperate stratagems such as few leaders would attempt today, and this applies equally to Joshua's thrust across Jordan water. Refusal to deal in rhetorical exaggeration does not make it necessary to minimize the miracles of leadership accomplished by Moses and his successor.

It is no wonder that men remembered the deeds of the sublime twain so vividly that records could be set down long after and the story told in such detail that even time and the blundering fingers of later chroniclers have failed to shake its validity. Memories of the Exodus and the Conquest had a vitality more enduring than if cut in tables of stone. From generation to generation ran the strange story of those awful days, the vague recollections of cloud and fire, faces and voices and miracles beyond nature, the sublime period of trial out of which emerged the Laws.

IV
THE BOOK AND THE MAN

MANY learned men incline to believe that Joshua himself "wrote" the record, or at any rate that it was made in his lifetime and under his direction. No doubt the division had to be imposed by his authority. But since, as we now know, only parts of this territory were reduced to possession by their new claimants, and some never were at all, much of this geographic exactitude must be attributed to the official and priestly revision of the early text that was made later. Taxation methods would, in any case, make imperative the precise descriptions, some of which are perfectly clear on our maps today.

There are a few doubtful passages, among them the famous statement that the sun and moon stood still at Joshua's command, of which more later. Aside from this dubious delaying of the sun and moon, however, *Joshua nowhere credits or blames the Lord for what He or the people under him do*. He does not seem to have felt compelled, like Moses, to justify his every act by the claim of express Divine authorization.

An exception should be noted here for Moses. His murderous rage at the golden calf seems to have been his own idea. At any rate, he did not, in this instance, lay it upon the Lord. Instead, he seems to have felt thoroughly satisfied, later apologizing to the Lord, not for himself, but for the people: "Oh, this people have sinned a great sin . . ."

This incident has recently done a good deal for Moses' reputation. The long-hallowed epithet "meek" is now considered an egregious mistranslation. We can see Moses far better in this description (when his brother and sister were criticizing his wife): "Now the man Moses was very *vexed*, above all the men which were upon the face of the earth." What, indeed, could be more vexatious? One feels that Miriam's leprosy and Aaron's terror served them both right.

Joshua's record contains nothing similar. We find, clearly enough, deep anger, a slow-burning contempt of the boaster who intrigues for others' help, and unhesitating assumption of command (after Moses had left him), but he never seems to have lost his temper, and only once was he really discouraged. As we shall see, this mood even sprang from no ignoble sentiments. Rather it was a reflection of his disappointment in himself, for what commander has not blamed himself for the defeat of his own troops? But of Moses' periodical outbursts, his passionate comminations delivered to the stubborn and "stiff-necked" people after their transgressions, his fire-breathing threats of eternal destruction and damnation unless they should mend their ways—not a trace. On the contrary, as when he trapped and mercilessly condemned Achan, the looter, or refused to spare the lives of his prisoners, such as the king of Ai or the five kings captured in Makkedah cave, Joshua wasted no time in explanations or appeals to precedent. He merely had them killed out of hand, hanged on trees, or buried under stones, such methods being an excellent form of deterrent advertising and thoroughly conventional, according to the manners of the time. His sole reference to the Lord, while dealing with these public enemies, came in his final judgment on the looter, Achan, which we shall consider in its place.

Otherwise the record before us is essentially a plain, square, straightforward tale of battle, conquest, and occupation, all under one man. It presents a leadership unsullied by personal vice, weakness, or greed, unmarred by dissatisfaction among the led, and maintained to the end without benefit of treachery, political chicane, or the "purging" of opponents. The story of David's rise to power, for instance, is an oriental horror tale. Besides all this, Joshua was not only completely successful in his objectives, but he established them on a solid and dignified basis, with the best of prospects for the future. "And Israel served the Lord all the days of Joshua, and all the days of the elders that outlived Joshua. . . ."

V
THE PERIOD OF TRAINING

JOSEPHUS, who has no doubts, says that Moses died in 1451 B.C., at the age of one hundred and twenty (following Deuteronomy), and Joshua in 1427. The Book recites Joshua's age as one hundred and ten. This would make him thirty-five years junior to Moses, whatever their dates may have been. Some historians and archaeologists, as we have already noted, set the invasion of Canaan at about 1400 B.C.; yet other authorities place it as late as 1000 B.C.; it is, after all, immaterial. Likewise, the generally accepted statement that Joshua was born in Egypt before the Exodus, while likely enough, is beside the point. Neither of these usually significant biographical details helps us to see the man himself.

What does count is the disparity in age between Moses and Joshua. Not that we can rely on Josephus alone. Scholars who have edited the smooth-flowing *Antiquities* left by that brilliant politician and administrator have often been pressed to explain his manifold divergences from the sacred text. It has been assumed that he had access to other and more elaborate sources, hence his

wealth of anecdote and description. But when one realizes that
this canny Jew of priestly stock, who maintained himself in favor
successively with Nero, Vespasian, Titus, and Domitian, took care
to censor from his account all reference to the Israelites' backsliding before Mount Sinai (a little matter of a golden image in
the shape of a calf), one wonders. No mention, either, of Moses'
rage, his breaking of the first set of tables (sometimes said to have
been made of sapphire sheets), and the murderous punishment
meted out by his relatives. "As to these matters," runs the glib
disclaimer, "every one of my readers may think as he pleases, but
I am under a necessity of relating this history as it is described in
the sacred books." Not too burdensome a necessity, it would
seem, either here or in other sections of his story.

Not Josephus, then. Other testimony must be followed, and
fortunately we have it: testimony far more convincing than any
patriarchal attributions of age or precise calculations based on the
years of Adam, who begat Seth at the age of two hundred and
thirty, "after which time," recites Josephus, "he lived another
seven hundred and then died." To begin with, Joshua is repeatedly
referred to as a "servant" or "minister" of Moses and always, until
Moses' death, as a young man. This would be, obviously, from
Moses' viewpoint. The difference of a generation sounds convincing. Moses, who spent his career outthinking his followers and
trying to save them from their own folly, must surely have looked
around him for an understudy. What a judge of character he must
have been! The account of the relationship of the two men affords
one of the most touching and inspiring pictures from the past.
Such affectionate, wholehearted, completely loyal co-operation
and comradeship between an older man, supreme in his field, and
the successor he is training is rarely recorded. Doubt and jealousy,
ambitious schemes, petty distrust, premature grasping for power,
and overripe retention of it—none of these are seen.

David and Jonathan, Damon and Pythias; the world has preserved some shining friendships between contemporaries, but full,
generous, unfailing collaboration between Ruler and Heir Apparent is something far to seek.

Moses, being Moses, had tested Joshua many times before
entrusting him with the command at Rephidim. The latter had

been singled out for unique opportunities to study his own methods and to learn his secrets of command. Joshua alone accompanied Moses up the Mount. The old chief told the others, Aaron, Hadab, Abihu, and seventy elders, no less, that he did not want them. He spoke in no uncertain tones. "Tarry ye here for us, until we come again. Behold, Aaron and Hur are with you." But "his minister Joshua" went with him, into the thunders and the lightnings and the thick clouds, and abode with his chief for the forty days.

Again, when Moses had spoken his mind in the matter of the golden calf to the "stiff-necked people" and had moved the Tabernacle outside the camp (but in full view), it was Joshua who stayed inside the holy structure while Moses came and went and made his second visit to the Mount. As the chronicle tells us, the cloudy pillar descended again and stood at the door of the Tabernacle through this period. Whatever the cloud and the fire may have been, it is plainly recorded that the Israelites regulated their movements upon them. All desert folk know the usefulness of smoke signaling and how far off even the smallest fire can be seen. It is proof of the high esteem in which Moses held the young Joshua that he left him behind on the second visit. No longer could complacent Aaron be trusted to restrain the unstable people, to guard the sanctity of the ark of the covenant. Joshua alone could be trusted, even though it meant the master had to depart alone into the mountain fastnesses.

Nor is it to be wondered at that the chosen lieutenant is not mentioned as leading in the battle which followed Rephidim. The tribes had flatly disobeyed Moses, reversing their decision not to invade Canaan and plunging unprepared into a fight with another body of Amalekites who were ruled by King Arad. Smarting under the persistent defeatism of their plaint, "Let us make a captain and let us return into Egypt," Moses may not have been unwilling to see them issue forth without their proper captain. A lesson was needed, and he may have been content to see them have their bellyful.

Joshua, clearly, had no part in that ill-starred venture. Canaan was not to be invaded by frontal attack along the desolate western

shore of the Dead Sea, the biblical "wilderness of Judah."* When
the time came later for him to lead the real attack he approached
by the eastern flank and struck westward at right angles with only
a few miles to go to reach his objective. It is legitimate to assume
that this was one of the many lessons in leadership which Moses
gave him. The keen eye of the young soldier could not fail to see
the fatal error of venturing across such dangerous terrain with the
Amalekites lurking in the foothills and ready to pounce upon
them at the right moment, and with equal certainty he would
unburden himself to his chief. One can hear Moses say, his eyes
burning with indignation at the folly of his followers: "Patience,
my son, patience. They are acting on their own counsel and they
will come to a grievous pass. The enemy will smite them and put
them to rout. Those who come back will hearken thereafter to
the word of command."

Which was how it fell out. The battle in the wilderness was so
complete a defeat for the self-willed tribesmen that they came
back thoroughly chastened and content from that day on to
listen, in military matters at least, to the wise commands of their
proper leaders. They had learned their lesson, and so had Joshua.

He does not appear by name in the defeat of the so-called Midianites who dwelt in the good grazing grounds east of Jordan, the
initial stage to the final approach. There is a geographic confusion
to be straightened out here since there is another Midian somewhere down in the tip of Sinai. It was to this Midian that Moses
fled from Egypt many years before the Exodus and married Zipporah, one of the seven olive branches of the priest Jethro. He
sent her back to the tent of her father and later married the wife
who is spoken of in the Bible as "the Ethiopian woman." When
the tribes came swarming across the desert Jethro heard of "all that
God hath done for Moses" and paid him a visit, bringing Zipporah
and her two sons. There was an affectionate reconciliation which
Moses turned neatly to advantage by persuading Hobab, one of
Jethro's sons, to stay and act as guide, something no traveler in
that country dare do without, even to this day, and perhaps

---

*Allenby by-passed it, sweeping up the coastal plain well to the westward
of the Lebanon massif while Lawrence rolled up the tribes on the eastern
side of Jordan.

thereby shortening the painful hegira of the children of Israel.

These obviously are not the Midianites whom Moses bade his people "avenge the Lord of" and spare none but the virgins, flying into another of his devastating rages because his officers did not kill the other women and all the male children. It is incredible that Joshua was not there, even though he may not have been in full command. Perhaps his master was putting him through another stage in the refining process from which he was to emerge the well-nigh perfect leader, teaching him willingness to forego ambition, to step aside, to divide the honor and the glory, the trials and the tribulations. Nor is he mentioned when the desert horde swept over the plains of Moab, pillaging and slaying as they went. The obstacles were tumbling now: Sihon, king of the Amorites and his city of Heshbon; Og, he of the fabulous bed; all the land of Gilead: the Promised Land lay straight ahead. Joshua was playing his part—of that we may be sure—an important part, without a doubt, because his leadership was accepted with no demur when the real work began, but of the nature of his earlier participation, the Word gives us no hint.

VI
LESSONS IN LEADERSHIP

ONE fact stands clear on the record, that Moses sought repeatedly for opportunities to impress lessons in leadership on the man he had chosen as his successor, and nothing we may learn from the Book about the great old man redounds more to his eternal credit than this. Men who wield despotic power come to consider themselves indispensable, to wish ill rather than well of those who take up the reins after them. But not Moses. That stern and unyielding patriarch asked nothing more than to leave his "stiff-necked people" in capable hands when the time came for him to stand on Mount Pisgah and bid the world farewell.

There was, above everything else, his careful remolding of the social organization of the tribes. The basic law of these nomads had been very close to a communistic order: every man for himself, each the equal of his fellows, each bitterly conscious of his rights. This had done well enough while they roamed in the wilderness, with no possessions to fight over save their pitifully small herds and such scant booty as fell to them. When they came into the Promised Land it would be a different matter. Then they would have the spoils of conquest to divide—land and the all-important water rights, privileges, and priorities, and the rich yield of a land flowing with milk and honey—and the deep trading instincts of the race would then flare up as never before. A new order must be found to hold them together in the contentious days ahead, and so wise old Moses, with an eye cast over his shoulder in the direction of the man who must see to it that any new regulations were observed, girded himself to the hardest task of all.

A way must be found, he realized, to settle the inevitable conflict between the claims of the individual and those of the group. He had suffered enough from untrammeled individualism to have any great respect for it and, as a result, his solution went far, very far, in the other direction. The group, or, better still, the state, must be supported. He was going to see to that, even if rugged individualism became an impossibility in the new order. Above everything, of course, the Tabernacle must be taken care of and a tribe consecrated to its upkeep with well-recognized rights and immunities. He felt the need for a social anchor. This would be a far cry from the unformulated communism of tribal life and, perhaps for that very reason, doubly acceptable to the leader.

Moses was far from perfect; he was not above the worldly desire to do well by his kinfolk. Consequently he saw to it that his own tribe got the plums. He appointed Aaron official lamplighter of the Tabernacle and devised a whole series of measures which set the Levites apart from the other tribes. In other words, he established a perpetual hereditary caste, with privileges as great as the feudatories of later ages, and he impressed it so deeply, moreover, that it lasted down the centuries without question or change. Everything that had to do with spiritual law and the ritual that went with it—the ceremonies of sacrifice, of purification, of commemoration—were in the hands of Aaron, his brethren and his successors. Theirs the sole right of ritualistic costume, the swinging of the censers, the easier ways of life—theirs and theirs alone. Aaron's breast was to glow with Urim and Thummim, and after him his son Eleazar, and, still later, his grandson Phineas. It was a tribal privilege entirely, and questions of personal sanctity or fitness of character did not enter into it; Phineas, indeed, was to figure in a cold-blooded and revolting murder without being judged unfit for his high office. Although the priestly caste retained always the sole right to temple control, it became later a struggle among the Levites as to who should rise to the top. The high priest of the Jews had to be a man of action, a diplomat, a scholar, above all else, perhaps, a politician; no mere saint could fill that parlous chair.

With a religious hierarchy to be supported, the need for group funds arose, and so Moses set his far-seeing mind to the vexed problems of taxation, well aware, no doubt, that he now trod on dangerous ground. What he managed to achieve was a lesson his successor could never forget.

He imposed first a poll tax on every person above twenty years of age. It was a true poll tax; all paid the same, rich and poor alike, being equal in the eyes of the Lord. Ability to pay, that bottomless Pandora's box, with its ever-multiplying jealousies, distinctions, evasions, punishments, and injustices, was carefully avoided. It must be noted at this point that the revenue on which the taxes could be levied was that of spoilation. The children of Israel had no opportunities then to profit in trading, their contacts with the outside world being almost exclusively on the field of battle. Moses reached a basis for imposing his general levies with which no one seemingly could quarrel. The spoils were divided evenly, one half for the men who did the fighting, one half for all the stay-at-homes. The warriors had to pay into the funds one fifth of one per cent, both in prisoners and bestial, the noncombatants a full two per cent. A perfect solution this: no man felt such a small draw on the possessions he gathered about him, the beeves, asses, sheep, and captured virgins; and the differential in favor of the fighting man was eminently fair.

But (O wise Moses) there was another provision which made the taxes, seemingly so easy and equitable, drastic to the point of confiscation. All other booty—the circulating media such as gold and silver, jewels, chains, bracelets, earrings, tablets—had to be delivered *in toto* to the Tabernacle and the privileged tribe in whose hands rested its administration! A one-hundred-per-cent levy! This meant, when the looting of the land of Canaan began, that a great store of wealth would be laid by against all future national needs and the perpetuation of the glory of the Temple. It was so cleverly devised that no protests seem to have been lodged. The men accepted it without a murmur, being only too happy to escape with a tiny levy on the things which seemed important in their eyes. If the women murmured over their exclusion from the gauds they coveted nothing came of it. The man was the head of the household, and his word was law.

This shrewd stroke was something for Joshua to ponder and benefit by in later days when he faced problems as knotty and hard.

Historical imagination is only too apt to overleap itself, and there is consolation, therefore, in finding in the records two more incidents which could not have failed to impress themselves deeply on Joshua's mind. These additional occasions which Moses utilized to give practical lessons in leadership may seem trifles on the surface, but actually they reach deep into the reservoir of raw material with which leaders work: human nature.

Moses and Joshua were coming down together from the Holy Mount. They had been gone a long time: forty days and forty nights, says the Book. Indeed, they had been given up for lost by the impatient and fickle tribesmen. "As for this man Moses," the rank and file were saying, "the man that brought us up out of the land of Egypt, we wot not what is become of him." Seemingly there was relief in the thought. Moses was a hard taskmaster: his eyes saw every fault; his tongue was bitter, his hand heavy in punishment. The two lean, bronzed, and ragged figures, returning with heavy feet but light hearts, were unaware of this. They knew only the hardships they had endured and the labor they had performed in the interests of these people.

For they had at last worked out and recorded on sheets nothing less than the Law—that amazing code which was to prove more enduring than stone, to engrave itself in the hearts of countless men. Josephus (who could speak with authority on this point) said more than a thousand years later: "There is still no one of the Hebrews who does not act even now as if Moses was present and ready to punish him if he should do anything that is indecent; nay, there is no one but is obedient to what laws he ordained, although they might be concealed in their transgressions. . . . Thus this legislation, which appeared to be Divine, made this man to be esteemed as one superior to his own nature."

Who can know what agonies and sweat, what soul-racking visions went into the framing of such a code there on the terrifying slopes of the mountain! The hand of Moses was in every line, but it is inconceivable that the man who sat by his side would have no share. Yes, these two men deserved well of their people.

It is not hard to picture them returning from their labors: the elder would be in the lead, a tall figure, a little bent undoubtedly, with something almost unhuman about him—a strange light shining in his wise, keen eyes. Ever since Lentulus, the contemporary of Pontius Pilate, endeavored to hand down a picture of the man Christ as he saw him (with little acceptance, it is true), there has been a temptation to draw likenesses of the great figures of Scripture. Now that we have started to visualize Moses, therefore, we might as well go a step farther, into details which must be drawn from the imagination and yet which seem both credible and even inevitable in the light of what we know of the man. Here it is, then: a great thatch of white hair, growing thin now, and unkempt after forty days of wrestling with visions; a wide brow above the compelling eyes; the predatory hooked nose of his race, bolder, however, and less retentive than in the set mold; a strong and sensitive mouth, accustomed to command, a determined and flexible mouth with lines of cruelty as well as understanding. The head would be held high in spite of age and the fatigue of the mountain sojourn. The stride of the old man might falter at times, but it would be set to the tempo of the conqueror. A stained mantle of the roughest wool (no cool linen to remind him of the bitter days of servitude), a tattered cord about his middle, worn thonged sandals; there is the complete picture.

Joshua must also have fallen into a pattern as inevitable as this. He would be shorter, with broad shoulders and powerful torso, his bare legs perhaps a little bowed, either by nature or the demands of his trade. A calm face; he was never to know the spiritual travail which enabled his leader to evolve such imperishable truth; a cold face, perhaps, and without a single line of weakness, but likable and comradely in spite of that. His costume would not differ in any respect save for the sharp and polished *chereb* hanging handy from his belt. He would undoubtedly keep a pace or two in the rear, it being a part of the discipline of the soldier to extend acceptance of leadership to such matters. His eyes would be fixed on the man whose word to him was law in everything, watching for opportunities to serve, to ease the path of the weary patriarch. The comradeship and affection between them would be manifest in every gesture.

Suddenly they halted and peered into the plain below. Darkness overhung the camp there, but through it appeared movement, excitement. Something was going on; something which the eager, exalted pair—descending, in more than one sense, from heaven to earth—had not been expecting. They questioned each other with their eyes. They were wary now, and watchful: old desert fighters faced with the unknown. They waited, and then they heard.

It was a strange, confused sound: hoarse yells, the chanting of women's voices, the shrill piping of the sacred ram's-horn trumpets. Yet it could not be in welcome for them. They were still too far off, and no man knew of their approach. Indeed, they themselves had forgotten how long they had been away. What could it be?

The younger man was the first to speak. "There is a noise of war in the camp," he said. War was what he understood best of all, and unconsciously his hand fell on the sword at his belt. He stepped forward eagerly.

But Moses held up a hand to check him. He was listening closely, wonderment and perhaps the first hint of anger in his expressive countenance. He shook his head. "It is not the voice of them that shout for mastery," he declared; "neither is it the voice of them that cry for being overcome." Moses had learned to draw such distinctions. He had heard much shouting among his stiff-necked followers and he knew this was not war.

"But," he added after a moment, and the reality seemed as strange to him as to Joshua, "but the noise of them that *sing* do I hear!"

Singing?

And so indeed it proved to be. All the people, apparently gone mad, were singing and dancing naked around a complacent Aaron and a small golden image of a calf. So the Book describes it.

Such was the welcome to the lawgivers, the heroes returned from the face of God. Singing!

Here we might as well pause ourselves to regard this strange scene. Artists and poets, as well as priests, have dwelt upon it at length during the centuries, and the "golden calf" has become imbedded in the language and the historic imagery of all Christian peoples. Possibly this is due to the dramatic shock of contrast. After all the elaborate preparations, the somewhat confused accounts of Divine visitations, fire and thunder and cloud and the fear of death, one expected the waiting tribes to be in an ecstasy of anticipation. Fear for Moses, fear for themselves, fear of the unknown Law that was to descend upon them should be the prevailing mood, to be kept at bay only by prayer and fasting.

But here, as so often in this deep-buried record of a long-dead past, we have but to clear away the sands, and the relic, the likeness of truth, emerges fresh, convincing, beyond our most careful reconstructions. The tribes, for the time being freed from Amalekite danger, and gathered in a space ample enough for relaxation and social intercourse, had turned to making merry. And why not? Had they not deserved it after their long and grinding toil through the desert? Their fanatic leader was away and perhaps would never return. With him might go, and welcome, all his strict rule and iron discipline. A new and kindly ruler, another and a more genial deity! Life should not all be stern and hard. Laugh, dance, eat, drink, shout, sing, be happy!

Who can blame them?

We may be sure that Moses and his companion took in the scene with all its implications of slackness and disorder. Scholars today, familiar with the world-wide priestly wisdom which encourages periodic sexual orgies among peoples living too close to the margin of subsistence to have extra strength for procreation, classify the incident as one of that kind. Such it may well have been, although of course the later Hebrew "redactors" allowed no such hint to appear in the text; and Josephus, normally so voluble, omits it altogether, as we have noted.

But, whether the affair was spontaneous or deliberately planned, it is surely no coincidence that it centered about a golden image of a calf. That is our translation. The more literal-minded experts say frankly "cow," for the cow-goddess, Hathor, a beneficent, mild-faced animal with a moon between her horns, was particularly identified with that part of the Sinaitic Peninsula. The turquoise and copper were mined under her especial protection from the very earliest times. Her subordinate connection with Astarte, the moon-goddess or queen of heaven (call her what you will), would amply justify her presiding over a feast of joy and exuberance, of temporary release from the never-ending march, fight, camp. We can perhaps measure the tribesmen's feelings by their having devoted what little gold they possessed to an image promising relief and pleasure.

As for the exact form of the dance itself, it may have begun as one of the astronomical measures they remembered dimly from Egyptian days, performed around the bull Apis, to represent the sun: a weaving series of steps to music made up of two notes, repeated twice slowly, then three times in staccato order. The Israelites had a regard for and a surprising knowledge of the heavenly bodies, as witness the seven-branched candlestick of gold, which was later one of the glories of the Temple of Solomon, representing the sun, the moon, and the planets then known: Mercury, Venus, Mars, Jupiter, and Saturn. It may have begun that way, but it inevitably degenerated into the wilder form of dance we see depicted in the Hypogea of Thebes. In the cool of the sudden evening, when cloak and headcloth were no longer needed against the sun, they abandoned for once their repression of instinct. Drunk with orgiastic excitement, naked and unashamed, they capered and leaped about the small golden symbol while Aaron looked on, blandly unconscious of the iniquity that Moses would see in it. Fire they must have had, for sacrifice as well as illumination, and above them blazed the same huge stars, wheeling in the blue-black night, that wheel there today. This was how the two weary men, returning from their lonely vigils and their long, deep discussions, saw them, invisible themselves on the darkened rocks above.

How furiously Moses punished his straying people is told in the Book. The point in estimating the effect of the incident on Joshua is that Moses prevented his young captain from rushing pell-mell to join in what he assumed was the defense of the camp. Had it not been for the restraining hand he would have arrived with drawn sword before the fires of the merrymakers and only then have learned what had brought him in such haste through the darkness. It might be formulated thus: *A leader must never act on impulse or without the fullest information and must never risk becoming ridiculous in the eyes of his followers.*

He succeeded in never losing "face" with the tribesmen, so it is clear he benefited by this and other lessons. In fact, there is no record of the rebellions or the "murmurings" during his term of leadership which so plagued Moses all his life. It takes more than tuition to explain this. There was something else back of it, something unquestionably in Joshua himself.

And now for the second incident. About a year after Rephidim the tribes were still camped in the Horeb section, somewhere near Sinai. The Law had been given them, but there was still continuous trouble and seditious talk which was to come to a head a little later in Korah's rebellion. The rampant Semitic individualism was never better expressed than on that occasion when the "princes of the assembly, famous in the congregation, men of renown," formed themselves into a committee to bait their leader with the truculent and perennial growl, "Ye take too much upon you, seeing all the congregation are holy, every one of them. . . . Wherefore then lift ye up yourselves above the congregation of the Lord?" It must have sounded familiar to the vexed spirit of Moses, for he had heard it even from Aaron, who had so much to be grateful for, and Miriam, his sister, who never missed a chance to seize her timbrel and fall into prophecy. It was from his own family that he heard the question, "Hath the Lord spoken only to Moses?" It is recorded that "Moses was very wroth" with Korah and his followers and that an earthquake fissure opened to swallow up the rebels shortly thereafter, a most convenient ending to the episode. Aaron and Miriam had escaped with a chiding.

But at the end of the year's stay at Sinai this was still simmering. The never-ending quest for food was, of course, at the bottom of the dissatisfaction. The tribesmen, finding subsistence difficult on the hot sands of the desert, were lusting openly for the flesh-pots. Long abstinence had sharpened their recollection of the fertile land they had left behind and no doubt dulled correspondingly their memories of oppression. Their mouths watered for the fish, "the cucumbers, and the melons, and the leeks, and the onions, and the garlick." Much later, at Kadesh-barnea for the second time, they were to taunt Moses that "this evil place . . . is no place of seed, or of figs, or of vines, or of pomegranates." The obvious lack of "milk and honey" was a standard complaint.

A year before the quails had appeared and manna had fallen from heaven in place of bread. Manna has been described for us as shaped like coriander seed, colored like bdellium (whatever that may be), tasting like wafers and honey, or like fresh oil, and amenable alike to baking and seething. If it was, as scholars now seem disposed to agree, the "munn" or gum arabic which exudes from the bark of the tamarisk tree (some say when stung by a certain insect), the tribal digestion could not have been weak. But manna, even when eked out by a fortuitous addition of quail, was not enough, and the mutterings were again mounting dangerously high. The tribes had just suffered a disastrous fire, apparently set by lightning, and were on edge. Moses heard them "weeping throughout their families, every man in the door of his tent." In his discouragement and disgust he was willing to have the Lord kill him "out of hand." He felt that he could no longer "bear all this people alone. . . . It is too heavy for me." He realized that he must, in the language of far later diplomacy, find a new formula.

He found it: spread the responsibility; let the elders and the head men carry some of the load.

So he summoned seventy (says the Book) whom he knew to be "officers" over the people to come out to a meeting at the Tabernacle. Presumably he sent around some writ of summons, since the group was described as "them that were written." All obeyed but two: Eldad and Medad. These remained in camp as a gesture of insubordination, such as many a chieftain has treated his king to, thereby enlivening the pages of history.

The point is that the seventy (or rather sixty-eight) summoned by writ proceeded to "prophesy." What this means we can only guess. Common sense forbids placing them in the same category with the later professional Prophets, graduates of Samuel's schools, who were trained to purify morals, advise the kings, and instruct the people. No. Moses had asked for their advice. They were there for that, and they must have taken their duties seriously, for it is stated that, after they began to prophesy, they "did not cease."

Eldad and Medad had refused to join the parliament, preferring to do their prophesying in the camp. One sees them, their elders and rivals safely out of the way, gathering the respectful and leaderless folk together and expressing *their* views on how the food crisis should be handled; all without hindrance or competition. And a runner (quite properly) slipped away and carried the news out to the Tabernacle.

Joshua reacted as might have been expected. A soldier does not tolerate disobedience. "My Lord Moses, forbid them," he entreated.

But Moses shook his head. "Enviest thou for *my* sake?" he asked. Another shake and perhaps a knowing smile. "Would God that all the Lord's people were prophets!"

In these few words he made it clear to his lieutenant that the time was not ripe for force. To muzzle two of the men selected for counsel because they had flouted him personally would have defeated his own purpose. "Divide the responsibility" was the new formula, and it must be tried out thoroughly or not at all. Moses undoubtedly explained at more length why he preferred to take no action to punish the dissenters. Perhaps he said something to this effect: "Are seventy tongues better than one? Contain thyself and soon they will see the truth for themselves, and the murmurings will cease. As for Eldad and Medad, they will talk themselves out of conceit with their fellows."

No more is heard of the gabbling seventy, or of Eldad and

Medad for that matter, except that no fissure opened to swallow
them. The murmurings died down. We may assume that the new
formula had proved successful. The pressure on the old leader's
spirit had been removed for the time being, and Joshua had
learned another and an important lesson. We may formulate it
thus: *Once you make a man or a group of men unimportant, you
make their actions equally so.*

The formula had received some aid, however, from the luck
which seems to have helped Moses in many times of crisis. The
wind brought more quails from the east.

Given the annual quail migration across the Mediterranean,
which we know about and witness to this day, and admitting the
space of a full year in Sinai camp, it would seem that Moses simply
caught two successive flights; no more miraculous than his finding
water at Horeb and at Kadesh-barnea. Water in the desert is
always a miracle—to the thirsty. But there was, after all, Guide
Hobab; and in the desert, if water is *not* found, there is no miracle
—and no history.

All might seem well settled with this second lot of game, but
such was not exactly the case. The results of the incident were
favorable, so far as the food crisis went. But evidently the quail,
so long absent from the tribal diet, disagreed most violently with
the people. Many throughout the tribes died out of hand. From
what we know of the almost moribund condition in which the
exhausted quail reach land, it may not be quite fair to lay the
sickness to sheer gluttony. The birds must have been pretty
"high" already.

The record is brief and brutal, however. Where the dead were
buried was named "Kibroth-Hattaavah," "The Graves of Lust."
Moses knew how to drive a point home.

VII
AN ACT OF KINGHOOD

AND one last act of kinghood shalt thou see Yet, ere I pass."

So, in the words of Tennyson, spoke King Arthur, gathering his strength for his final stroke against the traitor. The words come freshly to mind as we see Moses, at the end, also, of his life, gathering his strength for a final "act of kinghood." The patriarch's stroke is not with a sword but with his head, his wisdom—his kinghood, in short. Knowing as he does that he himself can never realize his life's ambition, cannot live to see the promise made good to his people, he turns, nevertheless, what looks like more trouble, more disunion, into what will prove probably the most useful single factor in his successor's career. With one last, generous gesture he not only settles the rising storm but creates for the man who is to succeed where he himself has failed those two utterly indispensable conditions without which no dictator, no ruler, indeed, of any kind, can function: a safe and contented home base of supplies (and of possible retreat), and a loyal and warlike personal bodyguard.

Many leaders have possessed both these invaluable adjuncts to rule, but almost invariably the elements of fear, of greed, of joint membership in a plunderbund, which disintegrates when the plunder fails, are present; and these, or a combination of them, invariably destroy the system which they have been invoked to support. The home counties revolt; the bodyguard plots; the ruler disappears.

Not so with Moses. At one stroke he both ensures for Joshua an armed and loyal force which agrees to act as the spearhead of invasion and establishes in the rear of that invasion-to-be a friendly, prosperous, and peaceful community. Moreover, this community is engaged in producing foodstuffs and in breeding, at peace, extra-potential sword fodder. It is also bound, by the closest ties of blood, religion, and tradition, with the invading forces, who therefore need fear neither treachery nor failure of rearward communication. Lastly, and perhaps most remarkable of all, this act of indubitable kinghood, which all subsequent rulers, bar none, could well have envied, holds good after his own death. It is not denounced, or violated, or reaffirmed only at the price of further concessions. Such evidences of structural weakness Moses left to later centuries. His own dispositions, *because soundly based on elemental human nature*, served his purposes, not only when made, but long after he had dreed his personal weird at Pisgah, on Nebo Mountain, and had been buried somewhere in a valley near by.

The dossier of this extraordinary diplomatic victory is fortunately very clear.

The tribes have arrived in Trans-Jordania, sweeping out the Amorites as they go. And this country, with upland valleys and plateaus rising eastward and northeastward from the great Arabah sink, between Mount Nebo and the north edge of Moab on the south and the River Jabbok on the north, was good grazing land. Once cleared of Amorites and other such heathen "without the Law," it was a place where cattlemen could thrive, they and their herds, and their women and babes.

Now in the tribes of Gad and of Reuben there were many good cattlemen who asked nothing better than to live and die as such. They—and, it seems also, part of the Manasseh tribe, a junior branch of Joseph's descent, Ephraim being the elder—had no stomach for foreign wars, for the loot of outlandish cities, for adventure and glory in Canaan. Milk and honey had no appeal for them. They were content to remain this side of Jordan, winding awesomely like a snake there in the hot valley.

So the Gadites and Reubenites sent a deputation to the old chief. One sees him, listening wearily, tired eyes closed on that past which, for him, is to have no future. What is this? More complaints? More backsliding? Reuben and Gad! Ha! This made a man remember.

The petitioners droned on.

"Ataroth, and Dibon, and Jazer, and Nimrah, and Heshbon, and Elealeh, and . . . and . . . and . . . is a land for cattle, and thy servants have cattle. . . . Let this land be given unto thy servants. . . . Bring us not over Jordan."

Bitter memories waken the old man's scorn. Reuben, Gad, even some of the Manasseh tribe. Yes, he remembers well. They, or their fathers, had helped to block the invasion of Canaan once before. Now, when the lean and painful years were overpassed and the Promised Land lay open, just across the valley, Reuben and Gad and Manasseh were again objecting. Cattle, indeed! They cared more for their cattle than for their own nation.

His words stung like scorpions.

"Shall your brethren go to war and ye sit here? Wherefore discourage ye the children of Israel from going over . . . ? Thus did your fathers . . . And the Lord's anger was kindled. . . . And, behold, ye are risen up in your fathers' stead, an increase of sinful men!"

The simple, single-minded cowherds were dismayed. This was something they had not expected. Their tribes had indeed voted against invading Canaan half a lifetime ago. But it was for the same reasons that now moved their own minds. Their families had no stomach for foreign adventure, then or now. They were not cowards. They would willingly fight if there were something to fight for—something like settled homes and folds and byres to shelter the stock at night. This constant wandering did the animals no good. Moses *must* understand.

So they crowded in a little closer—"came near unto him." They pleaded, explaining their feelings as best they might. They wanted to build "sheepfolds for our cattle, and cities for our little ones." But they were no shirkers. "We ourselves will go ready armed before the children of Israel, until we have brought them unto their place." More: "We will not return unto our houses, until the children of Israel have inherited every man his inheritance." And further: "We will not inherit with them on yonder side Jordan, or forward; because our inheritance is fallen to us on this side Jordan eastward."

Moses pondered. But not for long. He had already grasped the possibilities. These men were not, after all, obstructionists or skulkers. They were willing to serve for the duration of the conquest. Moreover, they volunteered for advance guard duty and would travel and fight without their families and baggage. All they asked was to be given the good pasturage already abandoned by the defeated Amorites, to have their titles to it recognized, and

to be released from service for return to their homes when, but
not before, the conquest was complete. Self-interest alone would
keep them loyal. And if by any chance the invasion should be
repulsed the other tribes could always fall back again across Jordan and be assured of a welcome among their own people, as well
as food from the cattle and strong points in the "fenced cities"
which the cattlemen would have built for their "little ones . . .
because of the inhabitants of the land."

Even the stupidest leader would recognize the overwhelming
value of such an arrangement. And all for some thirty miles square
of pasturage which nobody else wanted! (The Amorites did
not count.)

Nobody ever accused Moses of stupidity. We can imagine his
elation, the sudden hopes that must have flooded his thoughts.
But his face betrayed nothing as, finally, he broke silence.

"If ye will do this thing, if ye will go armed before the Lord to
war, and will go all of you armed over Jordan before the Lord,
until . . . the land be subdued . . . then afterward ye shall return . . . and this land shall be your possession."

That was the treaty. And again, in these less honest days, it
is a satisfaction to note that it was kept, on both sides, to the letter.

But Reuben, Gad, and Manasseh must not think they have prevailed too easily. There were penalty clauses for non-perform-
ance. "But if ye will not do so," continued the dread Lawgiver,
in his familiar but ever-impressive tones of doom, "if ye will
not do so, behold, ye have sinned against the Lord: and be sure
your sin will find you out." And the audience closed with his
dismissal: "Build you cities for your little ones, and folds for your
sheep"—provided only, comes the final warning, "ye do that
which hath proceeded out of your mouth."

To complete this, his "last act of kinghood," Moses summoned
not only Joshua, but Eleazar, the priest (his father Aaron lay
buried in Hor on the western face of Edom), and the "chief
fathers of the tribes." Before them all he published the fact, received confirmation of it from the Reubenites and Gadites, and
announced the allocation of the land, including therein the half
tribe of Manasseh. And then he added the master touch, the final
mark of supreme statesmanship.

To most minds the matter would seem to have been ended. But Moses had no ordinary mind. Suppose, he reasoned, that the invasion should fail. Suppose the other tribes, beaten back across Jordan, should return into Gilead and demand from their fellow nationals a share of the pasturage, camping and hunting rights, sanctuary for the ark and its attendant Levites; in other words, a renewal of the traditional unity of Israel. What then?

The highly probable answer from the established and now independent grazing tribes would be: "This is our land, not yours. Did we not buy it from Moses by surrendering to you all our rights of inheritance in Canaan? Is it our fault that you have failed to capture what you so greedily attacked? These are our cattle and our fenced cities. We alone have rights in this land. Go you and find yourselves some new inheritance."

We should note that our modern word "inheritance" hardly fits the Jewish meaning. "Proportionate share of loot" would be better. Possibly the technical term was used purposely by Moses and others in order to perpetuate the idea that, after all, the Israelites were only repossessing property which should have been theirs in the first place. Had it not been promised to Abraham? Driving out the present inhabitants and, if need be, exterminating them became consequently a simple act of justice. This easy delusion, probably the most ancient in the armory of mass deception, seems to be indestructible. So even if we do not quite follow the reasoning implicit in the Jews' claim to their particular "inheritances" in Canaan and to the cattlemen's sincere belief that, in renouncing their "inheritance" in that still unconquered land, they were giving up a valuable right, we can grasp the idea behind the expression as now translated.

In any case, Moses must have contemplated just such a confusion and clash of interests as has been described. The arrangement with the cattlemen was of the utmost value and would, *in all probability*, hold good. But in the last analysis it depended solely on the cattlemen. There was no way of compelling their performance, unless the fear that their sin would find them out would serve. Failure on their part—and a leader must consider every possibility—or even a repulse in Canaan without fault of Reuben, Gad, and Manasseh, would inevitably create some such confusion and clash, which in turn would mean civil war and the destruction of all the national polity which it had been his life-work to rear. This must not happen.

Therefore, before closing the record, Moses imposed upon Joshua and Eleazar and the chief fathers (all in the presence of the cattlemen themselves) this one surprising condition: "But if they" (Reuben et al.) "will not pass over with you armed, they shall have"—not a fearful visitation at the hands of a justly infuriated Lord, but—"possessions among you in the land of Canaan!"

Thus is the ground cut away from under any possible future secession by the tribes who surrender their "inheritance" in return for security in Gilead. Even if they do not keep their agreement they will still be on the same footing as the other tribes and so will have no grounds for refusing to share disaster and defeat with them in case of need.

How much the knowledge that they were not irretrievably cut off from the rest of Israel, or from possible possessions beyond Jordan, helped to keep the Reubenites and their fellow herders in line, we have no way of knowing. But it is plain that Moses, at one stroke, had taken a long step forward to that success which he himself was not to taste and had strengthened also a weak place in the national organization which might well, at the first check, have made ultimate success impossible. And all parties were satisfied!

By any and every standard, an "act of kinghood."

VIII
LAST INSTRUCTIONS OF MOSES

And now Moses was old. It is pleasant to read that "his eye was not dim nor his natural force abated," and to believe that the infirmities of old age never touched him. Death was to come suddenly to the old leader.

The factual account of his last days is meager and overlaid by the long restatement of the Law which makes up Deuteronomy (Repetition of the Law). This fifth book of the Old Testament is composed largely of farewell addresses by the patriarch, in which he proceeds as well to justify his own administration. But with the shades closing in he did more than make speeches.

He wasted no time in lamentation or sentimentality but called "all Israel" together and told them flatly: "I am an hundred and twenty years" (whatever that may have meant) "old this day; I can no more go out and come in." Undimmed eyes and unabated "natural force" he may have had, but he was too much a realist not to recognize that he could no longer measure up to the physical requirements of active nomad life. "Also the Lord hath said unto me, 'Thou shalt not go over this Jordan.'" No one knew better than he what the planned invasion would entail of dangerous and desperate campaigning. But he was far from that all-too-common mentality of lesser spirits which leads them to consider themselves indispensable. He foresaw no deluge after him. As, of course, "The Lord thy God, He will go over before thee . . . and Joshua. . . ."

Joshua's apprenticeship was done. Moses emphasized this in every possible way. He called Joshua and said to him, "in the sight of all Israel," those words which were to come back to the new leader in his hour of loneliness and fear, when for the first time he felt the weight of unshared power: "Be strong and of good courage, for thou must go with this people into the land . . . cause them to inherit it."

So much for the public investiture. But Moses did more than that. A private devolution of authority would carry great weight with the people as well. We can well believe that the long years of affectionate and loyal companionship sweetened the supreme mark of personal trust which Moses now supplied.

He and Joshua entered the Tabernacle, the rich folds of the blue-and-scarlet curtain falling behind them and shutting them off in the Holy of Holies from the gaze of the silent and awe-struck people, and again the Pillar of the Cloud stood before the door. A silence fell on Israel. Who could tell what was happening in that mystic shrine on which common eyes must never rest?

Had the spirit of the God who had spoken for forty years in the ears of Moses joined them there?

Probably, in that awful privacy, Moses unburdened himself of his searing doubts concerning Israel's future. He himself would be sleeping with his fathers, but "this people will rise up, and go a whoring after the gods of the strangers of the land." The invasion would succeed, but the people themselves would degenerate. Once in that Promised Land "that floweth with milk and honey," when "they shall have eaten and filled themselves, and waxen fat; then will they turn unto other gods, and serve them. . . ."

After all, however, this would be Joshua's responsibility. Moses had good ground for apprehension but could do nothing about it. All he could do now was to leave a testament behind him, a sort of lyrical warning in the traditional high-flown vein; the text calls it a "song." This, apparently, he later recited before the people, Joshua standing with him. Then, to fulfill the patriarchal canon, he blessed each tribe by name and attribute. And then he left.

"All men are curious concerning the bridebed of death," an age-old truth recently repeated by Rudyard Kipling; and biographies are always explicit, often painfully so, in this matter. Deuteronomy is no exception to the general rule. But there is another version extant of Moses' leave-taking, and we should examine both.

Josephus is certainly explicit. Gloom and tears overcome even the little children at hearing these last words of warning. So thick is the sorrow that, according to our veracious historian, "what the people did so overcame him, that he wept himself."

Somehow one questions this. Moses weeping? And in self-pity? If this were so, the stern moral fiber of the patriarch had weakened at the end.

But Josephus sweeps along. Moses restrained the people "that were remote from him, and bade them stay behind." Eleazar, the new high priest, and Joshua accompanied him, also the "senate" (Josephus was a very thoroughly Romanized Jew). On Mount Abarim he dismissed the "senate," and just as he was about to embrace Eleazar and Joshua a sudden cloud enveloped him, and he disappeared "in a certain valley." Josephus adds (perhaps to cover up his lack of definiteness about that valley) that Moses had already written "in the holy books," *in advance*, that he died—"out of fear, lest they should venture to say that . . . he went to God."

Note that, in all this staginess, Josephus refers to Mount Abarim only as "a very high mountain . . . that affords . . . a prospect of the greatest part of the excellent land of Canaan." And not a word about the dying man's reasons for going thither. Not an echo of the tragic drama that must have been unfolding in his heart during those last hours. Perhaps Josephus thought Moses chose Abarim (or Nebo, whereon lay the place called Pisgah) for the view.

Moses waving back the intruding common folk in favor of the "senate"? Moses faking an account of his own death out of excess modesty? Moses, after all that has gone before, choosing *both* Joshua and Eleazar as his last companions? Joshua, yes, as we shall see. But why Eleazar? There is no hint anywhere of a tie between uncle and nephew beyond the formal one of officialdom.

Yet Josephus, secure in his ancestry and scholarship, is egregiously willing to close his flowery tale with: "And this shall suffice for the declaration of the manner of the death of Moses."

In all the Pentateuch there are no such false notes. Simplicity and dignity mark every step of Moses' path to his expected end. Should they not mark that end as well?

IX
PISGAH

Moses had finished his warnings and his blessings. The Lord had made it clear to him that he could never enter Canaan, the goal of all his thoughts and plans since first he led his people out of the land of servitude a lifetime before. But he could at least overlook that passionately desired land and mark its features once before he died.

The Abarim mountains stand twenty-six hundred feet above

sea level, sloping west and northwest in abrupt declivities to the
twisting Jordan ten miles away. A series of limestone ridges,
these, sending a short spur directly westward, as though pointed
at the Promised Land. This one spur dissolves in a succession of
short wadies but provides a commanding summit called Jebil en
Neba, meaning "the mountain's back." Nebo, as we have come
to call it, is an ideal site from which to see not only all of Gilead
but the beckoning lands of Canaan across the Jordan.

This is what the fading eyes of Moses saw: to the north and
east, the rich grazing lands that Reuben and Gad and half-
Manasseh were to inherit, the gash of the Jordan valley stretching
and winding back to the Sea of Galilee (then called Chinnereth);
to the west, and certainly the beat of his slowing heart must have
risen for a brief moment when his eyes turned in that direction,
the slopes of high hills and the rich valleys of the land which had
been promised to Abraham and his seed. His eyes would rest at
once on the only sign there of the presence of man, a hillock
rising from the flat Jordan floor about seven miles west of the
river, with battlements showing faintly above its curtain of palm
trees. The walled town of Jericho!

There at Pisgah, which means "boundary" and beyond which
Moses must not go after all his desperate striving, he gazed at the
Promised Land. We are not told how long he remained there,
nor what, at length, stopped that noble, wise, and courageous
heart. We can be confident, at any rate, that whatever bitterness
and regret there was for him in that long-desired prospect, what
memories of the past, what forebodings for the future lay in the
cup, he drank without shrinking.

Was he alone in fact as he was in spirit? Can we believe that,
on the verge of dissolution, when he could no longer "come out
and go in," he would have climbed those flinty escarpments alone,
up one weary wadi side and down another, to reach finally a
difficult footing on the crest of Nebo? Hardly. Josephus for once
must be partly right. The man who had stood at his right hand for
so many years, who had gone with him into the Tabernacle for
the last rites, surely he would have been with him.

And there is one sentence in the record which must be considered: "*He* buried him in a valley." *Who* did? Only the Lord

is referred to previously. Possibly that is what the text intends and yet . . . Can we not fairly believe that this final act of friendship was performed by his greatest friend? Who else, moreover, would be so certain to keep the secret of his chief's burying place "to this day"?

Such considerations constitute the most disembodied, and therefore the most seductive, form of internal evidence. It is plain that whoever compiled the Deuteronomy account was familiar with the partition of Canaan between the tribes. This fact in itself confirms the modern view of that Book's relatively late origin, for this partition, of course, did not occur even in theory until at least five years after the death of Moses. Consequently, Moses himself could not have designated the lands he overlooked from Pisgah by the names of the tribes which later were to occupy them. Yet he is made to do this, and quite accurately too.

Here, then, is an obvious clue to interpolation, the kind of thing which lights scholars on their dubious way.

The triple snow peaks of Mount Hermon, rising over nine thousand feet above sea level and more than ten thousand above the Jordan floor, are one hundred and twenty miles to the north. Dan (once Laish, now probably Tell-el-Kady) is fifteen miles short of Hermon summit, which is so clearly visible from Pisgah; so Moses did see "unto Dan." The same fidelity to subsequent territorial nomenclature can be traced in Moses' horizon. The land of Naphtali comes next, counterclockwise, lying west of Jordan, between Galilee and Lake Huleh, hard by the "waters of Merom," and located in general some ten miles or so downstream from Dan. Then Ephraim, up to the westward crests which lie level with, or higher than, Pisgah itself, and beyond them, where Moses could not see. But the scribe knew what lay behind: Jerusalem, called Jebusi in those days. That great city clung to twin slopes thirty miles due west of the lookout peak where Moses stood. He could not see it, of course, for all those miles between were high and hilly, but his prophetic eyes must have turned and lingered in that direction, with a passionate certainty that the core of his people's subsequent history centered there.

Behind those grim, hulking ranges, back of Mount Ebal's three thousand feet, lay the sloping plains of Samaria, half-Manasseh's portion-to-be, but, to Moses, both out of sight and out of mind. Due southwest, completing the sweep around to "the shore of the salt sea," his glance could cover that cruel wilderness rising to Mount Hebron forty miles away, later to fall to Judah. This also the scribe names. But Moses knew nothing of the coastal flats beyond that wilderness, where the fierce Philistines were to block the marauding Jews and later lead them into bitter slavery.

The scribe is right. Moses must have seen it all. A look again at Jericho; what water must be there, with all those palms! And below it the little town of Zoar—its very name is "littleness"—where tradition even then had Lot escaping from the catastrophe that destroyed Sodom and Gomorrah.

Would Moses, *in advance*, thus describe what he was to see, and name the homes in which each tribe would settle, before his miraculous taking off? We cannot believe so. Rather is the entire account a wonderfully clear description of just what *can* be seen, standing where Moses stood, by one who had stood there and who later figured in the distribution of the lands. Yet even he, the describer, unlike Josephus, refrains from prying into Moses' thought.

It is the profoundest feeling for dramatic, human truth that has made "Pisgah-sight" a synonym for that vision of the unattainable which all men know. Underfoot is grim rock and barren desert, but beyond, to the yearning and disappointed heart, lies the Shining Land, flowing with milk and honey.

Happy the man who, in that last and bitterest hour, still can believe the Land is there. All the pain, the sweat, the sacrifice has therefore not been in vain. Did doubts assail the aged chief, resting in his aery niche above the sunken Jordan, as he scanned around and back the tumbled and folded rim of bare peaks shutting him so inexorably in?

"But," repeats Josephus generously enough, "let everyone think of these matters as he pleases."

"So," the high severe tale of Holy Writ finishes, "so Moses the servant of the Lord died there in the land of Moab."

Permit us, however, to cast forward for a moment into the future. The burying place of Moses became one of the most talked-of mysteries of all history. Centuries later Roman soldiers were to venture out from their cantonments in conquered Palestine to search for it, lured on by hope of treasure. Every foot of Mount Nebo was carefully surveyed. They ventured down into the tortuous wind of the wadies, looking for signs of a hidden cave where the sacred dust might lie. It was even supposed that a secret passage ran from the graves of the patriarchs in the Holy Land to the crypt where the leader of the Exodus was buried; and this fantastic supposition set the treasure seekers and the avid scholars on an even more eager chase. They did not progress very far with it because the burying place of the patriarchs was also a secret. Up almost to the present day biblical scholars have pondered the problem, not completely abandoning hope that the secret will be revealed. The tantalizing flavor of mystery clings even yet to the name Moab.

The burying place of that grand old man could never have been found because Joshua saw to it his bones were too well concealed. Somewhere on the slopes of Pisgah he buried his beloved chieftain, taking great pains that the spot could never be detected by roving thief or hungry beast, covering the body with all the skill of one trained in the rough necessities of the desert. Wherever it was, there Moses has lain, his head due west in the direction of promise, warmed by day in the hot blaze of the desert sun, swept at night by the raw winds which keep the summits of the hills so bare, the concealing cloak of stone his only winding sheet.

PART TWO

Crossing the Jordan

I

JOSHUA ALONE

JOSHUA was succeeding a chief without parallel in the memory of the people, a wonder-worker, a familiar of the spirit of God Himself, who had been his commander, his counselor, his constant companion, and his closest friend. How to fill the place of such a great one?

It is therefore completely convincing to us, at the end of so many veiled years, to read Joshua's thoughts as "the Lord spake" unto him in his heart. "Moses is dead. I, not he, must lead the people across Jordan." Moses had foreseen a great empire, stretching from the wilderness of "this Lebanon" east to Euphrates and west "unto the great sea toward the going down of the sun." This would be a tremendous task. "Can I do it?" Joshua pondered. "Will the people follow me? Will that Power which was with Moses be with me, and not fail nor forsake me?"

One thing Moses did leave: the Law. This at least could be observed, turning not "from it to the right hand or to the left," and meditating "therein day and night . . . according to all that is . . . therein," for so shall come prosperity and "good success."

In other words, here were the orders. One need but obey. Would that suffice?

Joshua knew it would not suffice. Joshua, the strong, sane, experienced leader in desert raids and expeditions, the well-schooled assistant administrator, the spiritual comrade of the greatest man of his day, was not lured into false self-confidence by any legal framework, however holy. Something more than obedience to the rules was needed in a ruler. And so it was that in the hour of his need there come back to him Moses' own high words, spoken not so long since in the sight of all Israel: "Be strong and of good courage."

Three times the call repeats, like a trumpet in the man's soul. Doubt and fear must vanish away. Great deeds await. "Be strong and of good courage. . . . Only be thou strong and very courageous," the single thought tolls. "Have I not commanded thee? Be strong and of good courage; be not afraid, neither be thou dismayed. . . ."

Thenceforth that admonition, together with the Law (which he does not seem to have had much occasion to call upon), was Joshua's creed. Strong he was, always. Courage he never lacked. And only once does it appear that he was dismayed—though not for long. What fuller proof of Moses' insight into the younger man's character could there be?

Moses had measured well the mental obstacles which his lieutenant would face. He had no doubts on the score of his industry or faithfulness. But he, the solitary chief, the sole bearer of his people's burdens through decades and generations, understood just what Joshua would need: encouragement. The feeling of being backed, supported (as at Rephidim), of being understood and approved and cheered on by those nearest—no man worthy of the name needs more. Joshua could rejoice in that supreme source of additional strength. Moses, at least, had comprehended and had bequeathed him the one necessary thought. Who shall say how often those words rang through Joshua's being as he faced, during the next few critical months, the crux of his life?

For what Joshua had now to accomplish was that quite definite, but yet undefinable, feat of leadership which every commander must prove himself capable of: namely, *getting the troops in hand.*

How he went about this formidable task is a model of military art, which is not, as popularly supposed, confined to acquaintance with the use of weapons or the invention of tactics. Fundamentally it consists in the training and molding of men—few or many, the difference is slight—to embody one purpose and to follow one will, the commander's.

The successive steps which Joshua took were these, and in this sequence: first, he issued clear and definite orders for action, naming the objective and allowing ample time for preparation; second, he formed a loyal bodyguard and an advance striking force; third, he secured his rear communications; fourth, he collected all possible information concerning the objective, and lastly, he prepared and performed an unheard-of exploit en route. We shall follow these steps as they come.

II
FIRST ACTS OF LEADERSHIP

THE transition period between changes of command is always packed with dangerous possibilities. Rumors fill men's ears. Some are sure they know the new leader's ideas and are already prepared to criticize them. Others are convinced that the good old days are gone, never to return, and that whatever the new dispensation turns out to be, it will suffer in comparison with the old. The great majority are sullenly watchful, ready to resent any changes in the accustomed order, more than willing to see the new man make some slip, and ready to take instant advantage of any sign of weakness or incapacity on his part. Surface friends and supporters are the most dangerous of all. Joshua's first official act, therefore, was bound to be important.

But his touch was sure. The first orders were clear, definite, sharp. Three days to get ready, and then—cross the Jordan and move into the Promised Land. No time was allowed for speculation and idle talk. The three days allowed for provisioning and getting into marching order would be too crowded with work. The new captain knew his own mind,

But a leader must look backward as well as forward. He must never mention the word "failure," but he must never let it out of his thoughts. And now was the time to put to proof the last diplomatic combination Moses had made: Reuben, Gad, and half-Manasseh. So while the tribes were clearing for action Joshua called in the cattlemen. It was no light risk he ran. Had there been a change of heart among these herders and drovers? Their pact was made with Moses in the shadow of his overwhelming prestige. It bound them only to him, not to his successor. What if they refused to ratify now, or insisted on changing, the treaty terms? Joshua had no force behind him: nothing but the prestige of nomination by the incomparable leader himself, a treaty that had no validity unless the other side wished it to have, and an agonizing doubt.

This last was soon laid to rest. The cattlemen and sheepherders remembered very well their contract with Moses. They had taken him at his word and were entirely ready to perform their part. One can imagine Joshua's intense relief in hearing the sturdy and honest reply: "All that thou commandest us we will do, and whithersoever thou sendest us, we will go."

And here Joshua had what might seem a piece of luck, for the drovers went beyond the letter of their covenant and volunteered what neither Joshua nor Moses had ventured to request. In essence they offered the most valuable service which any leader can enjoy, one which, indeed, no leader can afford to do without: namely, a personal guard. Whether it was the posthumous influence of Moses, or Joshua's own personality, or merely the native virtue of the simple and unambitious plainsmen, the pledge he received was as honestly performed, so far as we know, as it was spontaneously given: "Whosoever he be that doth rebel against thy commandment, and will not hearken unto thy words in all that thou commandest him, he shall be put to death." Brave words, these: the more impressive since the loyal tribesmen closed their pledge with Joshua's own personal formula, "Only be strong and of good courage." It is recorded that, when the time for action came, they "passed over armed before the children of Israel." A stout leader marches in the van, and so it may be assumed that Joshua crossed the waters of Jordan with the men of Gad and Reuben and Manasseh.

III
DATES, FACTS, AND FICTION

THIS is a study in leadership, not in oriental languages or archaeological research, and no effort will be made to trace in detail the
work that scholars have done on the Book of Joshua. It must be
stated, however, that the Book as we now have it has come to us
from various sources. Did Joshua write any part of it himself or
have it set down by learned men of the tribes? Experts claim that
an alphabetical system existed in Canaan at the time when the
invasion took place, and it is quite possible, therefore, that a record
was prepared which served later to guide the writings of later
historians. Barring such guesswork, the scholars believe they can
identify throughout the Book of Joshua two main streams of
original tabulation. One is distinguished by the habitual use of the
word "Yahweh" for God or Lord, the other by the use of "Elo-
him" for that purpose. The former, they conclude, was written
somewhere around 850 B.C.; the latter, a century later. These were
combined into a third version at some subsequent date. Later still,
when the Law was codified and given written form (in what we
know as the Book of Deuteronomy), the original stories were
enlarged with explanations and some additional detail. This edit-
ing, if it may be called that, occurred during the sixth century B.C.

After the captivity of the Jews the priests and scribes worked
over the records again and kept at it until about 200 B.C.; all this in
spite of Josephus and his serene faith in the Word's inviolate condition for five centuries. As a result there are certain passages
which even the experts cannot now identify. They have crept in,
no doubt, during the long generations of copying and expounding.

The text has been painstakingly combed out into the portions
attributable to each of these five periods and yet, after all their
labors, the learned doctors are free to admit that the later redactors, particularly those of the sixth century, have as good a foun-

dation for what they supplied as the early chroniclers. The fact
that the historians of the ninth century are credited with the story
of Joshua's deal with Reuben and Gad is not to be considered a
claim against its authenticity. The same group have given us the
details of his preparations for crossing the Jordan, much of the
story of Rahab, the raid to Shechem, which fulfilled the last wish
of Moses, and in particular the entire south Canaan campaign after
the relief of Gibeon; stories which convince by the weight of
evidence and their logical sequence. On the other hand, all the
parts which have put the stamp of the miraculous on the story of
the conquest—the vision of Joshua, the drying up of the Jordan,
the fall of the walls of Jericho, and the long day in the Valley of
Ajalon when he commanded the sun to stand still—are attributed
to the earliest sources.

Scientists have rendered another great service in the effort to
see behind the veil of time. Their excavations prove that many of
the walled cities of Canaan—Jericho, Ai, Bethel—were destroyed
at about the same time. They bolster this opinion with a convincing array of facts and inferences from Egyptian history and from
other sources, Syrian and Mesopotamian. What they tell us, therefore, may be accepted as something much more substantial than
mere theory or guesswork. Their findings lend us a basis for
material belief in the framework of biblical text, and there is no
reason why we should cavil at the evidence of so much addition
and subtraction in the compilation of the Book. Nor is there any
reason why we should not endeavor to winnow out the grain of
acceptable fact, rejecting such evidence as seems unbelievable in
the light of human experience.

Whether or not Joshua planned and fought and prevailed over
the enemies of Israel as set out in these long-ago recorded memories of men, the story we have of him possesses a value quite
aside from its historicity. Any man who did and said what Joshua
was reported to have done and said, under the conditions as laid
down and over terrain as described (which is there to be studied
today and serves as the most convincing evidence of all), that
man was great in the most lofty sense of the word. His leadership,
accordingly, may be studied in the light of the available records,
stripped of obvious mythology or factual impossibility, with as

much profit as though the records themselves were susceptible
of documentary proof.

But now we are back with him and his people, gazing at Jericho
across the narrow trickle of the Jordan, his mind concerned with
the problem of overcoming these first barriers to the Promised
Land.

IV
THE HARLOT ON THE WALL

Between the invaders and their objective lay a major military
obstacle, the bed of the River Jordan. For an individual to ford
or swim it in times of slack water is no great matter; it was probably not much more than a hundred feet wide then and not
deeper at the ford than four or five feet. But for a whole nation
on the move, six thousand souls or thereabouts with their flocks
and herds, their belongings, the sacred paraphernalia, the imple-
ments of war—that is a different matter.

The crux of the problem was that the spring floods were due.
Any day now, any hour, the flood crest might be spied, traveling
rapidly down the brown winding ribbon of the stream. Once
sighted, it would quickly be upon them, rushing with the impetus
of the great drop in grade between Galilee and the Dead Sea,
spreading out, washing everything before it. No one could cross
while the freshet was on, and when the first stormy hours were
over, the floor of the Jordan would be inundated to such an
extent that weeks might pass before the recession made mass
passage possible. If the crossing were started and the floods came
before it was completed, then the children of Israel would be
brought to a desperate pass. Their fighting forces would be divided
by an impassable barrier and might easily be wiped out in reprisal
attacks.

This was in Joshua's mind while he urged the people on to

hurried preparation for the crossing. Every minute now was precious. But another serious problem was also weighing on his mind. Their main objective, after all, was Jericho. That city must be taken almost immediately after crossing and, gazing at it in the distance, it seemed well-nigh impregnable. Just how strong were those high walls? How stern a resistance might be expected? There was only one way to find out.

Joshua sent spies across the Jordan.

The story of the two spies and of Rahab, the harlot who lived on the walls of Jericho, is another classic of clear-cut drama. The pair seem to have had no difficulty in passing within the one gate that the little city boasted and in mingling with the people. They had no difficulty in speaking with the Jerichites. The language of Canaan derived from the same root tongue as the Hebrew, the southwest Semitic. Variations had developed in the course of time, but they were not sufficient to constitute any bar to mutual understanding. The two strangers were directed to the house of Rahab. It was natural that they should seek out such a resting place. There were no inns in these days (in fact, there is no mention in the records of regular places of entertainment for travelers until a thousand years later), and so Rahab, without a doubt, provided food and shelter for the men who went up and down by way of the fords of the Jordan, as well as entertainment and gossip. Her house, moreover, was ideally located for observation of the state of repair of the walls, for estimating the number of fighting men in the place, for observing the preparations which had been made for defense.

It could not have taken them long to decide that Jericho was ripe for conquest. The outer wall was cracked in many places, and the fissures had been indifferently repaired with baked mud; it would be an easy matter to sap the foundations and bring these patchwork battlements tumbling down. The people, although in a state of panic over the presence of the fierce tribes on the other side of Jordan, were, nevertheless, indolent and far from alert, for they had allowed two suspicious strangers to come within their walls and to remain there unchallenged. An accurate estimate of the population of the place was easy enough: fifteen hundred at most, and only a small proportion of the men trained to the use of arms. The long years of Egyptian occupation had left them soft, unwarlike, lazy. Squatting there on the flat roof of Rahab's house, the two spies must have smiled confidently at each other in the growing dusk. The first step in the conquest was not going to prove as hard as they had feared. They would have the best of news to take back to Joshua: hard-pressed Joshua, spinning his plans on the other side of the water and laboring so zealously to prepare his people for their epic adventure.

But the sluggish suspicions of the townspeople had finally been aroused. Word of the presence of two sun-darkened, uncouth-speaking strangers had reached the ears of the king of Jericho, and orders for their apprehension had been issued. A loud voice at the lower door summoned Rahab below, and the two men, crouching in sudden fear beneath the low mud parapets, heard the voice of authority demand, "Bring forth the men that are come to thee . . . for they be come to search out all the country."

The two spies had found by this time everything that Joshua needed to know about the defenses of the city, but it must have been apparent to them that they would never get back now with their tidings. They were caught in a trap. Night was falling, and the gate had been closed. They could expect nothing better than a short examination and then quick death by whatever method the Canaanites employed for the punishment of spies.

But they were reckoning without Rahab. This quick-thinking practitioner of the oldest of professions had decided that it lay in her own interests to save them. To their amazement they heard her telling the officers of the law in natural and unflurried tones that the strangers were gone. They had been gone some time, in fact, since before the fall of dusk and the closing of the city gate, and by this time they must be well on their way to the Jordan ford.

The not overly zealous officers seem to have taken her word for it. Certainly, if they had made a search of the tiny house, they would have discovered the trembling pair beneath the flimsy covering of flax stalks which she had thrown over them before going below. They even accepted her suggestion as to the route the departing spies had taken. Almost immediately the clang of the opening gate could be heard and the shouts of the pursuers as they hurried off in the dark, searching through the shallow wadies and the clumps of stunted palms and ghurrah trees which lay between Jericho mound and the distant ford. An inefficiently guarded city, Jericho; a ripe plum, as the spies had already concluded, for the outstretched hand of Joshua.

Rahab is one of the most bitterly criticized figures in Bible records because of her seeming willingness to betray her townspeople at the price of her own safety. On closer consideration her attitude is easier to understand and even forgive. She may have been honestly sympathetic toward the two men who had sought shelter in her house and unwilling to deliver them up to a painful death. It is much more likely, however, that she viewed the situation with the complete realism she had learned to apply in the practice of harlotry. She undoubtedly realized that the death of the spies would not prevent the impending attack and that, on the other hand, if she saved them now she might exact a promise of immunity for herself and her family in the event of the city being taken. Selfish, yes, but eminently practical, this; and perhaps not an unexpected attitude on the part of a woman who existed as an outcast among her own people. A harlot living on the city walls, watched by the hostile eyes of housewives on the flat roofs below and in the crowded streets, the constant butt of bitter female tongues, making her meager living solely from strangers who stopped by, could not be expected to have any great degree of loyalty for the community.

She returned to the roof of her house, apprehensive of the fact that unfriendly eyes below could still see any move which might be made there. The Israelites remained under their stifling screen of flax stalks, afraid to move as much as a muscle for fear the telltale rustle would bring searchers back. The faintest whisper would have carried far on the hot, still air, so it was undoubtedly a long time later before she ventured to speak. The stars had come out and sleep had wrapped the city before she made her next move, and the few guards who paced the top of the walls of the slothful city were at a safe distance.

Permit us now a certain freedom in transcribing the words which the record puts into her mouth. "It was the truth they spoke," she whispered. "I know you are spies and that you came to

find out our weaknesses. And yet I have risked my own life to
save yours. I *can* save you. If you will do exactly as I say, I can
get you out of the city, so that you can return safely to those who
sent you."

Is that the step of a guard returning in their direction on his slow
and unwilling vigil? Silence falls for many minutes. The footsteps
die away in the distance. Then: "Yes, I want to be your friend.
I know that your people will attack us and that nothing we can
do will save us when you come. We know all about you, that you
are cruel and merciless, and that you will leave none of us alive in
all Jericho. We are a weak people. Our hearts have melted within
us. I have no hope left. And I don't want to die. I don't want my
father and mother to die, and my brothers and sisters."

She begins to seem less selfish now. The oldest of the children,
though still a young woman, attractive in some degree, no doubt,
courageous and coolheaded; Rahab is all of this. It is bare and
unfertile country around Jericho, no land of milk and honey certainly, and the standards of living are low. Most of the people eke
out an existence by reason of their position on the main route of
travel between Canaan and the east. Rahab's family are dependent
for their living on the wages of her sin. She does not want them
to die. So there is some honor in what she does. If her treachery
is discovered she alone will pay the price; if it succeeds they will
all live through the terror of death and destruction which hangs
over the city.

So she makes a bargain with the two men. In hurried snatches of
low talk, between the coming and going of the guards in the darkness, they come to an agreement. She will let them down over
the walls before daylight returns, and they will then be able to
make their escape to "the mountain," now called Jebel Kuruntul,
lying to the west of the city and, therefore, in the opposite direction from Jordan. There they must hide, she warns, for three full
days before attempting to ford the river. It seems a long time to
wait for the vigilance of the watchers to relax, in view of the carelessness that the leaders of Jericho are displaying, but Rahab wants
to be completely sure.

In return they are to exact from their leader a promise of
immunity for her and her family. The two men cannot give her

more than a conditional promise, for the decision rests with
Joshua; and the new leader, as we know, acts always on the bitterly uncompromising precepts laid down by Moses. This she
understands. It is the best she can get from them, and she is content to do her part in the hope that they will prevail. They agree,
then, on an identifying mark, red cords of string in the wall window from which they themselves are to be let down to safety. The
cords are to hang there when the furious horde of invaders come
swarming over the walls, and if Joshua has been won to compliance the edge of the sword will be turned away from this one
house in Jericho.

The spies succeeded in making their escape (another evidence
of the criminal sloth which marked everything the people of
Jericho did in their own defense), and for three full days they hid
somewhere on the face of Jebel Kuruntul. The hue and cry had
died down by that time, and they had no difficulty in making their
way to safety across the ford. Rahab had performed her part of
the agreement.

One can conceive of the satisfaction the new leader took in
the tidings they brought him. Committed to the gamble, a gamble
against the forces of nature which might unleash a mighty flood
against the venturing host, as well as against the forces of the
enemy, he needed the reassurance they brought him: that Jericho,
behind its high walls, was weak and impotent, her people amaz-
ingly careless, an easier prey than the desert fighters had dared
hope to find.

It is easy to see Joshua looking, first, up the long stretch of the
river—no signs yet of the delayed flood crest; then across the
normally ambling flow of the water to the walled town against
the background of the foothills—too weak a foe there to risk a
foray when the crossing began; and smiling for the first time since
he took it on himself to commit his people to this desperate effort.

V
THE RIVER OF JORDAN

THE WORD "Jordan" means "flowing down" or "the down-comer," which is distinctly appropriate, for it drops continuously after its rise near the snows of Mount Hermon until it empties in stifling heat into the Dead Sea, thirteen hundred feet below sea level. Above the Sea of Galilee this drop is achieved in roaring declines through Dantesque gorges and in churning, boiling rapids. From Galilee it runs south through a valley about four miles in width which opens out twice into broader plains, one of these being where Jericho stood. Here the river becomes sedate in its pace, even, at times of low water, a sluggish stream indeed. It is like life itself: a brawling, impetuous current in its early stages, a dull and ambling and very contrary old river as it approaches the point of dissolution.

It is the most sacred of rivers to followers of the Christian faith, but it may be stated at once that neither the Canaanites, nor the Jews themselves, nor the Romans who garrisoned the Holy Land for so long a time ever regarded it as anything but a geographical obstacle, useful only when it was most trying and dangerous, for then it overflowed its banks and made possible those fine crops of barley. They kept as far away from it as they could, and no city of any size ever grew up along its banks. Men went over it often, slowly and perhaps profanely, but they never went up or down its tawny water. A rather unpredictable stream, rising four or five feet in an hour of floodtime, twisting and turning and thus spinning out its actual length to nearly four times its crow-flight course, terrifying and unnavigable in its early reaches, slow and brackish as it nears its last stage, that strange white ridge of foam which appears at the same time each morning from the mouth of the river and strikes straight along the axis of the Dead Sea, a phenomenon which scientists have never been able to explain.

The scenery along the Jordan is curious rather than beautiful. The asphodel, flower of death, is found in white and yellow profusion along its upper reaches, as though in keeping with the fantastic and awe-inspiring shapes of its barren cliffs. Later, as it rushes toward the haze of the lower Ghor, the asphodel gives place to the oleander, with its lancelike leaves, and the acacia, called the shittah tree in the Bible. The tamarisk becomes common lower down, and the full ghurrah tree, with its silver foliage which has been described as ghostly in effect. Nor is there much life along the sacred river. Pigeons and cranes are to be found, of course, and the sweet-singing bulbul. They fly slowly, as though depressed by the intensity of the heat, and their cries, when heard in the full of a summer day, seem faint and far away. That is all that will be heard in all probability; sometimes a human voice, dreary and petulant, sometimes the pleasant interruption of a camel bell.

It is not a busy river. Solomon built shops for the smelting of brass on its banks when he needed that metal for his fabulous temple up in the hills, and the clanging hammers of the unhappy workmen must have sounded strange in that stillest of desolations. The barley crop is seasonable; later, when sugar cane was planted to some extent, the sleepy Jordan floor reached its most active stage. Time stands still there; the camel will be seen as often today as when Joshua led his people down to the Ford of the Partridges, and sweating farmers in flowing linen robes still winnow grain with huge-handled forks as in the days of Abraham.

When first seen it is easy to believe that the hand of Time has been deliberately stayed, that Divine will has intervened to retain in perpetuity the face of this bitter river where so much history has been made.

VI
THE LONG CONTROVERSY

Before coming to the story of the crossing of the Jordan it will be wise to review the many theories which have cropped up through long years of controversy and to dispel, if possible, the myths and misconceptions which hedge it about. It is bracketed in the mind of the fundamentalist with the crossing of the Red Sea, a twin miracle, a repetition in a smaller way of Jehovah's most spectacular intervention in mundane matters to help His chosen people. The Red Sea legend is far back in the mists of Exodus, and the place where the waves parted to let Moses and his people through is a matter of pure conjecture, even for literal interpreters. With Joshua's exploit it is different. The Jordan twists today through the Arabah as it did then; the same fords are used; we can locate and study the sites of Gilgal and Jericho. The same meteorological conditions exist, to reproduce year after year the same results.

Consequently the imaginative historian need not feel bound to the wheels of traditional acceptance. Josephus, of course, has everything worked out with his usual complacency. Joshua is "in fear," because the river ran with a strong current and could not be passed over with bridges, because, if you please, "there never had been bridges laid over it hitherto." One wonders whether the learned writer, in all his Roman experience and intimacy with Neronian court circles, had ever heard of one Julius Caesar and his bridging of another unbridged and strongly flowing river. One also wonders what language Caesar, seldom at a loss for words, would have used at any comparison between the two situations from an engineering standpoint: the deep, high-banked Rhine, rushing with a continent's water power to the sea, some fifteen hundred feet wide and thirty deep, and sluggish Jordan, its upper speeds and rapids left behind, weaving crazily between low banks, less than two hundred feet wide at most, and (where Joshua was prospecting) fordable in several places.

Not that we need deny Joshua equal ability with Caesar, but even Joshua could not be expected to build a bridge without timbers. Bridges over even smaller streams are not built of brushwood or dried reeds. As for ferryboats (of which Josephus says "they had none"), what would have been their like? David, three or four hundred years later, is said to have used a ferry when returning triumphant but saddened from crushing Absalom's revolt. If modern residents and travelers in Palestine are to be trusted, very similar craft still span the river at El Damiyeh, just below the confluence of the River Jabbok, some twenty miles, as the crow flies, north of Joshua's probable position. It is the familiar flat-bottomed affair, provided with a railing, and pushed by the current along slack ropes, such as still exist today in the more leisurely districts of England and Scotland and in remote parts of the United States. One boat can carry perhaps fifty people with a reasonable amount of baggage. Its rate of progress, in a generously curved line, may run as high as five or six feet a minute. If Joshua had possessed as many ferryboats as the bank would accommodate, he could not have transported all his people, and their herds and belongings, in less than three days.

There is a contradiction in the text which has often been noted. In the last verse of the third chapter it is said: "And the priests that bare the ark of the covenant of the Lord stood firm on dry ground in the midst of Jordan, and all the Israelites passed over on dry ground, until all the people were passed clean over Jordan." But in the eighteenth verse of the succeeding chapter we find, ". . . when the priests that bare the ark of the covenant of the Lord were come up out of the midst of Jordan, and the soles of the priests' feet *were lifted up unto dry land* . . ." The wording of the second passage would point clearly enough to a wet fording.

This same eighteenth verse concludes with the phrase, "the waters of Jordan returned unto their place, and flowed over all his banks as they did before."

As they did before! It is important to note that nowhere in the text is it stated that the Jordan was in flood before the crossing, and so this passage need not be accepted as proof that the floods ceased for long enough to let the tribes cross and then returned miraculously to their previous high level. "As they did before" could refer more reasonably to previous inundations, to the annual freshets along the Jordan which had occurred each winter or early spring since it had existed as a river and have been occurring every year since and will continue to appear as long as the laws of nature continue to operate.

Yet reputable scholars, seeking to put the story in other than the accepted language, have been led sadly astray. Witness one who describes how Joshua "marched the people down to Jordan, which now having overflowed its banks, lay broad, and apparently impassable. . . . It was now at its greatest width, lighted by the full Passover moon." It is a striking picture. "The multitude, miraculously aided by God, passed this seemingly impassable river . . . and again celebrated the Passover. . . ."

There are limits to imaginative historical reconstruction. To begin with, the Book mentions only one Passover, which was kept "in the plains of Jericho"; that is, *after* the crossing. Even Josephus agrees here, to the extent, indeed, that he puts the first day's approach to Jericho's walls on the first day of the feast, although he has previously followed the text by reciting the celebration at Gilgal. In either event he clearly conveys that the crossing was made *before* the Passover. Whence, then, the "full Passover moon"? Lacking a definite year, how are we sure that the moon was full on the fourteenth of the month Abib (about mid-April)? There is no warrant for one Passover before crossing and another after, if that is what the manual means. The Law, indeed, provides for a second feast, a month later than the regular date, for the benefit of those unable to keep the first, but there is no record in the text of any such event, nor any circumstances to make the second celebration necessary. Why not accept the plain statement, which is, after all, the best evidence we have, that the Passover was kept in Gilgal? This is not only clearly set forth, but it accords with reason. The Passover was, and is, a very sacred occasion. Would not Joshua want to attempt Jordan *before* the holidays, and so, if the attempt should succeed, allow that period of rest and religious observance as a time for reassembly and reorganization after the great adventure?

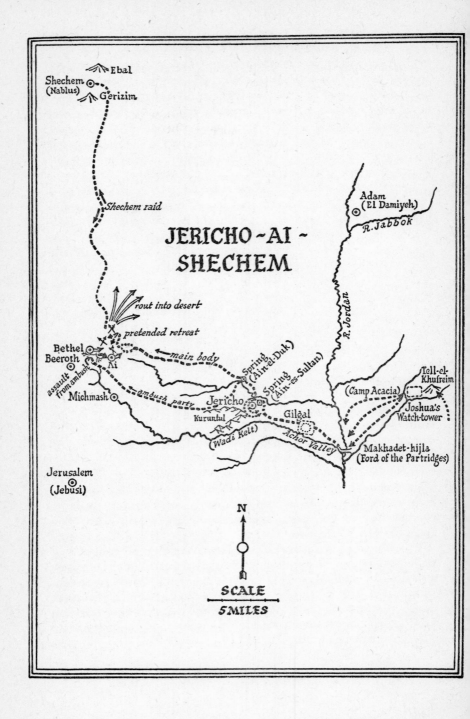

Ebal

Shechem
(Nablus)

Gerizim

Shechem raid

Adam
(El Damiyeh)

R. Jabbok

JERICHO ~ AI ~
SHECHEM

R. Jordan

rout into desert

pretended retreat

Bethel
Beeroth

main body

Ai

Spring
(Ain-el-Duk)

Spring
(Ain-es-Sultan)

assault
from ambush

Tell-el-
Khufreim

(Camp Acacia)

Joshua's
Watch-tower

Michmash

ambush party

Jericho

Gilgal

Kuruntul

Jerusalem
(Jebusi)

(Wadi Kelt)

Achor Valley

Makhadet-hijla
(Ford of the Partridges)

N

SCALE
5 MILES

Jordan floods between January and March, after the spring rains in the mountains. Barley, the earliest biblical crop, begins to ripen in April, the month Abib, just about Passover time. "Abib," in fact, means "green ears." For climatic reasons the harvest comes early around Jericho, before crops ripen in the plains of Moab. Surely Joshua would have taken this fact into account, for the people must be fed, and fed off the land. Indeed, this seems to have been just what was done. The story says that, after consuming "the old corn of the land" (presumably the local stocks), "they did eat of the fruit of the land of Canaan that year."

It is recorded, moreover, that Israel dispensed thereafter with their accustomed manna; why, we are not told. Maybe now that food was so plentiful they decided that they no longer needed any heavenly revictualing. Or, it might be, tamarisk trees were scarce around Jericho.

The business of trying to explain how and why the Israelites were able to cross Jordan has long been a thriving one. For example, we know that earthquakes are quite common in that part of Palestine. Naturally we have no seismographic records of the Late Bronze Age, but the *Song of Deborah*, admittedly of very ancient lineage, affords one possible reference: "The earth trembled. . . . The mountains melted. . . ." This, the exultation over deliverance from Sisera, captain of the hosts of Hazor, with his nine hundred iron chariots, refers, however, to the Lord's progress "out of Seir . . . out of the field of Edom . . ." Seir, or Edom, is the mountainous mass just south of the Dead Sea, around which the tribes were compelled to march on their way to Gilead. We read also how the earth opened up so conveniently for Moses, to swallow the troublesome Korah and his pestilential crew. But the texts are silent on the subject after that.

Records back as far as the thirteenth century A.D. show that landslips have occurred near the ford of the ancient Adam, now El Damiyeh, from time to time. The west bank of the river runs up there to cliffs as high as one hundred and fifty feet. As late as July 1927 a section of this high bank was shaken into the stream by a severe temblor, damming up the river and keeping the bed below virtually dry for a matter of more than twenty hours. The same thing occurred there in December 1267 with exactly the same result.

This has been seized upon by certain "experts" as the basis for an explanation of what happened in or before the month Abib, in the year of the crossing, after Joshua had moved his people from their settled camp at Abel-Shittim, "the meadow of the acacias," to pitch tents on the sandy, scrubby Jordan shore.

Deserted by the logical caution with which he surrounds every step of his own investigations, one of the most brilliant of these "experts" steps blandly into the same waters as he of the "full Passover moon." Thus: ". . . *he had reason to anticipate within that time some stupendous development which would materially facilitate the accomplishment of his task. It was necessary only to seize the moment.* . . . Once by the ford Joshua and the people *seem to have waited deliberately* for the anticipated development." (Italics ours.)

Seem to have? They waited just the three days set by Joshua; no more and no less. There is no other evidence. Yet our "expert," now well entangled, opines that, since any event at El Damiyeh "could have been reported to Joshua the same day," the cliff there must have been in imminent danger of falling, which explains the "acceleration" of Joshua's plan!—a complete *non sequitur.* There was no acceleration, as has been shown, and until the cliff should actually have fallen, there would be nothing to report. For some reason our author appears to think he is bolstering his "argument" by adding that, if Joshua were indeed "in a period of earthquake," he would have "all the more cause for watchful anticipation."

To anyone who, after an earthquake, has waited helplessly for the next unpredictable shock this last observation is a masterpiece, if not of historical reconstruction, at least of understatement.

Brushing aside all this baseless speculation, we find these facts, and these alone: earthquakes occur in Palestine and have, within historical times, dislodged portions of Jordan's high west bank, across from El Damiyeh, where Jordan's tributary, the Jabbok, flows in from the east. On these occasions the river above the slide has been dammed back and the bed below has been comparatively dry during somewhat less than a full day. But in order that these facts should explain Israel's crossing it is necessary to assume a startling series of other happenings. We must assume that it was in "a period of earthquake"—whatever that may be; earthquakes on the whole are no great respecters of the calendar. We must assume that Joshua had word of an earthquake which would cause, or had already caused, an incipient landslide across the Adam ford, so imminent that he was sure another shock would topple it. We must assume that Joshua felt confident that there would be another shock (or shocks) within a three-day period; confident enough, at least, to persuade his six thousand followers to leave their excellent and well-watered campground, where the shrub mimosa flowers to this day, and trek seven or eight miles into the hot, dry Jordan plain. We must assume that Joshua felt confident that the next anticipated shock or shocks would operate only upriver and would not disturb the tribes in their new bivouac beside the river or damage the ford they expected to use. He must have felt confident that such shock would indeed dislodge the overhanging cliff, or, at any rate, that it would fall within the necessary period even without benefit of earthquake. He must have felt confident that, whether shocked or merely slipped, the crumbled earth would fall clear across the river bed. He must have felt confident that, if it did so fall, it would be enough of an obstruction to block the current.

Furthermore, and to cap all, Joshua must have felt confident that he would receive news of all this concatenation of useful events in time to start the tribes moving and to reach high ground on the other side before the impounded waters could catch them. Jordan in flood, as has already been explained, spreads wide over the valley floor, overflowing the incredible arabesques of its normal meander. If the current, necessarily swift between the high banks at Adam, were suddenly cut off, the water below would not run off like an ordinary stream but would take some time to subside. Recent photographs of this condition, taken five miles or so upstream from Joshua's most probable ford, show a good half-mile sheet of sluggish water, one to three feet deep on the flat, with roads and fences submerged. Joshua must therefore have felt confident that the damming process would—if, as, and when it occurred—last long enough to allow the waters to recede and the sand and clay to dry out, so that the animals would not risk miring and the tribes could break camp and attain the far slopes under Jordan; and all this within two days of his arrival on the bank.

One readily admits Joshua's greatness, but such a combination of seer and human seismographic machine is merely fantastic. Rather than accept this pseudo-scientific rationalization of what occurred, it would be much easier to shut our eyes and swallow the whole affair as another miracle.

There is no need to strain so hard for a rational explanation. To cross the Jordan required no more than the exercise of common sense and the receipt of reliable reports on the condition of the river above. It was as simple as that.

Joshua knew that he was working on a very close schedule. The spring floods may come any time between January and March. A late winter, with a consequent late melting of snows on Hermon, would mean that the rise of the water in the flattening, dawdling river would be late. And here it was in the month of Abib, coming close to the extreme limit of lateness. The flood was inevitable now at any hour, any minute. A careful leader would have made arrangements to keep himself advised of what was happening upstream. Joshua had set up a system for securing intelligence about the behavior of the erratic river; that we may take for granted. The fact that the Jordan follows such a tortuous course made this comparatively easy.

To be more explicit, the River Jabbok, Jordan's last sizable tributary, enters above where stood Adam, or El Damiyeh, some twenty crow-flight miles north. But Jordan's course, slow and wandering, covers three times that distance in between. Good runners and a simple system of signaling along the straight and unobstructed valley would be amply sufficient. And just a little northeast of Acacia Camp—littered to this day with Late Bronze Age potsherds and pottery fragments—stands a small, steep mound. The ruins on it go now by the name of Tell-el-Khufrein and are not archaeologically interesting. But this ideal observation post must have been intensely interesting to Joshua. From it Jericho stands up clearly, fifteen miles away across the valley floor, and after rain, or before the daily heat haze rises and enfolds the horizon, one can see forty miles or so. Adam would be in sight from here most of the time.

Again, Jordan's overflow, though at times rapid enough to surprise dwellers on its flat banks, is not the "flash" type which speeds down a deep, dry course. It must spread wide across the valley floor as it proceeds. Sixty miles of river bed take time to fill up.

Calculations of time and distance: Joshua, like all great soldiers, was forever at it. Speed of the flood versus speed of the tribes. Distance the flood must come versus distance the tribes must go to reach ground above floodmarks. These were his elements, the ruling factors. Upon their resultant his decision must be founded.

The question of supplies, too, affected his timing. Each day more meant more filling in the barley heads across by Jericho; yet one day too long would block the invasion until after harvest, which would mean for a whole year.

Now we are on terra firma: no more assumptions at all. No superhuman divination, hand in glove with the Earth Shaker. We see beyond any doubt why Joshua moved to the river's edge: to time the crossing to the very minute. We know what he estimated his crossing time at: *a little less than the time it would take the flood crest to come down from the Jabbok.*

So, when "the waters which came down from above, stood and rose up upon an heap very far from the city Adam, that is beside Zaretan," Joshua had his people ready. The flood crest was still above the Jabbok. The undisputed fact that they got over, flocks, herds, and all, proves that the time it took to fill the valley for twenty miles was just about enough.

VII
CROSSING THE JORDAN

I t was, says the Bible, the tenth day of the first month. It was very hot—it could not fail to be at that time of year—and the early morning sun was beating down fiercely on the woolen-clad

shoulders of the shepherds and the crude metal helmets of the
fighting men. The din was incessant: bleating of sheep, lowing of
cattle, the snuffling protests of a few unhappy camels, mingling
with the cries of children already impatiently in line beside
mothers as heavily laden as the camels. Joshua was in the midst of
it, his eyes never still, his recollection clear on every small detail
of the marching orders he had issued. He was continually on the
move, now inspecting the van where the stout men of Gad and
Reuben and half-Manasseh were drawn up for the first advance
into the sluggish waters, now back with the green banner of
Judah, now in earnest talk with Eleazar and the priests who were
to play their part in a curious ceremony a little later. As far as he
could see, everything was ready. No warning signal had come
from the lookout man; the banks on the opposite side were clear
for miles; the scouts had returned from their hazardous trip to
the walled city.

It is not hard to identify the exact spot. There are several fords
in the vicinity, but the most often used today is Makhadet Hijla—
"makhadet" being the Arabic word for "ford." The plural noun
"hijla" takes in the singular the form of "hajal," or "hegla," both
of which mean "partridge." "Ford of the Partridges," then. Nothing seems to have changed at this particular spot through all the
centuries, and so it may be assumed that it offered then the same
advantages that it does today.

Now we are to see the first substantial proof that Joshua had
learned his lesson well from the old leader. Moses had been what
is called today a showman, a supremely great showman; in fact,
always ready to clothe in trappings of spiritual mystery what
would otherwise have been everyday events. The smallest command was given by him as though straight from Jehovah; the
discovery of fresh water was kept from the people until Moses
himself could march dramatically to the site of the spring and tap
the rock with his wand; the ordinary casualties of a forty-year
hegira were interpreted, when a lesson was needed, as acts of
Divine punishment.

Joshua could have raised his arm in the signal which would
have sent the first Hebrew foot splashing in the muddy waters of
the ford, and the crossing would then have proceeded to its well-

ordered conclusion without more ado. To do it as simply as that
would have robbed the new leader of his first chance to establish
himself firmly with his people as the new communicant of the
Divine will. Moses would have wrung from the events of this
historic morning the last drop of drama; Joshua, shrewd and well
schooled, proceeded to do likewise.

So when the signal came it was for twelve men that the leader
had selected, one from each tribe, the brawniest he could find.
They marched into the water in single file, each with a large
boulder on his shoulder. The people, trained to the histrionics of
Moses, watched silently, sure that the ceremony they were watching had been ordered by a Voice which spoke only in such far
places as the top of Sinai. Their conviction on that score deepened
when the priests followed, carrying on their shoulders the ark of
the covenant. Complete silence fell as the anointed few moved
forward, the gold-covered arms of the ark resting on their shoulders, their voices raised in a chant. Cautiously they stepped into
the water until they came to the boulders which had been placed
on the bed of the stream in a prearranged order. Each priest
stationed himself on one, their shoulders now well above the level
of the water. A trumpet sounded; every eye in the expectant
multitude back there on the sandy bank was fixed with fascinated
intentness on the scene below.

Undoubtedly this was the moment that Joshua chose to make
his announcement to the people. As long as the ark remained in
the middle of the stream, he declared, the waters would not rise.
If there had been doubts in any mind, they vanished; uneasy whis-
perings were stilled. This was what they were accustomed to, the
assurance that Divine protection hovered over them. Undoubtedly
it did, but we prefer to think it was manifested in such ways as
this, the perfect planning of divinely appointed leaders.

The crossing of the Jordan began. First came the men of Gad
and Reuben, their swords over their shoulders or held in their
teeth to keep the sharp blades dry. Joshua would be with them.
They had important work to do on the other side, and he would
not likely leave their disposition to anyone else. As soon as they
reached dry land they must push forward rapidly, fanning out in
an ever-growing half circle to fend off any attack which might

come from enemy forces lurking in the dense clumps of ghurrah trees. Joshua would be busy for the next hour, watching for signs of hostile sorties (longing, perhaps, for the aid of the upheld arms of Moses, as at Rephidim), taking advantage of every bit of terrain favorable for purposes of defense. Not until he had arranged his vanguard dispositions would he be free to turn his attention to other matters.

The crossing was going forward in the meantime. The Bible says that the people "hasted." They had every reason to haste; at any moment the word might come that the flood crest had passed the Jabbok, and so Joshua had demanded the utmost speed.

Looking down on what was happening there at the Ford of the Partridges, it would have seemed that a huge V-shaped mass was converging slowly on the eastern entrance of the ford. That would be the natural order of the undertaking, for the tribes must remain closely massed in case of attack from the rear and yet move in with the least possible confusion to a very small bottleneck where perhaps four people could cross abreast. There is no indication of the order in which they made the crossing, but it is certain that they proceeded in solid tribes, one at a time. There they were, waiting their turns, the men of Dan and Napthali and Benjamin and Ephraim and the rest. Now that the other side was screened from attack, the sheep and cattle belonging to each tribe would be herded over first. A noisy, troublesome business, this: keeping the stubborn, unwilling animals in line, urging them along, the "Ho! Youp!" of the shepherds drowning out the mutter of the uneasy people behind. Then the women and children, the women with pitchers on their heads and bundles on their backs, or carrying children in their arms. Even more difficult, this phase of the crossing, for the children would see no consolation in the golden figures on the ark and would shrink from the cold, yellow water.

Joshua was back now, sweating from his exertions in spite of the dampness of his garments. They were going over in the appointed order, moving out from the banks on the far side to the stations allotted to each tribe behind the screen of Gad and Reuben set so cunningly along the edges of the wadies and the palm groves. Simeon and Asher and Issachar: there they go, shouting, straining, keeping up to their schedule under the watchful eye of the new chieftain. The shoulders of the priests are sagging under the weight of the golden arms, but they keep upright nevertheless on the stones set for them, and the waters flowing by are still no higher than their waists. The Jordan is not rising.

Somehow it seems to have been done. Joshua had neglected no detail, physical or psychological. The push, the drive that he developed in the process, is far more to be wondered at than any presumed supernatural powers, greatly as some scholars are tempted to use them for explanation.

Everything, then, points to a carefully planned, completely successful exploit, such as had never before been seen. An entire nation had passed over a major topographical obstacle, without loss or confusion, and under perfect discipline. "On that day," says the scribe, "the Lord magnified Joshua in the sight of all Israel"; and we are not surprised to learn that thereafter "they feared him, as they feared Moses, all the days of his life."

There was still, however, an important part of the ceremony to be observed. Moses had never believed in half effects, and Joshua, as we have seen, was an apt pupil. The boulders on which the priests had stood were intended for a more lasting purpose than that. As soon as the tribes had passed over the priests stepped down to the bed of the stream and carried the ark of the covenant ashore, where, no doubt, it was soon hidden from vision again behind the blue and purple and scarlet curtains of fine, twined linen which draped the sides of the Tabernacle.

And now Joshua issued a command to the same twelve men: "Take you hence out of the midst of Jordan, out of the place where the priests' feet stood firm, twelve stones, and ye shall carry them over with you, and leave them in the lodging place, where ye shall lodge this night. . . . These stones shall be for a memorial unto the children of Israel for ever."

The voice was the voice of Joshua, but the purpose behind the command was straight from the teachings of Moses. There must indeed be a lasting memorial there on the plains of Gilgal, to keep what had happened in the minds of the people. The beneficence of the Lord, and the fact that He used his servant Joshua for the carrying out of the Divine will, could never be forgotten as long as these twelve stones stood on the edge of the Promised Land.

It had been accomplished, the first difficult step of the invasion. Tremble, Canaanites, Hittites, Perizzites, Girgashites, Amorites, Jebusites! Tremble, most particularly, men of Jericho, hiding behind your insufficient walls. The children of Israel have been led across the Jordan!

PART THREE

The Walls of Jericho

I

THE CITY

THE state of mind of Rahab as she sat, brooding and intent, on the roof of her house can be imagined. She had heard the shouts of the panting scouts who brought to the doomed city the first word of the crossing of the wild tribesmen. She alone had been sure that the blow was coming. The rest of the townspeople, sunk in fatalistic apathy, had lived on hopes. The Jordan would flood the plains; the Israelites would think better of it and move off to some less torrid spot for the balance of the summer season; something, at any rate, would happen to avert the blow. They had made no preparations to dispute the passage of the ford, and it is not even on record that they sent word to Ai, the nearest of the other cities of Canaan, for help in this grim emergency. Rahab, who had talked to the two spies and could judge the purpose of the invaders, knew better. And now that they had succeeded in crossing the Jordan she was sure they would strike fast and hard at Jericho, which stood in the path to the rich lands beyond.

Rahab, cool-thinking and completely realistic, had no illusions as to the outcome. These weak and ineffective people with whom she lived were no match for the tough, purposeful nomads, tempered to conquest by forty years in the crucible of the desert, filled with a fanatical belief in their destiny and the justice of their cause. The flimsy wall on which her little house rested would be a poor defense against men such as these.

She looked down into the streets filled with terror-stricken men and women wringing their hands and calling aloud on Astarte and Hadad for help. Scorn for such weakness stirred in her. Why had they not taken steps to defend their position? It would be clear to anyone as intelligent as she that the one chance to repel the invaders had been when the vanguard emerged from the waters. A vigorous attack then might have routed them and driven them back on the river in confusion and with heavy loss. The overdue flood would have done the rest, setting up an impassable barrier between the invaders and the land of Canaan. Did such weaklings deserve anything better than the fate which faced them? Let them shout themselves hoarse in appeals to their unheeding gods. They were beyond saving now.

Her mind was filled with bitter doubts, nevertheless. Had the leader, of whom the two spies spoke, confirmed their bargain with her? Even if he had done so, was it at all certain that the invaders, flushed with triumph, would pause long enough in the moment of victory to see a flimsy red string dangling on the walls? It was a slim chance at best. Rahab shuddered as she thought of what lay ahead. She was young and full of vitality; she did not want to die with a rough-edged blade in the cords of her firm white throat. And there were her father and mother, her young brothers and sisters, all of whom she seems to have loved. Rahab did not join in the wild clamor of supplication to heathen gods, but her heart was as full of deep fears as the most timorous of the shrieking townspeople.

What manner of city was this which the brooding eyes of Rahab surveyed? A small, dirty, flea-filled community, built on the top of an egg-shaped plateau with such indifference and sloth that the patched walls disregarded all engineering rules and followed the irregular contours of the land. Four hundred and ninety-nine yards in length, one hundred and seventy-five yards wide—a scant five acres, in fact—a home of fitting meanness for people of such poor spirit. From where the dying eyes of Moses had looked upon it, Jericho might seem imposing, formidable, rich; at close range it was no more than a wallow for bare and uneasy living, the last stopping place on the edge of the sweltering desert.

Jericho had been strong once and inhabited by people of more ambition than the scatterbrained lot who lived there now. This is evident from the fact that the first walls of the town had been well and truly laid with massive foundations which exist to this day, as sound as ever. On this splendidly escarped basis the walls of Jericho had been strong and high. Perhaps an earthquake had laid them low; more likely they had been razed by orders from Egypt. There is plenty of evidence that Egyptian levies garrisoned the town for a long period, leaving broken bits of Coptic pottery and even a few scarabs in the tombs beneath "citadel hill." Whatever the reason, those splendid walls had come tumbling down, covering the enduring foundations with a mass of rubble. It was on this rubble that the new walls stood. They are described in detail farther on, and now we know that they were completely inadequate for a long defense. It must have been a fearsome business living on the top of such tipsy masonry.

Fifteen hundred people, no more, lived in the uneven space thus enclosed, for the most part in one-roomed houses of the most primitive kind, flat-roofed and dark, with tiny slits for windows. The streets were malodorous alleys, as hit-and-miss in the matter of direction as the walls. There was, however, a sewer in the town, an open trench which carried some of the filth out under the walls and added a pungent note to the overpowering stench of the place. The houses had doors which swung on the most primitive of hinges, being no more than holes hollowed out in slabs of flint which served as sockets.

Life in Jericho was not as ugly and primitive as this first glimpse would seem to indicate. There were some dwellings of better size. If "citadel hill" existed then, as it may have (there had been so many successive phases of occupation that archaeological experts are still unable to determine where one ended and the next began), it may be taken for granted that in this favored high spot an upper class enjoyed a greater ease of living than the dwellers in the rabbit warren of clay walls which hedged it in. There was, we know, a king of Jericho. It must not be assumed that he lived in a palace and sat on a throne; he was little more than a ruling magistrate, and his grandeur consisted probably of a few rooms, one large enough to serve as court for the trying of cases. In passing it must be remarked that they were unfortunate in having a weakling for a king at this critical juncture, one lacking the good sense to order the gate closed when spies might be expected, too lackadaisical to guard the all-important fords.

One feature of the little city is completely puzzling. At intervals there were solid mounds of dried mud, shaped like drums and running to a height of twelve feet. They were isolated from the higgledy-piggledy houses with clay barricades around the top surface. What purpose could they have served. Were religious ceremonies conducted there? Were they used by the storytellers so popular in oriental communities? There is nothing about them to make possible more accurate conjecture.

The tombs of Jericho provide whatever tangible evidence there is of the everyday life of the place. Narrow shafts still lead straight down into dark crypts in which the dust of the long-dead mingle with broken remnants of pottery and crude objects of personal adornment. In one of these dank subterranean chambers as many as five hundred graves have been found, together with a great variety of utensils of various kinds: jars and pitchers of thick white glaze, with inscriptions to Hadad and other deities; cypriote bowls, lamps, rhytons of vigorous design, pyriform jugs, button-bottomed cups of drab ware; dishes on pedestals, wet-smoothed, showing unmistakable evidences of wheel finish; vessels with rims to facilitate carrying on the head in the daily visits the housewives must have paid to the well of Ain-el-Sultain, that beneficent spring, palm-fringed, which was nature's sole boon to sun-baked Jericho. There was, clearly, a tinge of culture to their life. They were learning to adorn their household utensils and, it may be assumed, their homes and their persons as well.

A few guides exist to the commercial side of the town. Round balls with holes through the center, some made of stone and some of clay, were used as commercial weights, a necessary adjunct to a people who existed largely on the traffic which flowed down from Jerusalem to the fords. Grain was ground in the most primitive way, however, with oblong frames slightly hollowed in the center, in which round stones were rolled by hand.

There it is, then, the Jericho of the conquest: nothing glamorous or exciting or colorful about it; crude, crowded, sundrenched, a huddle of miserable houses behind the craziest walls ever set up against aggression; a people sunk in idolatry, aware in only the vaguest way that life could be fuller and gentler in more favored lands; no more than one step above the life of the desert nomads, far below them in spirit.

Days passed and nothing happened. The timid scouts who ventured out along the roads and up into the foothills brought back word that the Israelites were sticking to their tents and that quiet reigned over Gilgal. The invaders had, however, erected a temple of glowing colors in the middle of their camp, where strange things went on—swinging of censers by men in rich tallithim and much bowing of heads and chanting. This, of course, was their way of worshiping that strange God of whose might and terror Canaan had heard so much, the God who had parted the waters of the Red Sea and caused water to gush from dry rocks and food to rain down from the skies. Clearly the invaders were supplicating more heavenly support in the attack they would soon launch.

The gate of Jericho was kept shut. Double watches were set on the walls at night, and men slept with weapons beside them. The king of Jericho tucked his robes up around his fat loins and made a belated inspection of the foundations of the wall, finding plenty of reasons for headshaking and increased worry. Women and boys carried rocks to the sentry walks, and men restrung slack bows and ground swords and lances feverishly.

No travelers passed up and down the trails from Jerusalem and Ai. Without guests to feed and entertain, Rahab had plenty of time for thought. She sat up there on the wall, her head turned toward Gilgal, wondering what the fruits of her treason would be.

II
KEEPING THE PEOPLE IN HAND

WHY did not Joshua move at once against Jericho? Why give them time to recover from the shock of the crossing, to prepare their defenses?

He had the best possible reason for delay. Care and good timing had served him well and earned the respect of his people. But he must still outthink them. And although they did not know it he was at another crossroads in the development of a leader. He was face to face with his first success.

Next to assuming a new command, the first victory is the severest test of a chief's capacity. Everyone acclaims him. Legends mushroom around the event and around his own part in it. Doubts and latent hostilities are no more, or, at any rate, are kept well covered. "What fools we were," his followers say, "to have imagined failure! And now, how about a little celebration in honor of our great captain?"

Some people in authority find it very hard, if not impossible, to dampen such notions. It seems such a waste of good will, of useful and spontaneous impetus toward unity, *esprit de corps*, loyalty based solidly on achievement. This is a capital mistake.

The commander's task is to tighten, not loosen, the sinews of discipline. The victor who basks in the plaudits of his conquering soldiery soon finds them convinced that they, not he, originated victory. The worshipers, not the god, have raised the temple. Therefore, at their fickle will they can tear it down, and the god with it. The process is as old as the herd.

It must never be forgotten, moreover, that Joshua was dealing with what Renan has called: "A race, incomplete from its very simplicity," whose "military inferiority . . . results from this total incapacity for discipline and for organization." They would not learn self-control from misfortune, as other races do. In fact,

they have never done so. The undiluted elements of Semite mentality among the tameless Arabian tribes exhibit today the very
same impermeability. Centuries of the cruelest oppression have
failed of any effect on them.

One thing, indeed, he had in his favor at this point: there was
as yet no loot to distract the people. We shall soon see how he
met that menace when it reared its head. But now the tribes are
still speculating about the fabulous plunder behind Jericho's
walls, so "straitly shut up." Their fear of Jordan flood is behind
them, like the flood itself. The priests must have their innings
and custom be observed with the Passover. But, these temporary
distractions once out of the way, there still remained the leader's
problem: *to keep the people in hand.*

Joshua ordered every male to be circumcised.

The true importance of this measure appears to have escaped
subsequent observers altogether. Josephus primly ignores it.
Others list it merely as a renewal of a religious rite fallen into
disuse since leaving Egypt and therefore to be considered merely
as a sort of spiritual reinforcement, another entry to Israel's
credit in the Lord's book. Viewed so, it must undoubtedly have
added to the overwhelming weight of Jewish holiness, before
which the walls of Jericho were later to fall flat.

Joshua's reasons for issuing this order are clear. All have been
told how Abraham initiated the rite and applied it both to Hagar's
son Ishmael and to Sarah's late-born Isaac, seven generations before. But the long desert wanderings had erased many of the
good old habits. Even Moses, as appears from various allusions,
was unmarked. The older men had mostly died off, and the new
crop had been neglected "by the way." It was time to revive the
ancient ritual—while yet the kings of the Amorites "on the side
of Jordan westward, and all the kings of the Canaanites, which
were by the sea," were still under the spell. Joshua's intelligence
had naturally reported that when these exalted ones heard of the
Jordan crossing "their heart melted, neither was there spirit in
them any more." He could consequently feel pretty safe from
attack, for a time at least.

Even today, when the greatest care is taken to protect the
health of closely grouped men, and science has advanced far

in ability to do so, disease is still the Great Killer of armies. The
strictest precautions still avail little against the ubiquitous louse,
and the commoner forms of sexual infection ride the camps of
all countries, although much mitigated in relatively unpopulated
lands like the United States of America. Ninety-nine per cent of
warfare, for the vast majority of men engaged, consists of hard
labor, exposure, undernourishment, fatigue, and unutterable bore-
dom. No more favorable conditions for the development of the
"social diseases" exist. Of course circumcision alone is no preven-
tive, still less a cure, and there seems to be no substantial evidence
that venereal disease, in any of its modern forms, had yet attacked
Egypt and Syria. But there were plenty of other good reasons
for the operation. In battle, for example, it was highly important
to be able to distinguish enemy corpses from friendly ones: all
would be lean, brown, black-bearded, beak-nosed, but enemies
were strippable, while friends should be dragged back for burial.
Identification of the dead is a problem in every war; under the
circumstances Joshua could hardly have chosen a better method.

His next move shows again how well he understood his people.
They have been reduced to a common physical level, marked
for life as a race apart. But Joshua, like all great leaders, knows
well that this kind of uniformity is not enough. Deeper moods
and reactions exist. Therefore, he proceeds to uplift the imagina-
tions of the people.

The successful crossing of Jordan must be fixed in the tribal
mind as an event of the utmost importance. He has already hinted
at what he has in view: "a memorial unto the children of Israel
for ever." The stones that supported the priests, carried up from
the waters, shall mark the spot and, shaped into a monument,
shall link for all time the names of Jordan and Gilgal with the
carrying out of God's orders and those of Joshua, His servant.

Scholars translate "Gilgal" as "a circle." Its exact location is
now accepted: midway between Jordan and Jericho. It is well
suited to tribal camping habits. On the south it is bordered by
the Wadi el Kelt, sometimes called the Valley of Achor, that
deep fissure in the hills which runs from Jerusalem to the Dead
Sea by way of Jericho and into which Elisha would retire much
later on in Jewish history and be fed by the ravens. Even in the

hottest season there is a trickle of water here, and at Gilgal it is
sometimes possible to sink wells. A good place to rest while the
men recovered from their enforced operation; a supremely wise
camping spot from military considerations, for the tents of the
invaders could be seen from the walls of Jericho, a constant reminder of the threat to that city; above everything else, the perfect location for the memorial.

The care he took to follow up and to implant in the minds of
all just what the memorial was to commemorate (the scribe repeats the admonition twice in one short chapter) may perhaps
be taken as a measure of his own price of achievement. It was as
near to self-glorification as he ever came. But this was only a part
of his motivation, if, indeed, it entered his mind at all. Symbolism
is grained in the Semitic nature. By some allusive or punning
trick of words Joshua transformed the description "circle" into
the concept of something that is "rolled away." Again we see (so
perfectly tuned is Joshua's sense) the most common rolling thing
in that country: a rolling stone. To this day caves and passages
throughout Syria and Palestine are habitually closed by rounded
boulders. Christ's tomb was so closed. Mark goes so far, in his
usual swift detail, as to describe that stone as "very great" and to
indicate that the three women could not have moved it by themselves: particulars well calculated to impress the factual-minded
Romans for whom he wrote, who had long ago graduated from
the rock-tomb stage of society. The image is sharpened by the
fact that, in the better tombs at least, the closing stone was *flat*
—like a thick, solid wheel. It moved in a groove and fitted in a
recess to one side of the opening when "rolled back." Many
remain today, and it needs but one glance to realize the felicity
of Joshua's metaphor.

The "circle" is, then, no longer a camp beside Achor Valley
but something that rolls—and preferably rolls away. For when
the stone is rolled away the door is opened, and the imprisoned
is free. The symbolism is apt, distinct, unmistakable. Josephus
skips all this, although willing enough in other places to explain
esoteric meanings with the scholar's serene satisfaction. He says
merely that "Gilgal" means "liberty"; the reason of this, from
the Israelite standpoint, being that "since now they had passed

over Jordan, they looked on themselves as freed from the miseries
which they had undergone from the Egyptians, *and in the wilderness.*"

Perhaps it is a trifle unjust to a busy and many-sided man of
affairs, doing his best, no doubt, to record in the intervals of more
important work what tradition has preserved of his earliest national history, to hold him too sharply on the bit of fact. But that
is the badge of servitude which every historian must wear.

All that Josephus passes on to us is a pedestrian relief from
former "miseries." Is that all? How could the people be sure
that even worse miseries did not lie ahead? The Jordan was in
flood behind them. Ahead loomed Jericho, and the barren mountains behind. Where was food? Shelter? Pasturage? Could this
be "liberty"?

Joshua's reasoning went far deeper. He knew that mental exal-
tation, a spurt of the spiritual and imaginative faculties, will take
the place of bread up to a certain point and for a certain while.
Not "liberty" (a concept, in any case, completely foreign to
people living such unfettered personal lives), but "delivery,"—
escape, enlargement, the rolling away of the imprisoning stone.
That was Joshua's theme. It is there in the record, plain for all to
read: "This day" (the Lord says) "have I *rolled away the reproach of Egypt from off you.*" Not a word about "miseries" or
the wilderness, but a trumpet call of enfranchisement. The "reproach" of former slavery is gone for good. The former subjects
of Pharaoh, the persecuted fugitives, the universally hated and
attacked and despised, are now a people, a nation, sovereign unto
themselves. What are past miseries, present pains, or future un-
certainties in comparison?

Modern psychologic terminology would summon the phrase
"inferiority complex" to fit the case. It will serve as well as another. Under any name Joshua struck it down, and all the subsequent enslavements and persecutions endured by the descendants of his people, from that day to this, have never served to
revive it. In their most hopeless misfortunes it has been, and still is,
the Jewish pride of race and intellect that has kept, and still keeps,
their peculiar spirit alive. So it is not unfair, when crediting that
spirit with the great debt owed it by European civilization at

large, to write down Joshua as due to receive the first dividend of praise. He saw to it that his people threw off their inherited and acquired fears and felt themselves in every way equal to the task ahead. Equal to the task and, therefore, superior to the enemy. That was all they needed. That was what he gave them in Gilgal.

And high time too. For the early harvest was ripening, and Jericho still barred the way.

III
JOSHUA SEES A VISION

Before he proceeds with the next great step in the conquest Joshua has a vision. The incident is treated lightly in the text: no more than three verses in the fifth chapter. It is of the greatest importance, however, in reaching a complete understanding of this forthright captain.

It would be very easy to accept Joshua as pre-eminently the man of action, a valiant captain, but lacking those fine spiritual qualities which so light up for us the figure of Moses; easy, if we were not afforded occasional flashes such as this. The incident of the vision opens a window into the inner feelings of this stern, aloof figure, permitting us to glimpse dreams molded in the shape of his own thoughts. Joshua, after all, has his share of the deep impressionability which always goes with true greatness of heart.

Here is how the story is told: "When Joshua was by Jericho . . . behold, there stood a man over against him with his sword drawn in his hand: and Joshua went unto him, and said unto him, Art thou for us, or for our adversaries?"

A sharp and vivid vignette. The commander, out alone on one of his continual reconnaissances, for the hundredth time inspecting Jericho and its surrounding terrain, suddenly sees a stranger. The stranger, moreover, is armed, his sword drawn as for attack.

The commander does not hesitate. Alone he advances and challenges: Friend or foe? The answer is equivocal and mystic:

"As captain of the host of the Lord am I come," but Joshua has no doubts of the meaning.

To him it seems to have been an authentic experience and a comforting one, for the scribe repeats the ritual admonition which accompanied Moses' vision of the burning bush. Both were told to loose their shoes from off their feet, as if entering a temple (a far-spread custom across the world), for "the place whereon thou standest is holy."

Those of us who have seen or felt visions of our own instinctively associate with them the spot where they have occurred. This indeed is done by all men. How else do places achieve holiness?

And Joshua falls "on his face" (only twice does he do this; Moses was constantly doing it) and worships.

The experience illumines his character by the light of two previous and like incidents in the lives of his two great predecessors, Abraham and Moses. Abraham's experience is described as entertaining angels. Moses saw a bush burning—something which might spell danger in the desert—promptly investigated, and heard a voice. Joshua spied and challenged an intruder. What makes these superficially unrelated stories of high interest is that, in each instance, *the visionary is promised what he secretly most desires.* His dream takes the form which most powerfully supports his prime ambition: Abraham to have a legitimate son, of whom he had long ago given up hope; Moses to return with honor to the land whence he had fled in fear of his life, to collect and weld his debased people into a nation once more; Joshua to be assured that victory would be on his side in the coming struggle.

In each instance the vision told truth. Hence their preservation, in all their delicate and highly personal perfection, fixed in the amber of the solid past.

IV
THE WALLS

AND now at last for Jericho and one of the most fantastic and yet ingenious sieges in military history. The facts about those walls must now be set down in more detail than has yet been attempted if we are to arrive at the truth.

Perhaps the unknown but fervent inditer of the Epistle "to Hebrews" is to blame. In listing the wonders worked by "faith" he included both the falling down of Jericho's walls and the preservation of Rahab. The latter incident, not requiring any supranormal explanation, seems to have passed relatively unscathed through the gauntlet of the higher criticism, but the former is different. Walls do not fall down of themselves, at least not the defending walls of a beleaguered town. "Faith," indeed, it must have been, and so the story has come "a-tumblin' down" the centuries since. To most people today it is the one event linked in their memories with Joshua's name. A miracle of faith, or an unexplained myth, Joshua led the children of Israel seven times around Jericho, and its walls fell down. "No instruments of war, nor any other force, was applied to it," says Josephus.

But the Book itself does not say this.

Bear in mind that, after all, we have still to deal with a very ancient record, and much of it cannot be entirely divested of legendary nebulosity. Yet Joshua's record is throughout so persuasively independent of the extraordinary that one feels reluctant to surrender Jericho without a struggle. Must we resign ourselves to believing only, with the devout manuals, that its walls "miraculously fell before these desert wanderers, who could never before have beheld a fortified city"? Is it so certain that they could not ever before have beheld a fortified city? How about Bashan, and Heshbon, and "all the cities of the Amorites"?

On the other hand, one should not minimize the impression which Jericho, as it then stood, must have created on the tribes. "Cities," indeed, they may have seen and must have learned to deal with in their steady movement north into Gilead. But there is no evidence that the Amorites, or any other of the peoples already occupying the land, possessed any such monumental fortresses as dotted the ancient, if now debilitated, country of Canaan. From earliest recorded times the desert dwellers, the Lords of the Sands, had built refuges of heavy stones. These were laid in low walls, surrounding a central camp and corral for the animals, and the walls were topped by *chevaux-de-frise* of acacia and thornbush. Against marauding wild animals and wilder marauding men these "fenced cities" were usually effective, but time and again the trained Egyptian troops stormed and destroyed them. Direct frontal assault seems to have been enough. Defenders, armed only with bow and sling, obviously would have been unable to concentrate enough fire at the point attacked to stop a rush in force.

As we shall see, it was a far cry from such primitive forts to Jericho, dominating from its scarred mound its spring-oasis and the cultivated fields around. But it is even farther from the Jericho of that day to what entrenched walls mean to modern thought. It is due, in reality, to this mistaken concept, that Joshua's story retains its miraculous aspect.

"Walls," to the modern mind's eye, mean castles: the sheer masonry of donjon and keep. What they could mean twenty-five hundred years later, under the rule of armed strangers, even in that stone-and-clay territory, we can still see: the breath-taking ruins of Crac des Chevaliers, Belvoir, Qurn-Surtubeh, in Palestine proper, and the group of huge Crusader forts in Syria, farther north, such as Rum Kalaat, Biridjik, and Urfa. No European vestiges of those dark centuries exceed in impressiveness this defensive line, which the joint tyranny of Church and State erected to guard a conquered but alien land precious to both. Their sheer size and the weight of the innumerable stone blocks that have been quarried, transported, and lifted into place high on those steep mountaintops are mute witnesses to incalculable human toil and suffering. This concept of "walls," which has ruled the English-speaking world since the mid-sixteenth century, when our Bible first became available outside of ecclesiastical circles, springs direct from memories of such formidable dressed-stone barriers. The mere suggestion of their like falling "flat" around Jericho in the face of an encircling force partakes so unquestionably of the miraculous that faith indeed was needed.

Later and less simple persons, faced with this difficulty, yet unwilling to pin so major a demolition on faith alone, have conjectured that perhaps the walls disintegrated because of the vibration set up by the marching Israelite feet. This odd fable is still widely current today, even among presumably enlightened and educated people. Aside from the fact that marching in step is a very recent* military invention, adopted first as an ornamental fad for picked troops, palace guards, and the like, then continued in use (chiefly by the Germans) for leg-developing purposes, the thing is impossible. Rhythmic vibrations may induce sway in delicately poised structures, especially if accompanied by the direct impact of weight, for which reason trained troops habitually break step over bridges. But a wall, even if not of squared stone, is not to be shaken by the shuffle-past of a few thousand unregimented desert walkers.

So we are brought back to the question: What were the "walls" of Jericho really like?

So far as the text itself goes, it appears that, in parts at least, they were wide enough to support a house, or more probably a room, for such as Rahab. Similar second-story chambers are common enough even now in the better houses of the country, and Elijah the Tishbite must have occupied one while he boarded with the widow woman in Zarephath by the sea. So must the prophet Elisha, "on the wall" of the house of the Shunammite, that "great woman," who moreover hospitably furnished with "a bed, and a table, and a stool, and a candlestick."

Then again, Joshua's spies could be let down from Rahab's window by such a rope or "cord" as was then woven: it could not have been a far drop. Nor was her window so high up but that

---

*Some authorities find the beginning of this custom in the old Roman marching step, noted by Vegetius (390 A.D.) and then neglected until revived with great success by Marshal Maurice of Saxony (1696–1750).

red strings in its shutters or bars could be seen from the ground.

These bits check any inherited inclination to visualize the walls of Jericho as comparable to the titanic medieval fortresses we have just recalled to view. Whatever they were, we realize that, to the Israelite marauders, fresh from the desert plains, and lacking in even the most primitive of siege weapons, such as battering-rams or scaling ladders, they must have presented a formidable-looking obstacle. Yet breached or scaled they must be: a problem for the commander and for no one else.

At this point the expert comes into his own. It is the glory of archaeology to continue patiently digging, measuring, preserving, classifying, cataloguing, until one fine day the hitherto impassable gates of the locked past swing wide, and a great light illumines our darkness.

So with the walls of Jericho. The very same investigator whose conclusions, when he stepped out of character, we have heretofore scouted now arises to solve for us a riddle over three thousand years old. His is a magnificent contribution to the reconstruction of history.

Ancient Jericho is as well fixed on the map and on the ground as ancient or modern Jerusalem. In Joshua's day it was already very old. Flint-using people lived there before the Bronze Age. It was a junction of paths or roads leading down the eastern face of the mountains to the Achor Valley and Jordan from hill towns like Jerusalem and Ai farther north. Thus it constituted a sort of halfway station or last gathering place before reaching the Jordan ford. The original town lay on a plateau, as already explained, at the base of the mountain itself. It was out of sight of both Jerusalem and Ai, and so beyond range of visual signaling in case it needed help. But successive centuries of occupation had gradually raised its level into a respectable mound. Three or four hundred years before Joshua saw it the place was girdled by a deep ditch, and the sloping sides of the hill were revetted with stone all around. On top of this glacis, twenty feet high or so, had stood a brick parapet.

But—still long before the days of Joshua—the city had been overwhelmed in spite of strong walls. The ditch was filled up and the glacis ruined. But again (the pull of water in the wilderness is not to be denied) men returned and built. This time the mound was higher because of the ruins, and the crown encompassed by the new walls was necessarily smaller. Fewer people could be accommodated, and the wall circuit was some two hundred yards smaller.

The walls of this new city must have been quite impressive to the eye: an outer one or "curtain" six feet thick at the base, and an inner one, the main defense, all of twelve feet thick at its bottom and from nineteen to twenty-five feet high. At the north-west corner rose a tower several stories higher than the walls. Inside the walls the ground level was much higher than outside. Houses were built against the inner face of the main wall, and even on timbers or transverse brick walls stretching across the narrow space (twelve to fifteen feet), between it and the outer "curtain." On such timbers, whose charred remains we can see today, Rahab's house must have rested.

In short, Jericho's great walls were a hollow sham. Owing to the previous fortifications and demolitions, the double walls in Joshua's time were very badly founded. Long security had recon-ciled the townsfolk to ramparts which were strong only in ap-pearance. So much rubble and waste material had accumulated over the mount that the wall foundations were dangerously flimsy. For the most part they rested on nothing more solid than the debris of the older walls. This was especially true of the western face, where some of the earliest Bronze Age ruins, still projecting aboveground, had been used as a base, but without re-newal or repair. The walls of Joshua's Jericho, therefore, rested on no firmer footings than the remains of previously ruined ones: a portent that does not seem to have disturbed the Jerichites, at least not to the point of stimulating them into any serious effort to bolster up their weakened protective system.

Furthermore, the new construction had been on the cheap and careless side. No doubt there flourished, in that day as in this, profiteering contractors even in matters of national defense. The bottom courses of that impressive twelve-foot-thick inner wall were made of native rocks, undressed, chinked with smaller stones. Where (as notably on the west side) these courses rested on ancient bases or on mere rubble they had naturally sagged and sunk here and there, and the Jericho contractors had merely chinked up the cracks in the upper brick layers with mud. The bricks themselves were of poor quality, made without straw. The outer or "curtain" wall rested mainly on the outside edge of rubble and dirt, pushed out from the center accumulation and leveled off, thus affording them no underlying foundations at all. And we must keep in mind that the old stone glacis and ditch had long ago disappeared. When Joshua appeared before it these conditions were already of some hundred years' standing.

Stretching almost north and south, the mound of Jericho, seen from the plain level looking west, almost eclipsed the barren mountain behind Jebel Kuruntul. Jericho's supplementary spring (now Ain-el-Duk), west of the town but dangerously unprotected in the open ground, was also hidden from that view. In the foreground the vivid green foliage which Moses himself had been able to see from Pisgah marked the Jericho spring, Ain-el-Sultain. In turn, that foliage masked Jericho's only gate with its small guard tower; beyond, and to the right, dominated the great corner bastion.

How many times, in his lonely and perilous jaunts, by day and by night, had Joshua estimated distances! Allowing for walls and slope, the city enclosure worked out to around a short two hundred and fifty paces by one hundred and fifty—what we should call a circuit of between six and seven hundred yards—enclosing some fifteen hundred people. This was approximately what Joshua's fighting force would muster, but the Jerichites had their walls.

So much for the mere physical aspects of the problem. The solution, Joshua found, begins to take on form. It is his approach to that solution which stamps him.

The one recorded piece of information brought back from Jericho by his spies concerned the public state of mind. Rahab, who could be depended upon to know, had reported it as already greatly terrified. This in itself was much. But he surely would have received other information as well: the strength of guards, the defensibility of the gate, the confirmation of what his reconnaissance had spotted as weak spots in the round of the walls, and so on.

That sapping was done during the period of active siege may be accepted as fact. One archaeological expert asserts that proof of this is coming out of the scientific work being done today on the ruins. Was it undertaken with the assistance of Rahab? Perhaps spies climbed the wall to visit her again and to cement the first bargain, on one condition, that she would go a step farther and allow them the use of her house, so conveniently suspended over the dark space between the walls, as a base of operations. This is pure conjecture, of course, but it is not unreasonable to assume that the anxious harlot would have agreed to such a suggestion.

We can be sure of one thing: sapping was done. How or when or where, we do not know for certain. But there yet remain very definite traces of a breakdown in the *west* wall. Keeping in mind that Rahab sent the spies to hide on Jebel Kuruntul, is it not likely that she did so because it was the nearest refuge—that is, *nearest to her room* on the wall? There are plenty of other scrubby, rocky hide-outs on either side of that grim and difficult pile. But the thing to do was to get away quickly and in an opposite direction from where the city police would be watching—that is, toward Jordan and the east.

The simple thing is the likely thing. May we not see, atop the nameless rubble (with its telltale westward slant) where, it seems sure, the walls were undermined and fell, the very location of Rahab's "house on the wall"?—only a little to one side of the breach, so that the red strings could be seen and, it is good to remember, respected.

There is no reason to doubt that Joshua used every weapon of siege, which would include, of course, treachery. We know that Joshua used that other weapon, called today (as if it were new) "the stategy of terror," "the war of nerves," and similar names. He understood that treachery is a double-edged sword, for a traitor is never dependable. Terror, on the other hand, can always be counted on to do its work. Joshua's spectacular conquest of Jericho's impregnable-seeming walls grows out of his use of terror as a weapon.

V
THE WALLS FALL

Down in the valley there was a disturbance. The camp of the invaders at Gilgal was still in deep shadow, but the darkness seemed astir: faint sounds, the lowing of cattle, a few spirals of thin smoke rising above the gray peaks of the tents.

The chilled sentinel on the tower stopped his pacing and gazed intently into the distance. It was very cold up on the walls, always particularly so in the last stages of the morning watch. He shuddered as he drew his woolen cloak around his shoulders, as much from fear of what might be impending as from the cold.

"Look!" he called cautiously to his companion on the nearest angle of the wall.

The other sentry joined him, and together they peered into the darkness. Dawn comes swiftly here, and as they watched a gray light began to appear on the eastern rim of the sky. Against this background it was possible to see the tents of the invaders more clearly.

"They've never been astir as early as this," whispered the first sentry. "Must we summon the captain of the watch?"

The other man shook his head. Better wait for a few minutes. The captain had been getting weary of the continual false alarms which had him tumbling out of his bed in the tower at all hours and rushing up to the walls for nothing. It had been a flock of birds in the trees at the well the last time, and the captain had sworn that, if it happened again, someone would feel the haft of a spear shaft over his stupid shoulder. Yes, better wait.

Lights sprang up in the camp of the dreaded nomads. The chanting of priests could now be heard, and a faint clatter of metal.

"O Hadad, save us!" said the first sentry in a frightened whisper. "They're coming against us at last!"

The hand of the second man fell on the outer surface of the battlement on which a stem stripped of its branches had been crudely carved. "O Asherah!" he cried in sudden panic. "We pray to thee! Lend us strength this day!"

Sentries on other parts of the walls took up the cry. "O Astarte!" "O Hadad!" "O Asherah!" The captain of the watch, his eyes red-rimmed from lack of sleep, appeared on the flat surface of the tower top, drawn sword in hand. He was muttering angrily, but it took no more than one glimpse at what was happening in the valley to change his tune. "Sound trumpets!" he ordered. "They're coming! To your posts, men!"

The whole city came awake. Men shouted as they emerged from the doors of their tiny houses into the crooked dark streets. Iron-soled feet rang on the cobbles, and the ends of weapons clattered against the surface of the walls. From the clay-enclosed top of one of the high mud drums a captain tried to direct the assemblying warriors, to get them to their proper stations with as little confusion as possible. The king of Jericho wakened and wondered if there was still time to send fast runners to Ai for help. It would probably do no good, he reflected bitterly; the great cities up the trail were little concerned with the fate of humble Jericho. "Wait until their turn comes," he thought, fastening a charm made in the shape of a coiled serpent on his cold arm. The cries of women and children came from everywhere.

Rahab roused at the first sound. She had not been sleeping well since the visit of the two spies. She went to the roof of her house which faced the still-dark slopes of Jebel Kuruntul. Turning to her left, she looked down the valley in the direction from which the attack would come. What she saw convinced her at once. She called to her family to get up and dress but on no account to leave the room where they all slept. Did she look nervously down into the dark chasm between the walls, straining her ears for any sound there? We can be sure of one thing; in her nervous fingers she clutched a ball of red cord.

Down in the valley the tribesmen were assembling. Joshua was issuing his final orders. They were to march slowly, and not a word was to be said under any circumstances. The best warriors were to be stationed immediately before and after the ark of the covenant, ready for a sortie from the town. And they must not forget that the eyes of God would be on them.

The men nodded slowly. They knew what they were to do but not why. God had spoken to Joshua. That they knew, and that was enough. The youngest of the priests, on whose padded shoulders rested the arms of the ark, looked up at the sky, which was now shot with streaks of light gray, fancying, no doubt, that they would be able to see, if they looked hard enough, the dread features of Yahweh as He watched them from somewhere up there.

"Forward!"

The order came. The children of Israel began to march, Joshua in the lead.

The garrison crowding the walls and the anxious harlot from the roof of her house watched the approach in silence. Nothing was heard but the *zing* of cord as the archers flexed their bow-strings and the hiss of bellows blowing on the charcoal beneath the pots of heating pitch.

It was a strange procession which wound into sight in the growing day. First came armed men in narrow files: ragged, lean, black-bearded, striding strongly, arrogantly, up out of the shadowed valley, evenly and without haste. There was something terrible, inexorable, about the purposeful ease of their gait. They were armed for combat: dark bronze on their breasts and shins, helmets drawn down closely over their wild black locks, swords in their hands, tipped lances on their backs, hand spears, short bows, dangling slings. Nearer flowed the column, still without haste, still without sound. The defenders could now see the cruel white teeth and flashing eyes of the marching nomads. There was something uncanny about the silence they maintained, the fixing of each pair of eyes on the crest of the walls. They were within easy bowshot distance now, but not an arrow was loosed against them.

When as near as a hundred cubits the van of the oncoming column checked and swung off to the right. Still maintaining the same distance, the marching horde began to follow the uneven

curve of the walls. Still not a sound from any of them, still every
pair of eyes fixed on the walls; not a stone slung, not a spear
brandished. The sun was up over the horizon now, and the steady
tramp of so many feet was raising dust which hung like a drifting
tent over the scene. Through the dust the anxious watchers saw
something that puzzled them more than the silent files of marching warriors: seven oldish gray-bearded men, with bits of tinsel
finery on their long garments, walking together. From time to
time these grizzled veterans raised small, crooked horns to their
lips and produced a high, thin, whistling sound. There was no
rhythm to the sound, no suggestion of music; just a penetrating,
unearthly screech.

Immediately on the heels of the seven old men, with measured
tread came a group of priests in costly vestments, carrying on
poles a shining oblong box. There was something about this small
vessel which drew each eye and held it there. It was made of gold
which caught and reflected the rays of the sun, and on each
corner were curiously wrought figures with outstretched wings.
It was perhaps no more costly than the images which the Canaanites had raised to their own gods, but a breath-taking intentness filled the morning air as soon as it came into view. Perhaps it
was the reverential air of the priests who carried it; perhaps it
was something still more potent, something unexplainable, which
made itself felt even by the idol worshipers on the walls. The
screech of the rams' horns fell off as the ark of the covenant came
into the full view of the doomed Jerichites.

After the priests came more fighting men, and after them a
mixed mob, mostly unarmed, old men, women, and children, following the same course around the walls, silent, also; all of them,
even to the smallest of the children, cast in the same predatory
mold, with bold and rolling eyes, an unblinking confidence in
their sun-blackened faces.

It was an uncanny performance. What did it mean? Was it a
preliminary to attack, a rite dictated by this strange and fearsome
Yahweh, of Whose power the Canaanites had heard so much?
Would the priests with their golden burden, the old men and the
women and children suddenly take themselves off to a safe distance while the fighting men plunged forward against the crazy

walls of the city? Was it nothing more than a ruse to throw the defenders off guard? Certainly the staring Jerichites had never seen anything like this before. They were baffled by the coolness and daring of the march, the serene confidence with which this mixed horde moved within range of the bows and the projectiles on the walls, as though saying, "Nothing you do can harm us while we walk in the protection of the one and only God." The archers above them felt no impulse to loose their bolts at the slowly moving circle; arms trained to the use of the catapults were curiously inert. They looked at each other and saw in the eyes of their fellows a reflection of their own fear: that Yahweh had cast a spell on them.

The unexpected silence had drawn the women of Jericho to the walls. They were crowding up behind the men, craning their necks and wondering, also, about the meaning of this curious march. The van of the Israelites had completed the circle of the town by this time and were filing off in the direction of Gilgal. The squeal of the little ram's-horn trumpets had faded into the distance, and the ark of the covenant was no longer to be seen.

The sun was high in the heavens, and the men of Jericho, who stood in the full heat of it while the rest of the slow procession completed the circuit, were drenched with sweat when the last of the Israelites moved off down the trail to Gilgal. The king, in the roped amber beads which set him apart from the rest, shook his head in complete puzzlement. Had this strange thing actually happened? Had it all been a dream? No, for there in the trampled sand was the trace of the marching Semite feet, girdling the walls as though made by a giant snake, leaving a disturbing impression on the superstitious townspeople that a cabalistic tracing closed them in from the outside world.

All day long sentries remained on the walls, watching for further movement in the camp of the besiegers. All day long tongues clacked in the crowded streets. Rahab heard what they were saying from her inner window on the wall, the anxious questions they were bandying back and forth. How many marchers had there been? They had seemed endless, with their fixed stares and cruel hyena grins. Were there more of them? Why had there been no attack? Would it come tomorrow?

Would they take any prisoners? Was it true that they would eat babies alive? Two questions were repeated over and over again: Would it still avail them to send runners for help to Ai or Michmash or Jerusalem? Would it be better now to surrender, to make what terms they could?

As the day wore on the talk became still more panicky in note. Where can we hide ourselves when they come? Is there time to send the women and children to hide on the face of Jebel Kuruntul? What can we do with our treasure? Where are our captains and priests? Why don't they *do* something? O Hadad, O Asherah, save us!

Nobody slept at all in Jericho that night. The war of nerves had begun in earnest!

The children of Israel slept soundly. They knew none of the answers to the questions the Jerichites were asking in such complete panic, but they did not care. They were following orders which came direct from God to His servant Joshua; the reasons for them they would know in His good time. They sat down cheerfully to their evening meal, dipping steady hands in the kettles for lamb bones and pieces of tender kid. Then they stretched themselves out under the spring stars with nothing on their minds save a sense of duty well done.

Joshua was busy, however. He had seen the walls at close range, had studied every foot, realizing that his spies had not exaggerated the weakened condition of them. Every dip and twist of the surrounding terrain was fixed in his mind. He knew now the exact spot where the frontal attack could best be launched and how his forces must be disposed on the appointed day, the spot where, in the meantime, some cautious sapping must be undertaken. Joshua had plenty to occupy his mind that night.

He was up long before dawn to send the summons through the camp for a repetition of the previous day's performance. The tribesmen assembled in exactly the same order, thinking among themselves, no doubt, that this was a curious way to go about the subjugation of a walled city. The seven old men blew the first thin blast as a signal to set forth.

The effect on the defenders can be imagined. Weary from lack of sleep, their nerves raw, they rushed again to the walls, certain that this time the attack would come. They could hardly credit their eyes when the march followed the same monotonous and yet fearsome course of the first day. Again they heard the eerie piping of the horns; again they felt the chill of the Unknown when the shining golden ark came swaying into view. This, they were sure now, was a symbol of the outlandish religion of the strangers, but there was no comfort for them in that. Their scholars had decided it resembled the arks used by the priests of Holy Egypt to enshrine the sacred boats of their gods, and when had Canaan been able to withstand the might of Egypt? Just out of spear throw the nomads marched, with their bitter raised faces, to retire as before to their lair across the trail down to the fords. No sleep for Jericho that night either.

Six continuous days of this. Only heavy, troubled sleep came to Jericho in all that time, with doubled sentries on the walls, with charcoal burning continually under the pitch kettles, with mad scrambles to the battle stations at every unaccustomed sound. Joshua, we can be sure, was calculating the time craftily. Opportunity must be allowed for the undermining of the walls, but not enough for the garrisons of Jerusalem and the other fortress towns up there in the unknown mountains to organize for a relief. He had watchers, without a doubt, on the trails leading up to Jerusalem and Ai and knew that there were no signs as yet of approaching help. His war of nerves would encounter the law of diminishing returns if unduly prolonged, sapping the fine edge of his own troops from the sheer monotony of it. At the end of the sixth day Joshua was ready.

Was seven a lucky number among the children of Israel, then? It had, we know, a religious significance for them, and Joshua would be sure to take advantage of that. One thing is certain: he waited until the most propitious moment had been reached for the blow.

His orders for the day were explicit. First, the circling of the walls was to be repeated seven times; yes, he must have been playing on the sacred significance of the number. Second, the same silence was to be observed until the signal for action came. A long blast on the rams' horns and then all must shout at the top of their lungs; conceive what that would do to the frayed nerves of the watchers on the walls! Third, Rahab and her household were to be spared; the original spies were detailed for this duty. Fourth, there must be no individual looting under penalty of a curse. All silver, gold, brass, iron "shall come into the treasury of the Lord."

There were other instructions, of course, details of a strictly military nature which are not mentioned in the Book. The attack could not be a hit-and-miss affair. It would be so contrived that the best of the fighting men would be massed at the spot where the frontal push was to be driven home. When the seventh and last encirclement began and the hypnotized gaze of the defenders had lost all capacity for sharp observation, the order of the march would be changed. The priests and all the old men and the women and children would draw off, as though wearied by the incessant toil, to be safely out of the way when that mighty shout of all Israel sent the legs of the shock troops rushing to the designated point of attack.

That was how it came about. The seventh slow encirclement had been completed. The sun was straight overhead, its blistering heat raising a haze through which nothing could be seen clearly. This much could be seen, however: that when that sudden, unexpected battle cry went up to the hot dome of the skies one section of the wall heaved and trembled and then fell!

The Book says: "The wall fell down flat, so that the people went up into the city, every man straight before him, and they took the city. And they utterly destroyed all that was in the city, both man and woman, young and old, and ox, and sheep, and ass, with the edge of the sword."

This much we have learned from the work of the excavators. A section of the "curtain" wall on the west had tilted outward and down, over a stratum of plain crushed earth. Here there was no foundation, and little preliminary work would have been needed to start the fall; it is easy, then, to picture a final loosening of supports as the fatal moment drew near, the "curtain" swaying out to slide down the slope in a roar of flying brick and billowing dust. It has been demonstrated, also, that at the same spot a section of the inner wall fell outward into the corridor, forming a ramp by which the besiegers could climb with ease to the top.

There it is, the scientific explanation of how the wall of Jericho fell, a perfect sapping operation.

Picture now the hand-picked warriors scrambling up that heaving mass of rubble, their swords in their teeth, the archers and sling wielders on the sides to keep a continuous volley of arrows and stones beating on the face of the broken wall, so that no defending force could concentrate there to meet the furiously climbing shock troops. Rahab saw it, the only one in the doomed city who had not been thrown into such an extremity of terror that observation was impossible. She saw the triumphant, sun-bronzed tribesmen gain the crest of the broken wall and then drop down the few feet to the rising slope of the crowded city. She saw many terrible sights that day, if her endurance was equal to it: the rise and fall of the flashing steel of Israel, soon dulled to grim black by the congealed blood of the butchered Jerichites; the pursuit of the terror-stricken women into the futile cover of one-roomed homes, even perhaps down into the narrow apertures of the underground tombs; the dashing out of children's brains against the sides of the buildings; the streets and the one sewer running with fresh-spilled blood.

It was thoroughly done, even as Moses had ordered it.

One thing remains to be told. The Book says: "But Joshua had said unto the two men that had spied out the country, Go unto the harlot's house, and bring out thence the woman, and all that she hath, as ye sware unto her. And the young men that were spies went in, and brought out Rahab, and her father, and her mother, and her brethren, and all that she had; and they brought out all her kindred, and left them without the camp of Israel. . . . And she dwelleth in Israel even unto this day."

PART FOUR

Next Step of the Conquest

I

THE FIRST SETBACK AND HOW IT
WAS REDEEMED

THE Book says: "So the Lord was with Joshua; and his fame
was noised throughout all the country."

The tale of the destruction of Jericho unquestionably was
"noised" throughout Canaan with all the additions and embellish-
ments that go with word-of-mouth stories of great events: how
the power of this terrible Yahweh had caused the walls to tumble
at the sound of trumpets and how the warriors under Joshua had
climbed the ruins to slay every man, woman, and child in the
city. No doubt the story grew the farther it spread, the terror of
the Canaanites growing with it, breathless details of sounds and
portents in the sky, of lightnings and tremblings of the earth as
this dread God of Battle sent his children into the fray.

Joshua's first fame would be augmented among the Israelites
themselves by the intimate view they had been allowed of their
great new captain in action. They had seen how skillfully he disposed them for the momentous capture, how he had worked out
every detail in advance. They knew him now, not only as the
appointed of God, but as a leader of remarkable parts. Still, they
were not yet prepared to accept his word in everything.

Semitic society always teems with politics, and Joshua's period can have offered no exception. Every westward step taken by the invading Hebrews was carrying them farther and farther into territory crowded with legends and memories of their own traditional past; land, moreover, rich in prospective spoils. Jericho was merely an obstacle; the sacred places lay beyond. No occupation of the Promised Land could be considered a success until those holy spots were taken under control. Joshua understood this, as Moses had before him. The problem had outgrown the field of tactics and become one of strategy.

Some thirteen miles due west and a little to the north of Jericho lay a very sacred town: Bethel, "House of God." Altars had been built there by Abraham; visits had been paid by Jacob; Deborah's grave lay "under an oak": Bethel was a marked locality. But Bethel possessed something besides religious importance, something older even than Abraham: a commanding geographical position. For this reason it was valued also by Canaanite kings. It overlooked and controlled the highway north from Jebusi to Shechem; that is, from modern Jerusalem to modern Nablus. Moreover, it was the last strong point northward.

Jericho, then, had been a mere tactical objective. Bethel was a strategic one. Its possession meant an open road to a still more sacred and significant place: the head of the pass into Samaria, between the twin peaks of Mount Ebal to the north and Mount Gerizim on the south. There Abraham had built his first altar. There, also, Jacob had hoped to settle down, going even so far as to lay out "an hundred pieces of money," though some say lambs instead, "for a parcel of a field." The base and murderous trick played on the seller's people by Simeon and Levi had frightened Jacob out of his newly acquired realty and driven him on south to Bethel, but the sanctity of the Hivite town called Shechem (like the young man who loved Dinah and paid with his life for his confidence in her brothers) was in no wise impaired. Indeed, in Joshua's day no place in Canaan was holier in tribal tradition.

Moses understood the lines of stategy Joshua must take. This was indicated by the elaborate instructions he left behind concerning the ceremonies which were to be performed at Shechem, *"when ye be gone over Jordan."* He seems to have entertained no doubt whatever that, Jordan once crossed, Israel would reach the Samaritan pass. There six tribes (or perhaps their representatives) were to take post on Gerizim, "to bless the people," and the other six "shall stand upon Mount Ebal to curse." The curses were to be pronounced "unto all the men of Israel with a loud voice"—and a very specific calendar they made. "And all the people shall say, Amen."

Thus the campaign presented to Joshua a personal, as well as a purely military, incentive. Shechem must be occupied, but it would be a deep satisfaction to know that in so doing he would also be rounding out one of his beloved chieftain's most cherished dreams. This element gave point to his extreme disappointment and dismay when his first move toward Bethel and the Shechem road was blocked. Too seasoned a soldier to be cast down by a mere minor setback, with the loss of only "about thirty and six men," some more rankling defeat than the one suffered by his subordinates in the field must have laid him, for the second and last recorded time, "upon his face before the ark of the Lord until the eventide." Bitterest of all regrets is brewed by consciousness of failure in a trust.

What had happened was a virtual repetition of the disastrous attack at Hormah, in the days before the wanderings. Moses, we know, had set his face against that rash attempt. Now, thinking ahead as always, but busied, no doubt, with the thousand and one details of mopping up after the sack of Jericho, Joshua sent scouts up the valley to reconnoiter the city of Ai. Any advance on Bethel must pass under the fortifications of that place. The cautious mountaineers must have kept themselves well out of sight, for the scouts reported back that only a small force would be needed. It was unnecessary to make "all the people to labour thither; for they are but few."

Small blame can be attached to the commander for accepting this report and sending out a relatively small party under one of his lieutenants. After all, the younger men must be given their chance just as he himself had been taught by Moses. One man cannot do everything.

Nevertheless, there was one sound reason why he should not have underestimated the men of Ai.

Although the people of Canaan had never been a unit but had developed into a series of small city-states, they divided ethnologically into two branches. We must not be deceived by the naming of so many varieties of them, the Hivites, the Perizzites, the Girgashites, the Jebusites. The first two are generic terms applied to people who live in villages and labor in the fields: farmers or, to adopt the Egyptian name, fellahin. Girgashite, on the other hand, is designated by some as meaning "city dweller," and we know that the word Jebusite was applied to those who lived in the city of Jerusalem. The occupants of the Promised Land were racially either Hittites or Amorites.

The Hittites were the dwellers in the lower lands, a not very prepossessing lot in the main. They were relatively small in stature, with brownish-yellow skins, prominent hooked noses, receding chins and foreheads. There was no mistaking a Hittite, for he set himself apart by wearing his coarse black hair in three greasy plaits. They lacked the stamina and the toughness of fiber for conflict. If none but the Hittites of that era had barred the way, the conquest of Canaan would have been a relatively easy matter.

The Amorites were a different kettle of fish. They lived up in the hill states and were supposed to derive from the giant people, the Rephaim. This giant strain crops out continually in all Old Testament records—Og and Goliath, the sons of Anak, the Zamzummim of Ammon, men of immense stature and great prowess. The Amorites, who had skin of a golden yellow and sometimes even blue eyes and red hair, were a tough and courageous breed.

Now the men of Ai were Amorites. They would be harder to prevail over than the feeble spawn of Hittite stock who manned the walls of Jericho.

The small force that was sent up against Ai (the Book says two or three thousand, but that must be accepted as nothing more than a translator's exaggeration on grounds already explained) were soundly beaten. Flushed with their easy triumph over the Jerichites, they seemed to have walked straight into a trap. The men of Ai smote them and chased them from before the gate even unto Shebarim, continuing to smite them "in the going down."

It was, in fact, a rout, followed by a headlong scramble down the hilly trails, with the descendants of the Rephaim howling on their heels and picking off the stragglers.

The Book says that "the hearts of the people melted, and became as water."

Joshua took this, his first defeat, very much to heart. He was learning that ultimate lesson for leaders: disaster often treads on the heels of triumph. Philosophize as we will; chide the gods for envy of our success; discover an eternal systole and diastole at the heart of things; postulate an everlasting flux and reflux, positive and negative, plus and minus, *Tao* and *Teh;* we see it happen all too often in the affairs of men. Only the leader who can learn and apply to himself that "high sorrowful" truth can master defeat.

For the first and only time that we hear about, or can deduce from the record, Joshua really was "dismayed." The people had failed him, as Moses said they would. Why, he asks himself (and the Lord), cross Jordan at all, if we are only to be destroyed by these Amorites? "Would to God"—the cry is wrung from him—"we had been content, and dwelt on the other side of Jordan!" And the captain's professional pride was humbled in the dust before the ark. "O Lord, what shall I say, when Israel turneth their backs before their enemies?" All the training and fighting, the discipline and exercises, even the recent exploits and the capture of a first-rate city—all gone to nought!

Naturally he was concerned chiefly with the practical side. News of the defeat would run like fire through the hills, bringing down all the enemy nations that had, up to then, gone in healthy fear of Hebrew prowess. They would unite now "and cut off our name from the earth."

Here Joshua appears, not as the invulnerable and imperturbable hero, but as a very human and disappointed man. We are not told that the noble words, "Be strong and of a good courage," came back to him just then, and in that form. But we are given, in so many words, the equally noble and springing thought that must have stung him to his feet among the elders, muttering of despair there in the dusky tent of the Tabernacle. Loud and clear he heard in his heart that Voice, known of old, calling him to action, not useless wailing: "Get thee up; wherefore liest thou thus upon thy face?"

Wherefore, indeed? The weakness, however humanly understandable, was unworthy. There was work to do. A twofold task: first, he must restore the morale of his troops. That accomplished, he must wipe out the stain of defeat by leading them to an instant victory. The strategic aspect of the problem remained unchanged. Bethel must be taken, which meant that Ai, blocking the way, must first be reduced. Characteristically he went at the imponderable factors first.

The solution he adopted brings Joshua before us in an entirely new light. He becomes the relentlessly logical leader, prepared to sacrifice the individual for the good of the mass. A scapegoat must be found to explain away that shameful route before the men of Ai. He did not have to look far.

One fighting man, and apparently one only, had disobeyed the order against keeping any of the loot of Jericho. It was an open secret in the camp. Achan, the guilty one, could not have carried such considerable booty away from the ruins without some eye observing his disregard of orders. The story had been whispered about, but if it had come to the ears of Joshua before this he had done nothing about it. Now he decided to use the incident without scruple as an easy way of restoring the morale of Israel.

No wonder the thrust against Ai had failed. It was not because of any lack of courage on the part of the men who fought in it. The face of God had been turned away from them because someone had disobeyed Divine commands. Find and punish him, and once again their God would be ready to smile upon them. Such was the reasoning he followed, the course of action that he adopted.

Joshua issued an order: "Sanctify yourselves against tomorrow." An inquisition was to be taken. He insisted on going carefully through all the forms of summons, arrest, and elimination, until the culprit should be detected and, possibly under some pressure, confess. Yet even before the chain of process was set in motion he was at pains to put the people's minds to work in the desired groove. He proclaimed: "Thus saith the Lord God of Israel, There is an accursed thing in the midst of thee, O Israel:

thou canst not stand before thine enemies, until ye take away the accursed thing from among you."

The trial began early in the morning before the closed curtains of the Tabernacle. The name of the offender was well enough known that his tribe, Judah, could be called first. Joshua, though still adhering to the established form of inquiry, did not unnecessarily take up the time of the rest. He called up the Zarhite branch of Judah first and focused the stern attention of the court on the participating representative of that line, Achan, the son of Carmi, the son of Zabdi, the son of Zerah.

It is difficult not to feel some sympathy for poor Achan, standing there in the eyes of all the people, shamefaced, tongue-tied, with no ready defense. He had fought well in the battle, being one of the very first, without a doubt, over the walls. The whelps of the lion of Judah were always in the van when fighting was to be done, and how otherwise would he have come upon such desirable loot so easily? Many Jerichites had fallen to his sword in the brief, frenzied flurry of fighting on the crest of the quaking rubble. He had plunged then into the dark warren of houses, and luck had led him to one of the few which had rich possessions, perhaps to the haikal of the poor booby king of Jericho himself. It was not unnatural that he lusted for the treasures spread before his eyes. Must all these fine things be turned over to the Levites? Latent resentment against the one-hundred-per-cent levy which Moses had imposed welled up inside him. That Babylonish garment, with its rich colors and its decorations in thread of gold, how well it would look on his wife! All that gold and silver, how rich he would be with it, a great man in Israel with wealth to pass on to his sons and daughters!

Well, he had sinned and now he must pay the price.

His guilt was easy to establish. It was written clearly on his flushed and troubled face. Joshua's steady questioning was laying bare his transgression. "My son," intoned the leader, "give, I pray thee, glory to the Lord God of Israel, and make confession unto Him; and tell me now what thou hast done; hide it not from me."

Achan seems to have broken down at once. He answered, "Indeed I have sinned against the Lord God of Israel." Further questioning elicited the whole truth. The treasure he had kept for himself was hidden in the earth under his tent. Messengers were sent at once to dig it up, and when they returned and laid it in full view of all the people a gasp must have gone up from the assembled tribesmen. It had been a noble find, rich enough, certainly, to raise covetous longings in any but the stanchest heart: the Babylonish garment, fit for a queen and perhaps once worn by the queen of Jericho, two hundred shekels of silver, a wedge of gold of fifty shekels' weight: a great haul indeed!

Joshua lost no time in pronouncing sentence: death by the most severe method known to the tribes, stoning. Harsh punishment for the offense, but not too harsh if what the people had been told was valid, that only by the washing out of this crime could the favor of the Lord for all His people be regained. One likes to think that Joshua said the words which sent Achan to death with inner qualms. It is certain, however, that he did not hesitate. He knew these people. Only in this way could they be rehabilitated in their own eyes.

The sentence was carried out at once. Achan was taken to the Valley of Achor. The silver and the wedge of gold, and his sons and his daughters, and his oxen, and his asses, and his sheep, and his tent, and all that he had; everything remotely connected with the crime was taken out with him. The condemned man was stripped of his clothes and stretched out on the hot, burning sand, his legs and arms pegged down so that he was incapable of movement.

Joshua then spoke the final words, clearly for the effect they would have on the assembled people: "Why hast thou troubled us? The Lord shall trouble thee this day."

It is a cruel way to die. The first stones which fall on the body do no more than stun and bruise and then break the smaller bones; it is not until the weight of the growing pile becomes too heavy for the body to withstand that the framework gives way and the lungs collapse and the heart stops. Death comes quickly then in most cases. After the pile has been raised to the proper sacrificial height, it being the custom for each person present to throw one stone, the people leave, it being assumed that the price of wrongdoing has been paid. But sometimes the stones continue to heave slightly for a long time afterward with the labored breathing of the dying man.

The gold and silver and the Babylonish garment and the tent were, presumably, buried under the stones with the unfortunate Achan; none of the heinous evidence could be left. Whether his family and his livestock also died is not specified. Let us hope not.

Now the campaign could be renewed by a confident people, reassured as to their omnipotence and the favor of their Lord. A scapegoat had been found, the stain of defeat wiped out. The Book says, "So the Lord turned from the fierceness of His anger. Wherefore the name of that place was called the Valley of Achor" (which means "troubling") "unto this day."

II
THE TAKING OF AI

In the capture of the city of Ai we see clearly for the first time Joshua, the general, the able strategist. The fight at Jericho had been a minor engagement, a frontal assault over mined walls. It required a much higher degree of generalship to outwit the Amorites of Ai and capture their city up in the hills.

Ai was no inconsiderable place. It had a larger population than Jericho and a strategically strong location. It dominated the little valley which ran up from the Jordan to the hill cities, sitting astride the roads which traversed it. Watchers on the walls of Ai could overlook all the approaches, not only from the fords but from Michmash and Jerusalem. Full in their line of vision was the outline of Rock Rimmon across the valley. Jericho, or what had once been Jericho, down three thousand feet or more in the haze of the Jordan flats, could not be seen from Ai; but the roads which attackers must use, whether they came up the trails from the river or swooped down from the hills, could be kept under observation.

Ai served in a sense as an outpost for the much larger and more important city of Bethel, which was out of sight to the west, around a boulder-strewn hill. There seems to have been an alliance of sorts between the Amorite people of the two cities. Ai lacked water while Bethel had a bountiful spring, which flows amply to this day. The men of Bethel carried water to Ai; the men of Ai stood guard against aggression aimed at either place; that, probably, was the basis of their partnership.

Leading up through the hills was a narrow path. It exists today, probably without change: a winding path, steep and hard to climb, more suited to mountain goats than the feet of men. It ends on a hill to the west of Ai, in a nest of great boulders. No sensible foe would think of marching to the attack up this insignificant and difficult footpath; and, in any event, it had many open spaces where the climbers would be exposed to full view. Unless, of course, they took the precaution of moving by night.

Joshua had reconnoitered the country between Jericho and Ai with his usual thoroughness. When he discovered this little-used path to the back door of his objective the strategic conception of his campaign took form in his mind at once.

He marched his main body by the northerly road, taking two days to do it and breaking the journey at the fine spring of Ain-el-Duk. Scholars explain thus the statement in the Book that Joshua "lodged that night among the people," and later that he "went that night into the midst of the valley." It is not easy marching, and he undoubtedly saw the wisdom of taking his time so that his troops would be fresh for the work which lay ahead of them. It is clear, in any event, that at the end of the march he "pitched on the north side of Ai," at which point there was a valley between his camp and the Amorite city.

The statement in the text that he had thirty thousand men with him is so obviously an impossibility that it hardly merits correction. It would take a long succession of days to move thirty thousand men up the narrow roads between Jericho and Ai, with water available for no more than a tenth of the number; and to send such an army against a small outpost would be tantamount to razing a mountain because a tree barred a path on its crest. Again, the translator's exaggerations: as we recall, the Hebrew character for "thousand" being the same as that for "family."

The second night a picked force, comprising about one sixth of the total strength, reached the west side of Ai after negotiating the narrow path. There they went into hiding behind the rocks and in gullies.

The rest was beautifully simple. Joshua counted on the impetuosity which had already served the mountain men so well. When he was assured that "they had set the people . . . and their liers in wait on the west of the city," he moved out of his own camp, and presumably dawn discovered his forces in position to attack. This, of course, was just what the men of Ai had been hoping for. Had they not already smitten these marauding dogs and chased them back to their kennels? This time they would destroy them utterly.

So out they came, the tall men of Ai, shouting their exultant battle cries. They were so confident that they issued out in full force, leaving no one behind to guard the city. Never was there easier prey; the gates open, the walls unmanned, the women massed outside the city to cheer their men on and see the final extermination of the hated invaders.

Joshua took advantage of the situation with consummate skill. He dropped back before the impetuous Amorites, drawing them farther and farther away from their base, with this difference: that he retreated, not down the valley as before, but to the north, toward Bethel and the dread stretches of the Beth-aven desert. The men of Ai could hardly credit their good fortune. The Hebrew dogs had been thrown into such a panic that they were cutting themselves off from their one line of retreat. All that was needed now was for the forces of Bethel to come out and take them on their other flank, and the disordered Israelites would be driven over into the desert, where such as were left of them would soon die of hunger and thirst. So fast runners carried the amazing news to Bethel town, and soon (so small are the distances) these good neighbors joined in the hunt, for it is recorded that "there was not a man left in Ai or Bethel that went out after Israel."

It was indeed a classic.* Joshua waited until the right moment and then "stretched out the spear that he had in his hand toward

*Many centuries later Alexander the Great, who had never heard of Joshua, captured the city of Tyre with a similar ruse.

the city." The men hiding to the west of Ai were high enough to command a view of the battle being waged to the north of them. When they saw the designated signal from their chief they came out from their hiding places with a rush which carried them down on the defenseless city before the women could close the gates. It was easier than the taking of Jericho. They hacked their way in through the screaming people, and the first intimation that the Amorites had of disaster in their rear was when flames and smoke filled the sky behind them.

They turned and hesitated, not certain whether they should complete the rout of the main Israelite body or hurry back to save what they could of the city. This was the moment Joshua had been waiting for. He turned and struck, and in a trice—so fast can the fortunes of battle veer—the pursuers became the pursured. The Amorites ran. Now they were caught in between, for the ambush force, fresh and keen for their full share of the victory, came out from the burning city. The text describes it thus: "And the other issued out of the city against them; so they were in the midst of Israel, some on this side, and some on that side: and they smote them, so that they let none of them remain or escape."

The inhabitants of Ai were "utterly destroyed," only the "cattle and the spoil" being saved. The record says that "Joshua burnt Ai and made it an heap for ever, even a desolation unto this day."

One prisoner at least was taken alive, the king of Ai himself. He was brought before Joshua, weary and bloodstained, his long red beard a strange thing to see in that country of dark-skinned men, and the Hebrew leader gave him short shrift. The unfortunate ruler was hanged on a tree, and his body was not cut down until eventide, so that all the victors could see him dangling there. Joshua then commanded that they "should take his carcase down from the tree, and cast it at the entering of the gate of the city, and raise thereon a great heap of stones, that remaineth unto this day." A great believer in stones as monuments and reminders, this man Joshua: the circle at Gilgal, the stained heap under which lay the body of covetous Achan, now this grim burying place of the hanged Amorite king. Undoubtedly he knew how potent they were in keeping certain lessons fresh in the minds of his people.

There is no record of what happened to the city of Bethel. In the Book of Judges it is stated that the city fell to the tribesmen of Ephraim and Manasseh, and it is generally assumed from this chronologically distant recording that the capture of the city was much later. But there is no such proof. The site of Bethel proves that its fall was contemporaneous with that of Jericho and Ai. Joshua, moreover, was of the tribe of Ephraim, and did not the agreement with the three sheepherding tribes specify that they would retire to their happy grazing grounds beyond the Jordan as soon as they had played their part in the conquest? The men of Manasseh would not have been fighting on that side of the river if the fall of Bethel had been in the late period generally assigned to it. Never would Joshua have a better chance to settle with the Bethelites than on this occasion when they had ventured out to be in at the kill, leaving their city wide open, their walls unguarded. Nor would he have risked by-passing a town of such strength, leaving the Bethelites free to plague him in the rear through the rest of his hard campaigns.

It is plain common sense to assume, rather, that Bethel fell the same day as Ai, the flames from its burning homes raising a second flare that night against the dark sky.

The next we hear of Joshua is at Shechem, his final objective in this campaign.

There he scrupulously fulfilled all that Moses had desired: altar, inscribed stones, half the tribes on Ebal and half on Gerizim, cursings, blessings—everything. "There was not a word of all that Moses commanded, which Joshua read not before all the congregation of Israel, with the women and the little ones, and the strangers that were conversant among them."

This act of fulfillment must have brought lasting satisfaction and solace to Joshua, now increasingly alone and apart in his leadership.

His visit to Shechem is a late redaction, one of the most recent additions to the Book. But imaginative reconstructors of history should be allowed some freedom, not to guess, but to deduce. No reasonable explanation appears anywhere in the Book of Judges, nor can the scholars offer one, as to why the Israelites were permitted to gather in peace at Shechem. That town was far bigger

and more important than Jericho or Ai or Bethel—the key to
Samaria and the Plain of Sharon.

Moreover, as will be explained later, the astounding march
which Joshua made the next year along this same north-south
road, to strike down the Northern Coalition under the Jabin of
Hazor, could scarcely have been made across the front of a large
and well-fortified town like Shechem. Quite apart from the psychological factors we have discussed, would it not have been the
shrewd and farsighted thing for Joshua to have staged a quick
raid immediately after the elimination of Ai? His men were
flushed with victory; no important defenses barred the way, and
in any future conquests, based as all must needs be on the north-
south line of communication, Shechem would inevitably be of
extreme importance. Would not a great leader reason so?

This, the first real campaign of the conquest, had been a
resounding success. The Israelite forces retired to Gilgal to rest
and prepare themselves for the heavy fighting later, when Joshua
would lead them again to the completion of their task. The
Canaanites left them undisturbed. They had bitter reason now to
fear the hard-striking nomads.

III
A CLOSER LOOK AT CANAAN

A STUDY of the country of Canaan becomes necessary at this
stage if the subsequent course of the conquest is to be understood.
Not all the cities of the Promised Land were as small and poor as
Jericho, and most of them maintained a higher degree of culture.
Canaan had been quite prosperous and even powerful before the
heavy hand of Egypt fell on the land. Thutmose, now lying in
mummified state with a text from the Book of the Dead on his
breast, had reduced all the cities to vassalage by his great victory
at Megiddo. He took back with him after that decisive battle a

catalogue of spoils which can be used as a measuring rod in considering the resources of Canaan: chariots of silver with massive iron wheels, tent poles covered with gold, carts piled high with the gold and silver rings used then for money, armor wrought out of iron, handsome vessels of copper, and pottery decorated with carnelian and amber. For several reigns after Thutmose the cities of Canaan sent yearly tribute to their absentee masters: weapons, tents, mares and stallions, cattle, sheep, goats, male and female slaves, grain, wine, incense, oils, fruit, objects of gold and silver and copper, the finest woods.

The Bible offers this evidence: "For the Lord thy God bringeth thee into a good land; a land of brooks of water, of fountains and depths that spring out of valleys and hills; a land of wheat, and barley, and vines, and fig-trees, and pomegranates; a land of oil, olive and honey."

. It is believed that the Egyptian exactions had ceased before the host of Israel came up, but by that time it was not the land of milk and honey that it had once been. The population was impoverished and weakened; its wealth had been levied on so seriously that a reflection of the poverty and apathy of Jericho was found, in some degree at least, everywhere. The departure of the Egyptian levies had brought not relief and recovery, but anarchy and chaos. The land was ripe for conquest. The timing of the drive was perfect.

. It must have looked desirable to the wanderers fresh from forty years of painful travel in the Negeb, in spite of its many drawbacks. There was not a great deal of water in the mountains; so little, in fact, that the existence of springs explained the selection of most city sites. Bethel had water and was a great city as a result, and Shechem was rich in springs. The land was bountiful only in the valleys. The people of Canaan depended for whatever wealth they had on the fact that their compact little stretch of mountain country lay squarely on the only feasible trade route between the two greatest countries in existence at the time, Egypt and Babylon. Back and forth over the narrow Canaanite roads went the travelers from each country, always glad to stop and refresh themselves and their asses and camels after the hardships of desert trails. The Canaanites inevitably had become a race of traders, keen at a bar-

gain, well versed in money and the value of goods, filled with
book learning, and skilled in writing. In all the larger cities there
were schools and libraries with clay tablets on which had been
set down in cuneiform what man knew then about astronomy and
the geography of the limited world and the laws of Dagan and a
host of other gods.

The cities still lying ahead on the conquering hosts numbered
seventy. Hidden in the folds of the hills and in narrow passes,
crowning all the important crests and dominating the roads, they
stood, large and small, ranging from important and populous
cities such as Jerusalem and Hazor to tiny walled hamlets which
had no excuse for existence save the presence of water. Sometimes
local conditions or deposits had led men to build in curious and
unlikely corners; a mine, or salt flats, or a pool of pitch.

In spite of the exactions of Egypt, the larger cities retained some
of their previous greatness. The walls of Megiddo, as Joshua would
discover later, were twenty-six feet through. The High Place of
Gezer consisted of ten large monoliths, in the Egyptian manner,
on a finely paved court. Other temples of worship were imposing,
with outer courts and elaborately decorated inner sanctuaries,
each with its *parakku*, or mercy seat. There were haikoloth
(palaces) in most of the cities, ornamented in the Babylonian
manner with the rosette, the winged cherub, and the sacred tree.
The murex fish, caught off the Mediterranean coast, supplied the
people with dyes, and so, for ceremonial purposes, they clad themselves in robes of rich purple. They were skilled makers of cloth,
employing spindles and weavers' weights and pins and needles
of bone. They had come even to the making of buttons, which
must have caused the invaders to open their eyes in wonder. They
were sufficiently well supplied with the luxuries of the day to be
able to afford the burying of lamps and rich bowls with their dead.

The nature of the land, however, kept them in a loosely organized state. Canaan had all the advantages and likewise all the
disadvantages of a bridge country. It had no large rivers, with the
exception of the Jordan, which served as a geographic boundary
and played little or no part in commerce. The mountains divided
the land into small tillable pockets and made communication difficult. Canaan had drifted for this reason into a series of weak city-

states, completely independent of each other, fiercely retentive of their small rights and possessions. The fact that each city had its own king aggravated the situation, for kings are the last to see wisdom in any kind of union which destroys or diminishes their own authority. It was this lack of cohesion which made it possible for the invaders to prevail over them. Had they been in a position to combine their strength from the first, it would have been difficult, if not impossible, for the tribesmen to gain a foothold this side of Jordan.

The kings of these little *urus,* or cities, saw the dire need for concerted effort later. Joshua had leveled Jericho to the ground and had burned Ai (and perhaps Bethel) and so had established himself as master of the Ghor and all the passes up into the hills before they could bring themselves to the idea of concerted action. Then it was too late; too late, at any rate, to make headway against an invading force under the leadership of a great soldier like the modest son of Nun.

Joshua realized the advantage he enjoyed from this lack of union among the Canaanites. The course of his subsequent campaigns shows how shrewdly he capitalized on their disorganization, striking first here and then there, appearing unexpectedly on the main roads to cut their communications, gaining for himself opportunities to strike at single cities and to destroy them, giving the bewildered kings no resting spell, driving his fierce tribesmen to ever-greater marches, doubling back to guard his own lines: a supremely fine series of strategic moves against forces of much greater strength.

IV
THE APPEASERS OF GIBEON

THE sun shone down now on a Tabernacle which never had to be moved and in front of which no cloud of fire stood. The children of Israel were at home in the Promised Land. They had reason for content there in Gilgal. Their losses had been slight although the victories had been great. The heat was so intense that the lion of Judah and the aurochs of Ephraim with its twisted horns hung limply on their standards, but the barley crop had been gathered and threshed, and there were bulging sacks of it in every tent. They could enjoy this plenty, for a time at least, in peace.

Joshua knew that the lull would not be forever. When he sat in front of his tent, which opened to the north to catch any wisp of breeze blowing across the steaming Ghor, his mind was full of plans and speculations. Where should the next blow be struck? Should he wait for the Canaanites to make the first move? How long could he hold his quarrelsome tribesmen in the narrow valley of the Jordan floor without bringing their rebellious tendencies to the surface again? He was sitting there one day full of such thoughts when the news was brought to him of strangers in the camp.

This was hard to understand. Not since the tribes had dared the floods by crossing the river had any travelers ventured down the roads to the ford. He asked questions of the men who brought him the word: were the strangers Hittites or Amorites, or did they perchance come from more distant lands? Were they prosperous? What reasons did they give for their presence in the camp?

The answers he received added to his surprise. The newcomers spoke the familiar tongue of Canaan and yet they were footsore, as though their journey had been a long one. They were not prosperous merchants; they were ragged and hungry. They were not spies, for they had come limping into Gilgal in the full light of day, asking for audience with the Israelite leader.

Although the men had been thus described to him, Joshua found food for speculation in the appearance of the strangers when they came before him. Their robes hung on their backs in ragged shreds; the sandals on their feet were worn and broken; the waterskins they carried were patched and leaky. Even the saddle pads on the rumps of their asses were mere rags from long use. They were indescribably dusty and undeniably weary.

"Who are ye? And from whence come ye?"

"From a very far country thy servants have come because of the name of the Lord thy God."

They went on to explain the mission which had brought them such a long distance. They had heard of what He did in Egypt (very old news now, forty years and more), and what He had done to Sihon, king of Heshbon, and to Og, king of Bashan (more recent, but still well back in the past). Because of what they had heard they had taken counsel and had come to make a league with the servants of such a powerful God.

It was not a convincing story. If they lived so far away, what was the need for a league, and how could it operate to the advantage of either party to it? Even the details they hurried to supply in collaboration were suspicious. They pointed to the bread they carried; it had been hot when they left their houses and now, behold, it was dry and moldy. The bottles of wine were whole when they set out and now they were rent. They pointed to their robes and their sandals, calling attention to the condition of them. They were supplying the answers to questions which had not been asked.

Joshua saw through them at once. That is certain from the shrewd course he adopted. Although it had been his custom to make decisions for himself, he decided to share the responsibility this time. He called in the princes of the congregation and let them consider the plea of the strangers.

The reason is not hard to find. Moses had warned against any dealings with the Canaanites. They would become "pricks in your eyes and thorns in your sides." Over and over he had driven the point home, "Thou shalt make no covenant with them, nor with their Gods—nor show mercy unto them." Joshua had no desire to go against the command of the inspired leader, and yet he sensed what this was all about. If the strangers came from the lands just beyond Ai and Bethel, as he suspected, and their purpose was to win immunity for themselves before the next blow could fall, he was prepared to meet them and "make a league" as they begged. The advantages of the plan were clearly manifest to him. Such an alliance would bring him doubtful support, but it would provide him with what he needed most of all, a neutral zone which would mask his own movements and give him both a screen and a base for his operations and which, moreover, would act as a cushion against any surprise thrusts on the part of the hostile cities beyond. A perfect arrangement, this, with all the advantages apparently on one side. Joshua's intention must have been to accept from the very first and yet, in so doing, he would be running counter to the dictates of Moses. No decision, therefore, for him to make alone. The responsibility must be shared by all. For that reason he summoned the princes of the congregation.

The princes, proud to share again in the direction of affairs, considered the offer of the strangers and decided to accede to their request. A league was made with them, by which immunity was assured to all the people of the country from which they came. This was duly sworn to; it is a safe assumption that Joshua saw to that.

Joshua then took the direction of things back into his own capable hands. The emissaries, he decided, must remain in camp. They had come such a great distance that now they must rest—with guards over the tents to which they were assigned. There must be no departure, in fact, until everything had been straightened out and the true basis of an alliance decided upon. In the meantime he sent out some of his trusted men to see what they could find.

He had told them, without a doubt, where to go, for they were back in three days with the proofs he needed. The emissaries were not from a far country; they came, instead, from the four little cities which formed the confederacy of Gibeon, just as he had expected. The dusty robes, the worn sandals, the moldy bread had been part of a shrewd scheme to trick Israel into an alliance which otherwise would not have been granted. Gibeon, in fact, lay no farther distant than twenty miles across the divide, in the path of the next Hebrew thrust. It was to be reached by crossing the valley south of Michmash and the main road between Shechem and Jerusalem and then on a mere mile or two to the spot where the good tracks forked.

The northern track followed the ancient caravan route, skirting the southern slopes of the cave-infested hills, Beth-horon the Upper and Beth-horon the Lower; the southerly one slanted down, along a trace later to be surfaced by the Romans, six or seven miles farther to the "city of woods," Kirjath-jearim, overlooking a four-cross road, one branch of which led back southeasterly to Jerusalem itself. More than that: they had discovered Gibeon to be "a great city, as one of the royal cities . . . greater than Ai," even claiming lordship of a considerable territory, including not only Kirjath-jearim, in its highly strategic location, but the mountain fortress of Chephirah, about halfway between the two westward roads already referred to, and even Beeroth, another town overhanging the Shechem road, about five miles northeast of Gibeon itself and only three miles beyond Bethel.

Israel had indeed been tricked! This fat and fertile quadrangle was the objective of the next campaign, and here the princes of the congregation had granted immunity to the people who dwelt there. It is recorded that "all the congregation murmured against the princes." Wily Joshua!

Now he had things in his own hands and could make the terms he had wanted all along, not only with his own people but with the Gibeonites as well. He summoned the princes a second time.

The deliberations must have been painful for the scapegoat princes who now bore the burden of the alliance into which Israel had so blindly rushed. Joshua, who kept his own counsel and alone seems to have realized the advantages to be gained even though it went contrary to the commands of Moses, was determined that there should be no backing out. He based his decision on the ground, however, that the honor of Israel was at stake. The princes had pledged their word to the strangers, and there could be no repudiation of that. So the unhappy princes reported to the congregation that "we have sworn unto them by the Lord God of Israel; now therefore we may not touch them." There was more murmuring at that, without any doubt; nothing would have pleased the tribesmen more than to take these hypocritical emissaries and stone them to death, as they had done with poor Achan, or to hang them on high trees like the defeated king of Ai. It went against the grain to find their hands tied by the bungling of these stupid princes. What did it benefit them for the warriors to win battles under mighty Joshua if the old men threw away the fruits of victory?

Joshua, who could never be accused now of going against the word of Moses in getting what he wanted, took the next step. He went to the trembling ambassadors to force a rewording of the treaty. It is not hard to picture the scene: the shaken Gibeonites, white now from a very real fear and not from simulated fatigue, hauled forth from their tent to face the consequences of their treachery; Joshua, grim and unrelenting of visage, backed by the princes of the congregation, and behind them again the savage faces of the discontented tribesmen; the stern voice of the leader charging them with their deceit.

"Wherefore have ye beguiled us?" demanded Joshua.

The ambassadors surrendered immediately, humbly, completely. The people of Gibeon, they confessed, had been "sore afraid of our lives because of you." Now they were in his hands. "As it seemeth good and right unto thee to do unto us, do." Abject surrender; they had gambled and lost; now they expected to pay the penalty.

In announcing his decision Joshua went a step beyond what the princes had decided in their deliberations. It had been their intention to make the people of Gibeon hewers of wood and drawers of water unto all the congregation, but that was not enough for their leader. Joshua had not sat for so many years under Moses for nothing. He added a small clause. Just seven little words— barely noticed, no doubt, in the general negotiations and given, indeed, no prominence in the record, but, unless we grossly misjudge both Joshua and the situation, of really great importance. The folk of Gibeon were to be "hewers of wood and drawers of water for the congregation, *and*" (this is Joshua's addition) "*for the altar of the Lord . . . in the place which he*" (Joshua) "*should choose.*"

In its way this is quite as far-reaching and subtle a stroke of diplomacy as Moses' handling of Reuben and Gad. Not private slavery (dangerous in any case with people so closely related in blood and speech, which was why Moses eschewed such relations), but *public service* was to be the lot of Gibeon. Supplies, a base of operation inhabited by people under heavy obligations, willing and even anxious to do his bidding, and plentiful common labor: what more could a commander want who was preparing for a new campaign against greater odds than he had before faced, and in an unfamiliar land?

Now it is in order to consider in detail what Joshua had gained by his handling of the Gibeonites. In case of retreat the going was easy to the Shechem–Jerusalem highway. Then, once over the crest, the tribesmen would again be on familiar ground, the kind they were well used to. In those narrow goat tracks and stony defiles twisting down to former Jericho and Gilgal the skilled desert fighters could hold their own against almost any pursuers from the western plains. That much was clear.

For offensive operations the advantages were equally apparent. The roads of Gibeon were essential to any forward movement; by no other route could Israel march to the conquest of the lands beyond. At one stroke Joshua had won for himself safe conduct over these tortuous trails in the choppy, treacherous hills. Now no hostile bands would lurk in the woods above to harry them in their advance, to swoop down on them in the event of a retreat. Here was the real danger spot in the terrain of still-unconquered Canaan, and it had been turned over to Israel with no stipulations, no heavy price, nothing more than a promise to spare the lives of the Gibeonites in return for their co-operation on terms which amounted to slavery.

PART FIVE

The Sun Stood Still?

I

JOSHUA FACES A DECISION

WORD came down from the hills that the kings of Canaan were ready to strike. It came from Gibeon but also from the scouts that Joshua kept at work up along the deep Wadi Larith and in the mountain passes beyond; he was still not too sure of his new allies and did not depend upon them for his information. The hostile forces were gathering: five kings, no less: Adoni-zedec of Jerusalem, Hoham of Hebron in the mountainous north, Piram of Jarmuth in the valley of Elah, Japhia of Lachish, and Debir of Eglon from farther west on the border of the Philistine coastal plain; a formidable combination.

The combination of the five kings was no mere tribal feud. The Worek River (today the Wadi-el-Surar) is one of the chief landmarks and natural dividing lines of that region. It curves gently southwestward from near Gibeon, then turns west and northwest again past Makkedah, and so cuts off the Hivites of Gibeon from the Jebusites and the other communities southwest from Jerusalem —Jarmuth, Azekah, Lachish, Eglon—all the way to Gaza. Whoever the Hivites may have been, it is clear from modern discoveries that they stemmed from the Hittite power in the far Mesopotamian

north, which was constantly opposed to Egypt. It is easily seen
that their alliance with the invading Israelites, on however humili-
ating terms, threatened to open the gates of a well-defined and
fertile little territory to spoilers who were not of the Egyptian
brand.

Gaza was then, and long before and after, the chief Egyptian
administrative center for Palestine. Jerusalem, rather an outlying
post, nevertheless represented Egyptian authority in its neighbor-
hood and bore a good record of loyalty to the far-off Pharaohs.
The line between it and Gaza must be kept open, and no such
threat on its northern flank as a joinder of rich Hivite with savage
Hebrew could be permitted. Hence the punitive expedition,
gathered by the ruler of Jerusalem, and enlisting contingents from
the main cities down along the Gaza road.

It follows that, in presuming to rescue the Gibeonites, Joshua
was openly colliding with no less than Pharaoh himself—Pharaoh,
that distant and immitigable Power. Moreover, if the plea for
help were a trap, Joshua was facing sheer disaster. Gibeon of the
Hivites was an important traffic station on the highroad from
Jerusalem to Joppa (now Jaffa, near the modern Tel Aviv). Its
water supply and reservoir were famous; its surrounding fields
were fat, and its population was larger than Jericho's. Its three
allied or vassal fortress towns—Beeroth, Chephirah (with its seven-
teen-foot-thick walls), and Kirjath-jearim—mustered, from their
known areas, enough fighting men to bring the total Hivite battle
strength just about level with the Israelite.

Joshua waited. How could he be sure that the mission of the
men with the moldy bread had not been a ruse? How could he
know what was going on today behind the border of Gibeon?
Would they allow the five kings to march secretly across their
land and then strike down the valley before Israel was ready?
Might they not even join in the offensive movement, swelling the
Canaanite army to still greater strength? Could he dare to send
his own men into the nest of Gibeonite towns until he knew what
reception they might expect?

Then runners from Gibeon came panting into the Gilgal camp
with an urgent demand for help. They did not seem to be acting a

part this time. They were covered with dust and white with fear; they had left in such mad haste that they carried no bread of any kind, and there were no wineskins on their backs. "Slack not thy hand from thy servants!" they cried. "Come up to us quickly, and save us!"

Still Joshua could not be sure.

If the proffer of Gibeon had been a ruse in the first place, this might be the final move to draw his army to destruction. Why should they have wanted an alliance with Israel at all, accepting terms which amounted to labor enslavement? If, as the runners said, the five kings were already encamped before Gibeon, would they risk destruction by holding to such a one-sided arrangement? They would be more likely to make terms, and an essential provision of such terms might be this effort to lure the Hebrew forces up into the hills.

On the other hand, they might be making an honest effort to live up to the alliance, preferring servitude and security under Israel to the uneasy independence which was all they could hope for if the five kings prevailed. If they were honest, then the strategic advantages were great. The besiegers would be caught between Gibeon in front and Israel moving up on their rear. In that event quick action should be taken lest the perfect opportunity be lost.

And if they were not honest? When the children of Israel crossed the Jordan it was for the purpose of fighting the whole of Canaan and in supreme confidence that the hand of their dread Lord would direct them to victory. Not until Gibeon held out the olive branch had they hoped for a division among their enemies. If, then, the worst construction was to be put on Gibeonite motives, the invaders were no worse off than they had expected to be in the beginning. That was certain enough. If the country of Gibeon could now be cleared with the assistance of its people, Joshua would have the advanced base he needed for all subsequent campaigning. It had to be cleared eventually, with or without their aid, or there would be no Promised Land to inherit. Israel could not be content with the small triangle of land already conquered. The eastern slopes of the mountains overhanging Jordan did not flow with milk and honey, and the crops that could be raised on the baked river floor would not suffice to support them very long. The hills beyond and the fertile valleys which nestled between them must be taken.

But should the struggle be joined on terms set by his opponents? Joshua suspected that the five kings would not be rash enough to attack Israel in the valley. Perhaps it would be wiser to let his tired tribesmen rest before taking up the gage. Joshua could well afford to bide his time and strike when he was ready, even though the city of Gibeon fell to the armies now camped before it. This was a more important matter from a purely military standpoint than any considerations based on the intentions of the Gibeonites themselves.

Joshua knew, moreover, that he was under no compulsion to go to their aid. The terms of the league, as reported, had not guaranteed them help against outside attack. Nor, for that matter, was Gibeon bound to fight for Israel. It might be a costly gesture if he moved to their assistance now.

But was this a decision which could be made on purely military grounds? The humble Hivites of Gibeon had sent down to Israel for help in their extremity, confident that the might of the Twelve Tribes would be unleashed. "Slack not thy hand from thy servants!" There was all the appearance of honesty in that impassioned plea. If they had placed themselves in jeopardy by entering into the league could Israel selfishly leave them to their fate? "Thy servants," they called themselves; could the master hold back and see them perish?

All these conflicting considerations ran through the swift mind of Joshua as he listened to the men of Gibeon. He made no pretense of calling in the princes of the congregation this time; his was the decision in all points of war, and his alone. We believe it did not take him long to make up his mind.

The summons must be heeded! Action now, not calculation any more. What if he had not intended to measure his strength so soon against the armies of the five kings? They had forced the issue, coming up to give battle on their own. So be it!

Up, banners of Israel! The rams' horns sounded through the tents of Gilgal as the fighting men donned their armor. The anxious women, who had hoped for a long period of peace before their men sallied out again, stifled their fears as they filled bags with meat and bread for the warriors to sling over their shoulders. Behind the curtains of the Tabernacle the priests were swinging censers and lifting their voices to Jehovah for the aid which had been promised them.

Israel would strike hard and strike fast.

II
THE DEFEAT OF THE FIVE KINGS

There is little recorded about the victory over the five kings; little, that is, to help in arriving at any conclusions as to how this very complete victory was won. It is clear that Joshua employed the element of surprise, for the Word says, "Joshua therefore came unto them suddenly, and went up from Gilgal all night." That is all we have to go on from a purely military standpoint.

We must endeavor to fill in the outline from what we know of this leader and his methods.

The five kings were sleeping in their tents, and silence wrapped the whole encampment. Sentries had been posted, of course, but only on the side facing the beleaguered city; there was nothing to be apprehended from the other direction yet. The five kings had retired to their slumbers in a mood of complete confidence. They knew how weak the Gibeonites were. In the morning they would launch an attack up those steep slopes on which the city perched, so thickly planted with vines and olive trees. There would be ample cover for the advancing platoons, and the siege ladders could be planted against the walls with less than the usual risk. Yes, it would be an easy matter to drive those weak-spined renegades from their battle stations and gain an entrance into the city. The kings slept soundly.

There was a complete lack of confidence in Gibeon. High up on their hill the night guards, pacing nervously along the tops of the walls, could look down over the whole of the hostile camp. They looked beyond it more often, however, straining their eyes for the first signs of approaching relief. The Gibeonites, as we have reason to know, were not a fighting lot. They shared fully the conviction of the sleeping kings. They had one hope only: that their new allies—their masters, rather—would arrive in time.

The vigil of the anxious pacers on the top of the walls was rewarded sooner than they had dared to hope. Dawn was breaking. Was something moving there in the eastern breach of the hills? They peered in that direction, their heads together in huddled speculation. Yes, someone was coming. Was it only the runners they had dispatched in such desperate haste to Gilgal, returning to report—failure? No, the signs of movement in the pass indicated the approach of a considerable body. Hope sprang high in the hearts of the watchers, changing to an exultant certainty when the first rays of the sun glinted on the metal points of spears: many spears, filling the faintly traceable ribbon of trail, spreading out on each side. No sound reached the city—the approaching army was still too far away—but to the peering eyes up there on the cold walls it was clear now what had happened. Israel had hearkened to the plea of Gibeon! The fighting tribesmen had marched all night up the winding roads, and now here they came, spreading out over the edge of the plain, ready to strike.

Dawn showed the besieging army still unaroused: men sleeping in the open, their spears stuck in clumps into the ground, the canvas flaps still drawn over the openings in the tents of the slumbering kings, no smoke yet rising from breakfast fires. The sentries, strolling wearily along the base of the hill, could not see what was happening back there in the east. They had eyes only for the walls above them, speculating, no doubt, on the loot that the day's fighting would bring.

The silence held. The hosts of Israel drew closer. And then it came, the sound of trumpets: not the faint tooting of priestly horns as at Jericho, but the full-pitched, brazen, rousing blast of the call to battle, shattering the morning calm, throwing the sleeping camp into a complete panic. The gleeful watchers on the walls could see how complete the panic was: men springing to their feet, staring stupidly in the direction of the sound, the tents bursting open to emit the overconfident kings, the screech and whinny from the horse lines.

Israel had indeed "come unto them suddenly."

Clearly the battle began that way, for the more complete details that are supplied of the pursuit indicate that the rout was an early one. The beaten remnants of the Canaanite hosts streamed past Beth-horon, which is a full five miles west of Gibeon, in the early hours. They were being driven through the Valley of Ajalon before nightfall, and that lies ten miles west of Gibeon. A running battle over those twisting roads and sinister hills would consume many long hours. It may be assumed, therefore, that Joshua's attack was launched with sufficient suddenness to turn the battle into a retreat without prolonged fighting under the walls of the city.

The basic principles of tactical warfare were unquestionably the same then as now. A good general would understand the advantages of concentrating his forces on a given point. He would be wide awake to the possibilities of outflanking, of holding his reserves to be thrown in at the crucial moment. We know that Thutmose, who was a very fine leader, won the battle of Megiddo by throwing a part of his army around the west of the walled city, catching the Canaanites on their exposed flank, and then leading a general advance against the center, his tufted helmet showing high above the press as he drove forward in his glittering electrum chariot.

Having caught his foes unprepared, Joshua's problem was a simple one: to strike hard with all the forces at his disposal, putting everything into the initial blow. It was not too difficult, apparently, to effect the rout, sending the armies of the five kings in full retreat for the caves of Beth-horon and the Vale of Ajalon straight ahead.

In that limestone land of steep weathered hills and narrow valleys there were not many routes for the fugitives to take. Some went northwest by Beth-horon, Upper and Lower, on the old caravan trail, and some southward toward the Elah River. Still others escaped westward by the way of the ancient hot springs at Emmaus, two or three miles beyond the city of Ajalon and the pass through the hills to the Sorek River. On the northern horn of this pass lay a strong place called Gezer, whose king seems to have sympathized with the allied five but who had been unwilling, or perhaps had not been invited, to join them in this operation. Later he came into the war, with consequences which will be related in due course. Down the valley six or seven miles stood Makkedah.

The five defeated kings ran away faster than their unfortunate followers, or else they started to run sooner. At any rate, they kept far enough ahead of the avenging blades to reach what they hoped would be a safe hiding place in a cave near the city of Makkedah. It can be assumed, moreover, that not one of the five was down in the heat of the fray, directing and leading the troops that he had marshaled for the campaign. An unworthy lot, these five craven kings. Apparently they had viewed the fighting from some vantage point and, when it was clear that the day was lost, had gathered up their kingly robes and led their men in flight.

Their hiding place could not have been too wisely chosen, for their presence in the cave was promptly discovered and reported to Joshua. Welcome news to a victorious leader! He paused to think and to wipe the perspiration from his brow, being the kind of leader who was always in the thickest of the fighting. The thought may have run through his mind, How would the Master have turned this happy circumstance to best advantage? Perhaps by this time he had developed in himself the ability to capitalize and dramatize such fortuitous happenings.

He issued an order at once: "Roll great stones upon the mouth of the cave, and set men by it for to keep them."

A wise decision, this, from two standpoints. The pursuit must not be slackened to witness the capture and delivery to punishment of the beaten kings. The enemy must not be suffered "to enter into their cities." Furthermore, the treatment of the runaway leaders must be reserved for a more spectacular setting, when all Israel would be there to see.

The battle over, the weary fighting men returned to the rallying point of Makkedah. Their swords were black with blood, and on their backs they carried the spoils of victory: armor and weapons and the trinkets they had hastily snatched from the bodies of dead foes, most of which would find its way at once into the coffers of the Temple. There were no Achans here. *That* lesson had been well learned. They were bone-weary after a night of marching and a day of incessant fighting, but there was much exultant shouting and a buzz of loud talk. A great victory had been won, and it must have seemed to them that all of the Promised Land was now theirs for the taking.

The noise died down when Joshua advanced to the open space in front of the cave and gave his second order, addressed to the men who had stood guard outside the entrance:

"Open the mouth of the cave, and bring out those five kings unto me."

It is difficult to feel any sympathy for the craven captives. Out they came, blinking their eyes in the sudden light, cringing when they found themselves confronted by the whole of Israel: an unkingly lot, though they wore on their arms the gold bracelets of anointed authority and helmets of silver and gold on their heads—Adoni-zedec, Hoham, Piram, Japhia, and Debir, the five leaders who ran away in a body and hid.

The wise psychologist (showman, in modern phrase) now peers out at us from under Joshua's helmet. He had planned to make the most of this episode, to use it as an aid to Hebrew morale. First he called up the captains of his men of war and said: "Come near, put your feet upon the necks of these kings."

The captains obeyed the order. While guards held the five prostrate bodies each tribe leader placed his foot not too gently on each royal neck in turn. Marauding dogs, were they, uncouth robbers from the desert! If they had ever accepted these epithets, if any sense of inferiority still lingered in their minds from the days of servitude in Egypt, this ceremony put an end to it for all time. A mere captain of an Israelite tribe had been good enough to set his tired heel on the squirming necks of the kings of Canaan. The circle of warriors pressed closer to watch, laughing and jeering, absorbing the lesson which Joshua had prepared for them.

Then, of course, he hanged them. Adoni-zedec, Hoham, Piram, Japhia, and Debir were led in turn to separate trees and hanged on the highest limbs so that all Israel could see them suspended there. And they were not cut down for a day.

Perhaps Joshua had a still deeper purpose in thus punishing the kings who had made the first concerted attack of Israel. Since

Thutmose first overran Canaan it had been incumbent on the kings of all the cities to send their first-born to Thebes as hostages. A young man thus held was never permitted to return home until the word was received that death had vacated the throne, and he was then sent back in state to assume whatever authority and trappings went with such petty kingship. Word of the killing in one day of five kings would reach Egypt in due course and would accomplish the purpose of serving notice on the absentee suzerain that a new order had come about, that the children of Israel were taking Canaan as their own, and that the rule of Egypt was definitely over.

This effort to tell in plain and common-sense terms what happened that day will appear strange to readers who have been firm in their belief that the defeat of the five kings was not only the most spectacular battle of all time but the most miraculous event since the beginning, when God created heaven and earth, for it was during the struggle which began under the walls of Gibeon and ended in the Valley of Ajalon that something very extraordinary was reported to have taken place. It was in the course of this crowded and eventful day that Joshua raised his arms (at least he is always so depicted by the many artists who have painted the scene) and cried, "Sun, stand thou still upon Gibeon; and thou, Moon, in the Valley of Ajalon." And, as the Book records, "the sun stood still, and the moon stayed, until the people had avenged themselves upon their enemies."

To have left out from the foregoing description of the battle all mention of this great upheaval, by which the world ceased its endless spinning through space and the moon suspended its majestic course across the night skies, by which, in fact, the whole of the then-known universe became static and expectant while two small bands of sweating men fought out their issue with sword and spear and arrow and sling, is not because it was intended to let the passage stand without question or attempted explanation. So many issues are involved, however, that a full section must be devoted to the discussion.

III
DID THE SUN STAND STILL?

It should be pointed out, first, that the Bible quotes in this instance and does not *record*. Immediately after the direct passage set down in the previous section these words appear: *Is not this written in the book of Jasher?*

The Book of Jasher! That is a different matter. In the days of King David, or later, there existed a collection of songs or stories about the heroes of the past, a Hebraic laudation on the order, no doubt, of the northern sagas, the *Song of Roland* and the fables of the Knights of the Round Table. "Jasher" means, literally, "upright men," and we may assume that in it was recorded all the brave and noble deeds of the great fighting men of early Semitic history. The book unfortunately has vanished, although its importance as a collection and a source cannot be minimized. That it was of first importance once is evident from its numerous progeny, all rejected now by scholars as spurious.

One other quotation from the Book of Jasher appears in the Bible. When David was resting at Ziklag after the slaughter of the Amalekites a man came to him with news of the death of both Saul and Jonathan, bearing with him for the new king the crown that had been on the head of Saul and the bracelet that was on his arm. David rent his clothes and pronounced that incomparable threnody over the dead leader and his son, beginning "The beauty of Israel is slain upon thy high places; how are the mighty fallen! . . . Saul and Jonathan were lovely and pleasant in their lives, and in their death they were not divided." Injected into the text before the opening of the lamentation are the words: "Also he bade them teach the children of Judah the use of the bow: behold, it is written in the book of Jasher." It is a very obvious interpolation; so obvious, in fact, that the reverend divines, who are responsible for our form of Holy Script, went so far as to decree that this piece of extraneous information be segregated between parentheses. It is worth noting, however, because it indicates how unerringly the author, or authors, of the Book of Jasher seized upon the most dramatic incidents for their pages. What a great pity that it is lost! What brave tales have been riven from our knowledge by its disappearance: romantic and colorful detail, no doubt, from the lives of unhappy, troubled, courageous Saul, of greathearted Jonathan, of Samson the mighty, of the sons of Anak. Deeds as great as any we have heard are lost forever in those vanished pages. Perhaps, and this is hardest of all to accept, Joshua's contribution to Hebraic history would burgeon into a well-correlated and detailed story if all the evidence from the Book lay before us now.

Even without benefit of the vanished Book this one legend has laid heavier imaginative toll on Joshua's memory than any other, except possibly the walls of Jericho. One can, if one so desires, accept it as written and translated, without thought, consideration, or explanation. Many have done that; many still do. Hear Josephus, probably at or near the beginning of the devout chain: "Moreover it happened that the day was lengthened, that the night might not come on too soon, and be an obstruction to the zeal of the Hebrews in pursuing their enemies. . . . Now, that the day was lengthened at this time, and was longer than ordinary, is expressed in the books laid up in the temple."

Thereby hangs the whole tale: upon a reference to a lost record, the only other quotation from which refers to a circumstance irrelevantly interpolated in a dirge over deaths occurring some four hundred years later! For Joshua to wish for more time, for more daylight in which to consolidate his victory, was but natural. The apostrophe to the sun and moon, whoever said it or thought it, is magnificent in its simple grandeur. But is it imperative to its effectiveness, or to Joshua's fame, that we postulate astronomic compliance? Surely not. The records of all great battles are spiced with admittedly fictitious sayings and orders delivered by the great captains. Granting that the same liberty in dramatic recording may have been taken in the case of Joshua, we may again free our contemplation of his achievements from the shackles of miraculous origin. Defeat of the five kings by a surprise night march, and covering over twenty miles in a four-thousand-foot climb, cutting loose from the base at Gilgal, is miracle enough. The rout beginning at Gibeon must have been confused and painful. By Ajalon Valley it has obviously become a ghastly riot of bloody death, "a very great slaughter, till they were consumed."

We know that the attack must have come in the very early morning. Some resistance was surely made, both on the ground and during the retreat. Ten miles by air; say a good fifteen on foot, with hot and dangerous work every step of the way. A fair day's work for retreating men under pressure to reach Ajalon stream by nightfall.

Is not this exactly what Joshua (or someone, recording his exploit in the Book of the upright men for him) tells us? "Sun, stand thou still *upon Gibeon;* and thou, Moon, *in the valley of Ajalon.*" When Gibeon was left behind and the victorious tribes plunged into the ravines and broken ground to the west, every rock and cave (the place is full of caves) hiding an enemy at bay, the sun was already up. All that day they fought and struggled and followed after, until eventide, when they reached the stream. And behold! the great moon rose at their backs, then, over Ajalon. It swam high in the heavens before they broke off and made camp so they could sleep.

Such is a reasonable reconstruction. Yet again certain experts have explained the joint astral performance by postulating a waning moon, which would therefore still be visible, "smote by the fresh beam of the springing east," at Gibeon "in the morning." Once more, why? Supposing Joshua (or some other poet) to be addressing this dual phenomenon *at Gibeon* in the morning, what grounds would he have had to expect the show to be still visible *at Ajalon,* nearly ten miles away? Why not (if he were prophesying, or even only guessing) choose Azekah, or Jarmuth, or Makkedah? Why stop at Ajalon?

Common sense supplies the answer: because that is where the poet himself stopped. Yet this half-baked idea, without straw, like the political bricks in Jericho's walls, leads its promoter to feel confident that Joshua made his night march from Gilgal in "light from the waning moon, as appears from the further details of the narrative"; said details being simply and solely the poetic phrase under discussion, which, as we have already seen, is highly suspect, clinging as it does to only the most shadowy of textual coattails: the lost Book of Jasher.

Now, no practical man would for one moment believe that Joshua would wait on the moon to carry out an urgent relief. The rough, steep path he probably took slips in between the ridge fortress of Beeroth to the north, which was presumably friendly, or at least subject, to Gibeon. Men using it would, it is calculated, be invisible from each. No moon at all might have suited Joshua better; on the other hand, with safe defilade on both flanks, light would be welcome on that rocky path. Anyway, the poet says there was a moon over Ajalon the next evening. What of it?

What neither experts nor pious commentators seem to have insisted on enough is the way in which this whole incident brings out a major characteristic in Joshua: his boldness. We know he was careful, never reckless or indifferent to any advantage. But we may wonder whether, in taking his men on that punishing all-night scramble and committing them at the end of it to an unknown length of desperate fighting, without rest or sleep, he knew all that we do.

That, perhaps, is beyond the point. We know that Joshua had taken the risk. We know that sun and moon, as the poet sang, spanned that day. Do we need this interpolation, from a vanished record, with its magnificent imagery of the universe standing still that Israel might improve her victory, to complete our conception of a great exploit?

With or without benefit of Divine interruption, Joshua had smitten his foes so mightily that thereafter, for a time at least and in that territory, "none moved his tongue against any of the children of Israel."

IV
PALIMPSEST OF HISTORY

MILITARY men are notorious lovers of precedent. This is only human, since a soldier must train himself for one end only: success. And success, moreover, in the most dangerous, most complicated, and most risky business that men can undertake. At first glance it seems odd, to say the least, that so uniformly successful a record as Joshua's, such easy mastery of terrain, such precise adjustment of effort to the obtained result, should not have been studied more closely by the professionals. His exploits have, in addition, the very great advantage of a locale almost unchanged since his day. Fenced cities may have vanished, but their sites remain. Railroads and motor highways must still follow the same contours as did Hivite, Jebusite, and Israelite. Lebanon and Anti-Lebanon still grimly guard the weird gash in the earth's crust from Mount Hermon south to the Dead Sea. Compared to most, the theater of war is astonishingly small and astonishingly well preserved.

Several obvious factors contribute to this neglect. The semi-sacred patina acquired since the Christian era by the ancient Jewish tribal records, due to their continuity with the story of Christ, has almost entirely protected them from profane scrutiny. Once the accumulation has been accepted as the "Canon of Scripture," its contents are admittedly of Divine origin and authority. They are beyond question or correction. Josephus relates that no one had dared to add, subtract, or change, for some five hundred years before his day; that is, since the time of Ezra and Nehemiah. The thirty-nine "books" now used as biblical divisions were then grouped into twenty-two, corresponding with the twenty-two letters in the Hebrew alphabet, the five double letters coinciding with the five double books: Samuel, Kings, Chronicles, Ezra, and Jeremiah; an ingenious and convenient arrangement, whether or not divinely inspired.

The Book of Joshua, although not rated among the Pentateuch —the first five—and so not considered, by Philo Judaeus, for example, as a part of the integral teaching, was very early included in the Canon and has partaken ever since of its privileged and immutable character.

So the admiration and respect which should long ago have been Joshua's, from the very class of men he best understood, the statesmen-soldiers, has been withheld. He was lucky, it is assumed, to have been assisted by miracles just when he needed them most. And if they were not miracles they could not have happened at all.

The brief, bald chronicle of sacks and marches that we find in his Book brings no message to the student. Better stick to Lee in his wilderness, or young Bonaparte's successful bluff in Italy, or even Caesar's pedestrian and dog-eared daily catalogue.

Another obstacle is the familiar textual one. An instance meets us at this precise juncture in the campaign. Immediately after the pursuit to Ajalon Valley and the scattering in other directions of the allied forces it is stated that "Joshua returned, and all Israel with him, unto the camp to Gilgal." This does not make sense. The next twenty-eight verses, outlining the operations which we are about to consider, are specific and detailed. The map confirms the text at every essential point. Joshua "mopped up" at Makkedah and roundabout, then started south to smash the centers of resistance there, and afterward returned to Gilgal. There would be no point whatever to his re-entering Gilgal *beforehand*, only to retrace his steps to where the five kings were hiding in a cave at Makkedah, and *then* move down-country. He was as detached from his base, after the victory at Gibeon, as was Sherman in Georgia. Return would have been a complete loss of the initiative. It would have wasted precious time and have allowed the allied leaders to escape. They could not, after all, be expected to let themselves be bottled up in their cave, even behind "great stones," until it might suit Joshua to come back after them. Most important, perhaps, of all: such a move would have confessed weakness, or timidity, or doubt of his strength for further attack.

But there stands the statement. It is awkward until we note, in the very twenty-eighth and last of the following verses, its word-for-word repetition: "And Joshua returned, and all Israel with him, unto the camp to Gilgal." Clearly the first exemplar is out of place. The second alone properly and naturally closes the account.

Earnest scholars, charged with instructing the laity in these matters, have traced out Joshua's movements on the map. Yet the map itself shockingly confutes them. Printed schematic plans exist, showing him to have reached as far as Gaza, thence to Hebron (which he did do), and from Hebron all the way to Kadesh-barnea, some forty miles *south* of the southern tip of the Dead Sea! Then they indicate his return to Gilgal along that sea's western shore, under the mountains, through that same wilderness of Judah which had blocked the tribes in Moses' time—something which no traveler in his right mind would try to do, when the perfectly good main highway, trod for uncounted centuries between Syria and Egypt, lay open only fifteen miles to the west.

Such carelessness would elude our comprehension were we not on guard against the power of the text. And this time our vigilance is well rewarded. Right after reporting Joshua's return to camp the sacred text summarizes the campaign. This is entirely normal and usual. "So Joshua smote all the country of the hills, and of the south, and of the vale, and of the springs, and all their kings. . . . And Joshua smote them from Kadesh-barnea even unto Gaza, and all the country of Goshen, even unto Gibeon." But it does not say that Joshua *attacked* Gaza or Kadesh-barnea; only that he "smote" the "country." The summary is in general terms; the details have already been given.

The inclusive expression "from Dan to Beersheba" is familiar throughout the Old Testament. It indicates what we might call the "length and breadth." Modern maps still use it, and the limits which it names, to frame their Palestines. Dan, we have seen, originally Laish, was situated on the southern slopes of Mount Hermon. Beersheba was a station on the caravan route to Egypt, twenty-five miles or so south of Hebron. The two places were simply geographic pegs or markers, easily identified as coinciding with the extreme north and the extreme south.

So of Gaza and Kadesh-barnea and all the land of Goshen, between Philistia and the lower Dead Sea; not to be confused with some other territory, said to be in Egypt, for which the Hebrews used the same name. Joshua's campaign seems, indeed, to have subdued the land between: roughly, Gibeon on the north, Gaza on the west, and the lower Dead Sea on the south. But there is no justification whatsoever for confusing a brilliantly clear series of tactical moves by tying them to impossible and absurd objectives. The text is indeed strong, but it should not now be too strong for us.

One of the keenest of human pleasures must be that vouchsafed to those persons who are able to resurrect long-forgotten beauty. The restorer who watches, inch by inch, some masterpiece of painting reveal itself under the peeling layers of later botch-work; the expert whose instruments disclose some vanished manuscript under the palimpsest: these are privileged souls whose feelings we cannot hope to share. But we can perhaps guess at them as we apply ourselves, map and Bible page in hand, to searching back through three thousand years. Under the age-old phrases, left so long undisturbed in even their probable contradictions, and between the dry monosyllables marshaled in their majesty of "purest English undefiled," we begin to see, or can believe that we see, emerge a flawless product of human forethought, courage, and achievement. No doubt the long weathering of time has obliterated many details that, in more recent instances of applied military art, compel us to admit the often paramount influence of chance or luck in these matters. Many times the winner clearly should have lost, and vice versa. But, as with the classic Greek buildings and statues, where the lapse of years has washed away the paint and gilding which we know their builders doted on, leaving their perfect proportions to stand out only the more clearly for being naked, so it is here. The problems of supply Joshua faced, the effects of weather and temperature, the accidents of march and bivouac, the specific orders of the day he issued—we are spared all these. What remains is the bare but utterly sufficient and convincing outline, and a deepening and solidifying impression of a man.

PART SIX

The Campaign Proceeds

I

JOSHUA HAD NO MAP

THE five kings are dead, but their cities remain: Lachish, Eglon, Jarmuth, Hebron, and, above all else, Jerusalem. At this distance in time it is impossible for us to reckon the relative importance of these little hill towns. Much less can we tell why, at this point, Joshua neglected Jarmuth, which lies only a few miles east of Gath, and apparently ignored Jerusalem entirely.

At the risk of undue repetition, we must give warning at this point that some of the scholars reject as a much later contribution the entire campaign which we are about to consider. So, we have seen, do they reject the raid on Shechem. Possibly the uniformity of the victories reported indicates a subsequent glorification of the affair. But, as with Shechem, the story makes so much sense and illustrates so well the qualities of leadership which the man who conducted the operations must have possessed, that one feels justified in accepting what is, after all, the only evidence we have.

There is, besides, the highly probable incident of the Gezerite pursuit, which the scholars thus calmly ignore, although they admit the great contemporary importance and power of Gezer, as well as its close Egyptian connections. If Jerusalem, up at the far end of the branch road from Gaza, felt bound to punish the

Hivites for allying themselves with the invading tribes, how much more would Horam, King of Gezer? He was far more of a political and military factor than the Jebusite Egyptian puppet. His town was virtually Egyptian, in religion and culture. Its walls were fourteen feet thick, with no less than thirty towers and a subterranean water channel. He dominated both the coast road from Gaza, from a distance something under ten miles, and the Jerusalem–Joppa road to his own north. It seems most unlikely that such a ruler, so placed, having failed to fall upon the pursuing Hebrews as they passed below his city, would not have felt it due both to his loyalty and to his own personal pride to turn out after them. Which adds another reason for our trying to pierce the many veils between and for preferring to accept as it is given the rest of Joshua's southern campaign.

There is still another reason, more nebulous, perhaps, yet equally compelling. If Joshua did return direct to Gilgal, after driving off Gibeon's enemies, what would he have accomplished? No more than another raid. What position would that have been for a claimant to suzerainty over Gibeon and all its vassal territory? The thing would have been absurd. Joshua, if he returned at all, must return with more than just a surprise victory to his credit.

At first sight, as already stated, we cannot see why, at this juncture, Joshua apparently neglected the troops of Jarmuth and Jerusalem, particularly the latter. Jarmuth was a rallying point in the heart of the territory he was planning to subdue, and the Jebusite people of Jerusalem were presumably the least knocked about by the Gibeon fight. The Israelites had pursued to the west and south, not to the southeast. Consequently the Jebusites could have retired in fairly good order around the headwaters of the Sorek and down the highway to their citadel. Was not Joshua violating a fundamental military precept by not following up and destroying the enemy's main field forces while still in being? Was he not also risking further trouble by leaving Jarmuth on his flank?

Not that Joshua seems ever to have hesitated over mere risk, but what he does now seems almost foolhardy, even for him.

We can guess that Jarmuth would be, in his judgment, overawed or at least "contained" by what he was planning to do to its western neighbor, Gath. We can also guess that Jerusalem gave

him and his victory-flushed fighters no trouble at all on their triumphant northward march back to Gilgal, for which reason the
place, though strong, cuts no figure in the subsequent record of
the campaign. We must also admit, if we study the map, that
Joshua was perhaps justified in leaving Jerusalem to be dealt with
later. Hebron, twenty miles south of it on the highroad, was the
obvious key. After that only Jerusalem would bar the way home,
and the Jebusites could be dealt with then.

As to Eglon and Lachish, however, we have no way of entering
Joshua's thoughts. But in considering the question, we have one
advantage: we have a map. If we press that advantage we begin
to appreciate how completely sound was his decision. His conception of the strategic situation and his faultless handling of it on
the ground become things only the more to admire when we
realize that, unlike us, Joshua had no map.

Eglon and Lachish lay at the southwest corner of a quadri-
lateral. The north was bounded by the westward line, Gibeon–
Makkedah; the west by the southward line, Makkedah–Eglon; the
south by the eastward line to Hebron; and the figure is closed by
the northward line up the highway along the backbone of the
mountains, through Bethlehem and Jerusalem, back to Gibeon.

This quadrangle contained about all the useful territory in
Joshua's southward purview. It lay entirely on the westward
watershed and comprised much desirable land: witness its many
fine cities and the numerous streams irrigating its mild slopes.

On all four sides, furthermore, this nearly perfect square was
bordered by far less promising country: to the north, the forbid-
ding mountain mass later named for Ephraim; to the east, the
frowning heights and barren shores along the Salt Sea; south, the
all-too-familiar deserts of the wandering; and west, the profitless
plain where dwelt a fierce and rapacious sea people, the wandering Philistim. Whoever ruled that square ruled all of southern
Canaan that Joshua's people could use. More of it they did not
need, and more of it Joshua did not plan to take.

Few, indeed, are the conquerors who, in full tide of success, can
recognize the limits of their effort; not the military limits, but
those within which their chief object, the well-being of their
people, can be attained. Joshua, it would appear, was one such. At

least the appalling tale of bloody ruin and bitter slavery which is Israel's, following upon its subsequent overlapping into, or being overlapped by, the lands and peoples outside Joshua's quadrangle, down the centuries to this day, seems to underline the wisdom of his restraint.

This, then, was the tactical theater: a square some twenty-five miles on a side, cut by many westward-flowing streams, filled with jumbled valleys growing deeper and steeper as the ground rose to its eastern edge. Joshua's force was at the northwest corner. The north side was already held. Clearly, the southwest corner was next: Eglon and Lachish.

Today a good road runs south from Makkedah along the very track that Joshua's men must have trodden. It leads across the Sorek Valley to high ground, then dips to the Elah River, a few miles downstream from where stood the important city of Libnah, or, as some think, Gath. This city Joshua promptly attacked and carried, with the usual consequences to its king and its unfortunate inhabitants. Tactically this must have contained Jarmuth, as doubtless Joshua intended, for he moved on south again without delay.

But not even Joshua could carry on a war unmolested. We have noted the inactive Gezerites, whose city flanked the Gibeonite route beyond Ajalon but who, for some reason, took no part in that fight. Now, for another equally unknown reason, they suddenly entered the scene; not in a flanking attack (which, if made earlier, might have made much trouble for the pursuing tribesmen and possibly even have saved the five kings their heads and their reputations), but as pursuers in their turn. Like trailing hyenas, Joshua found them following him from the sacked ruins of Libnah.

Now, with the topography laid out for us on a nicely colored piece of paper, we can overlook the whole problem with a cool eye. From Libnah a main valley saddles the watershed to the next east-west river—two rivers, in fact. Bear west across these, and south again, five miles or more, with steep hills to the right and left. Once through these guarding heights a little plain slopes to a third river. Turn sharp left up this (now the Wadi-el-Hesy), and there, on the south bank, stood a city, one of his two objectives.

Tell-el-Hesy, "the mound of Hesy," is all the name we now have for it, and under that name it has sparked many bitter controversies in learned periodicals. The probabilities are that it was Eglon, rather than Lachish. In any case, it was part of the southwestern king post of Joshua's strategic problem.

Lachish, we believe, lay to the east-northeast, where an old Roman road and the travel diary of Eusebius locates it, between the chief valley of Zephathah and the north fork of the Wadi-el-Hesy. It was a big and well-fortified place and closely tied in with Gezer and the Egyptian powers.

So here was Joshua's problem. Both cities must be taken. Somewhere back along the line of march the men of Gezer were coming. And Joshua, remember, had no map.

II
LOGISTICS AND THE GEZERITES

THE best a map can do for us is to help us realize how wonderfully well Joshua did without one. Our engraved knowledge may bite into our thinking certain errors that become well-nigh ineradicable. Those same drawers of maps of Joshua's campaign, who would have him take Gaza and trek all the way down to Kadesh-barnea, merely because of a routine phrase in our text, are outstanding examples. One of them assumes, because Lachish is said to have been attacked before Eglon, and also because the king of Gezer is said to have been vanquished by Joshua in the course of operations, that Lachish lay well to the west, between Gibeon and Makkedah. This last, as we have already realized by weighing Joshua's alternatives after the Gibeon fight, would be virtually out of the bounds of possibility. In any case, the record itself supplies a far more reasonable version.

Unfortunately we are not given the basic elements of what, to a commander in the field, would be the biggest question mark of all: how about the Gezerites? We can only judge by Joshua's actions. Clearly he solved his logistic uncertainty in favor of his having a sufficient head start of King Horam to allow time for the handling of Lachish or Eglon, which means that he had to consider, all together, the distance to be covered, the condition of the roads and the water supply, his marching speed, the condition of enemy troops and his own, the probable power of resistance of Eglon.

"Logistics" is a "portmanteau word," if ever one was, and mastery of the supremely complex calculations which may be rolled up within it marks the supreme commander. Politics, not logistics, is the greatest lion, however, in any military leader's path. Possibly this explains why Joshua, who had only internal politics to contend with and who seems to have been completely emancipated, at least by this stage in his career, from responsibility to, or control by, any other person or authority, lived to a ripe old age and died in the fullness of honor.

So at this point we can only guess at what logistic factors influenced his decision. Perhaps a certain measure of procrastination and delay was to be expected from King Horam anyway. At any rate, he had missed a very obvious chance back at his home city. For whatever reasons, Joshua decided that he had time to deal with Lachish (or Eglon) before Horam could intervene. And as it developed he was right.

This decision made, another arose: which city first? Eglon or Lachish?

Since even now scholars disagree as to which place was which, it would do us little good to reconnoiter the terrain in detail. If Eglon be taken as the present Tell-el-Hesy, it would have to be attacked either from the river, where it would be strongly fortified, or from the land, after crossing the river far enough up or down the stream to be unmolested during the operation. And its walls—real ones, dried brick, twenty-nine feet through at the base —were no trifle. "Lachish," in fact, means "impregnable." This may have been something of a vainglorious boast, but the place was a well-settled community of some three thousand population, an important outpost of Egyptian influence and culture, and the scarp of its ramparts rose sixty feet in air. Just as hard a nut to crack as Eglon.

To attack a city of such great strength in the short breathing spell which remained before he would have to turn and face the oncoming hordes of King Horam would have been foolhardy in the extreme if the men of Lachish had not figured in the great defeat. King Japhia was dead, his neck first trod upon by the feet of common soldiers and then broken in a fall from the gallows tree. A defeated army drifts home gradually, and those who had already arrived must have been a panic-stricken lot, with little spirit left to make a stand against the conquering Israelites. Joshua doubtless counted on this, or he would never have launched his men against those towering walls.

A far cry from the tottering masonry of Jericho to the stately battlements of Lachish! There is no hint of the need of another miracle at the sound of trumpets; Joshua had learned his lesson well and knew how to deal with walls, no matter how strong. The defense, we may assume, was not a vigorous one. The city fell easily, and the Hebrews swarmed in to sack it with all the thoroughness Moses had commanded: wrecking the haikoloth of the wealthy, destroying the "high places," as Canaanite temples of worship were called, ransacking the citadel, razing the once proud ramparts. Death, rapine, destruction! Lachish had ceased to exist, and all in a short matter of two days.

Now we can envisage, if only dimly, the timetable at work. Obviously the men of Eglon had no time to interfere and unquestionably lacked the stomach for interference. While still a factor to be reckoned with, they seem for the moment to have been contained. Perhaps had Debir, their king, been on the ground, instead of sealed in shameful death, the story would have been different. While they remained so was the time to meet the still uncontained threat. A question of logistics again, but again Joshua estimated his situation correctly.

All we are told is that "Horam King of Gezer came up to help Lachish; and Joshua smote him and his people, until he had left him none remaining." Which is to say, a complete victory was scored.

Note that this victory was in the field, not a siege and storm of a "fenced city." We place the encounter in the flatter ground north of Eglon, assuming that Joshua would have had time to reach that territory after finishing with Lachish, and we do so for several reasons. An unsupported and unbased field force needs room to maneuver, especially in the loose, undisciplined, hand-to-hand combat conditions then obtaining. Fighting as individuals, armed for the most part with weapons of contact, or at best (like the primitive bow) with very short effective range, the Israelites would be cramped if crowded into narrow defiles or valleys. Joshua must have been very wide awake to the danger of being caught by Horam in the valley occupied by Lachish. Surely he hurried out of that trap and back into the open before the Gezer-ites broke the horizon. And since they were following him he would inevitably meet them somewhere to the north, where we accordingly place him. At any rate, we are left in no doubt concerning the outcome.

Once more, now that Gezer was eliminated, the pression of the inevitable move weighted the situation. Joshua still had Eglon to deal with. We do not know how he reached the place, but it is very certain that he and his men had to climb.

To his footmen their first dawn rush against Gibeon would perhaps come back strongly to memory. How long ago was that? It seemed a lifetime. Here they were again, pushing upward through the stony and prickly dark, struggling to reach positions before daylight. Had all since Gibeon been a dream?

No dream to the Eglonites, though, but a nightmare of carnage and destruction. As with Lachish, so with them. "And they took it on that day, and smote it with the edge of the sword, and all souls that were therein he utterly destroyed. . . ."

Two days for Lachish. An undetermined number to back-track and destroy King Horam, though an easy two days' march from Lachish through the defiles to open country. Say two days and a night to break off and climb to the assault and capture of Eglon. Allow a good week for the entire thing, not counting time spent on the road from Makkedah, and the southwest corner of Joshua's square was safe. A whirlwind campaign, this; certainly the most impressive military feat accomplished so far by this iron commander.

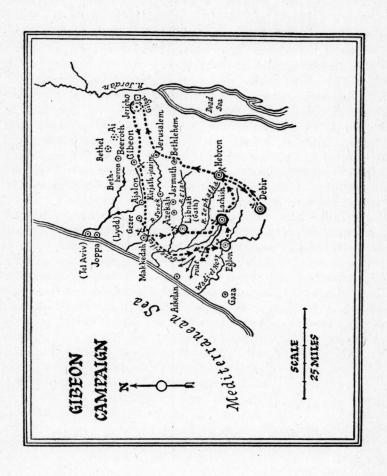

GIBEON CAMPAIGN

N

SCALE
25 MILES

R. Jordan

Dead Sea

Mediterranean Sea

Ai
Beeroth
Bethel
Beth-horon
Gibeon
Jerusalem
Bethlehem
Hebron
(Lydd)
Ajalon
Gezer
Kirjath-jearim
R. Sorek
Azekah
Jarmuth
Azekah
Debir
R. Zephathah
Lachish
Libnah (Gath)
(Tel Aviv)
Joppa
Makkedah
Gezer
rout
Wad-el-hey
Eglon
Gaza
Askelan
Jericho
Gilgal

Joshua had indeed moved like a thunderbolt of God, but the tempo of his final moves showed a still greater acceleration. From the smoking ruins of Eglon he marched to Hebron. In doing so he was doing more than pegging down the southeast corner of the map he carried in his agile mind. Hebron was a strong point, a station on the caravan highroad, and its inhabitants were fighters with a reputation. Kirjath-arba, the city of Arba, was its ancient name; and Arba was the father of Anak, whose sons, the Anakim, the "long-necked men," have given a generic label to all giants and powerful men of their hands, "unto this day." Joshua did not want to leave this nest of stout, stiff-necked fellows on the main highway. Hebron, besides, blocked his way home. He knew that country well. The brook Eshcol, one of the many waters rising on the mountain, had been a point of call on traveling back through Canaan to report to Moses. Hebron obviously was next.

And Hebron, approached by the most practicable route, a valley called Zephathah, which means "watchtower," fell as all the others had done, the ancestors of the Anakim finding themselves powerless against the hammer strokes of Joshua.

Still he was not content. All this country must be cleared for the occupation which was to come later. It was not enough to defeat the sons of Anak; the power of Israel must be felt in their outlying possessions as well. The frontiers of the Promised Land must be pushed back as far as possible. The farther they were pushed back, the wider would spread wholesome awe, and the more secure would rest Israel's new and hard-won boundaries.

So the city of Debir, sometimes called Kirjath-sepher, must also be eliminated; and eliminated it was, in another day of scrambling over walls and death in the streets below.

Back to Gilgal, then, along the high-lying track: through Bethlehem on its plateau (the "house of bread") and Jerusalem of the ineradicable Jebusites, with its hills and pools. We are not told just how Joshua went, but there seems no good reason why, with all the land quiet in his *Pax Hebraica*, he should not have cut off the triangle and taken the easy and immemorial road from Jerusalem through Jericho to the Achor Valley. No point now to the hard and narrow paths his people had trodden up to the ridge, northward yonder, when they had first set out for Gibeon and the great unknown adventure.

Again we see him, therefore, in the midst of his lean and battle-hardened followers, their gear stripped to essentials but bright for instant use, their clothing ragged and patched but very serviceable. They carry themselves with a swing and sureness more noticeable than in the run even of their tough and self-sufficient desert breed. They do not straggle. They make no unnecessary noise. The long plodding train of pack animals, laden with the choice loot of Canaan, is closed up in the middle of the column and efficiently herded along. Their guards are in place, front and rear. The ranks, irregular but obviously well in hand, bear the indescribable but unmistakable stamp of made and seasoned fighting men. And there is a spring to their step, an eagerness in their sun-blackened faces. Joshua is leading them home.

Although they made no unnecessary noise it is certain that they sang on the way. The musical strain has always been deep in the race. That it existed then in a remarkable degree is made clear all through the sacred records. The edicts of Moses were uttered in the form of prose poems of extraordinary quality; when Miriam felt the gift of prophecy coming on she reached for her timbrel; the minstrelsy of David soothed the strange moods of Saul; Solomon made harps and psalteries from the wood of the almug tree. The pages of early Scripture are filled with references to the use of the kinnor (a three-cornered harp), the ugab (a primitive wind instrument), the dulcimer, the cithara, the khabil (a reed pipe), and the nebel (which seems to have been the earliest ancestor of the Scotch bagpipes).

There is no way of discovering what songs the battered warriors sang on the way back to Gilgal. Perhaps they intoned chants which were turned later into those wild battle hymns of the Maccabees. Perhaps, as the words of Moses were sacred in the minds of them all, they sang snatches from his vengeful battle poems as they swung along, weary and bandaged and laden with spoils.

I will make mine arrows drunk with blood,
My sword shall satiate itself with flesh,
The blood of the slain, and of the captives,
With the head of the chief of my enemy.

They make a picture which should be graven for all time on the pages of history: Joshua's victorious men coming home. Down the trails they march, their tribal banners heading each division: the lion and the aurochs, the eagle of Dan clutching a serpent in its claws, the upright man on the pennon of Reuben. The Kohathites of the tribe of Levi are not there to carry the ark before them on their shoulders, but the spirit of their God goes on before.

The time has come to pay just tribute to these men who fought under Joshua's orders. They have been given little praise in any chronicles dealing with that day, and none in the Bible itself. The victories they won are almost without exception described as miracles. The purpose of this narrative is to define these as miracles of inspired leadership rather than manifestation of Divine help, and even there the whole of the credit falls on the shoulders of their leader.

Let us pause now to say that they must have been fighting men of real caliber. Joshua directed their amazing marches, but it took strong and willing legs to climb the trails from Gilgal to Gibeon in one night. His planning caught the enemy unawares on countless occasions, but in the bloody melees which followed it took the stoutest of hearts to prevail over such heavy odds. Rebellious at times, stiff-necked always, prone to murmur and dispute, avid for plunder, but when they had their orders they carried them out as swiftly and surely as any band of fighting men the world has ever seen.

PART SEVEN

The North Is Up

I

THE CAMP AT GILGAL

Twenty-five hundred years after the conquest, in the days of
the Crusades, when men's thoughts had turned as never before
to religion, the flatlands on the west bank of the Jordan became
of such interest to the Christian warriors and the holy palmers
who followed in their wake that fees were charged for the right
to visit there. It is said that the Knights Templar, to whom the
commercial rights to the plains were allotted, drew an annual
revenue of five thousand pounds from them, a very considerable
sum of money in those times.

Let us pause for a moment to look at Gilgal as it was in the few
jubilant days of rest when Joshua led his fighting men back
from their victories in the hills.

It had changed greatly from the first stage when the newly
crossed tribes camped there and Joshua raised the monument of
stones to commemorate the safe passage of the Jordan. It had
grown, of course, beyond recognition, in spite of the fact that
there were fewer people to fill it. The campaign had taken its
toll of fighting men, and there would be scouts still in the hills
and representatives in the cities of Gibeon to co-ordinate the
efforts there. The increase had come from the spoils of war which

were heaped everywhere, swelling the limits of the camp. At night the lowing of cattle and the bleating of sheep came to the camp from all directions, for out on the plains, as far as the eye could see, were the great herds and flocks taken in the rape of Ai and Lachish and Eglon and Hebron and Debir, making the question of pasturage a serious one with which the princes of the congregation had to cope. The sound fell gratefully on the ears of the resting tribesmen, with its promise of plenty for all time to come. The share of the Temple had become a great and unassorted mound of treasure, kept in extra tents pitched around the site of the Tabernacle and carefully watched by the sons of Levi, making it necessary for the other tribes to move still farther away from the sacred center.

They were living well, with whole oxen roasting over fires, the steaming kettles filled with the choicest cuts of lamb and kid, and the wholesome loaves of barley from the harvest which was to have fed the people of the slaughtered cities. A far cry from the days when anxious eyes sought in the mornings for the fall of manna! They had stores of wine to keep in their porous vessels or to cool in the low waters of the river; the cellars of Canaan had been well stocked with fine varieties that the thirsty nomads had never seen before, wines from Cyprus and the vineyards of Damascus, which sparkled in gold and amber and were very grateful and mellow on the palate.

The talk around the heaping kettles was cheerful and confident. Stories were retailed by the warriors: how craftily they had taken El Tell, "the heap," as they called Ai; how the five kings had trembled when the captains set thonged sandals on their necks; how Israel had put the taste of Jebel Usdum, the mound of salt, in all Hittite and Amorite throats. Big talk, full of plans for the future, of the division of the land, boastful and contentious, with hushed references at intervals to the might of Yahweh and as often, perhaps, praise of the captain who had led them. The acquisitive instinct of the people was coming out strongly. There was much argument among the different tribes as to their respective shares of the beautiful land, the seed being laid for bitter controversies which Joshua himself would have to settle later.

Individual spoils had been enormous, of course. The sweeping tax, craftily imposed by Moses, had been ameliorated, in all probability, now that the loot of great cities was to be divided. Certainly the unlimited supplies of household goods brought down from the hill country had been parceled out for family use: grindstones and weavers' weights, clay measuring balls, bronze knives and weapons, kettle-shaped and neckless vessels for storing grain and wine (but none with inscriptions to false gods on their rims), lamps and oil jars, unlimited quantities of cloth and silk. Already the everyday life of the Israelites was easier and richer.

With the grind of incessant wandering a thing of the past, the daily pack-march-unpack, the people naturally had fallen into more comfortable ways. Things they could not afford to carry on their toilful hegira were now collecting in every tent. Memories of the household luxuries they had enjoyed in Egypt were flocking back, to be matched from the spoils of Canaan. In the Tabernacle the laver of glass was spouting water like a fountain, and handsome lamps swung at the corners of the enclosure, filled with burning oil when the shadows of night fell. In the tents of the people there were smaller lamps standing on pedestals. Couches had been acquired, for no longer was it necessary to roll up in blankets on the ground for a few hours of uneasy slumber. Rugs were spread on the ground, and there were gratefully soft sheets and covers.

The people had blossomed out in better raiment than the useful but plain garments they had worn in the desert. Men stalked about on the holy day and for evening prayers in tallethim made from the rich materials taken in the captured cities. They were proudly wearing "uquals" on their heads, tied in front with bowknots of colored silks and most handsomely lined with the same materials. The women, if not garbed in Babylonish robes, were wearing fine linens as well as the men.

In the evenings the sound of music rose around the campfires and in the tents with their stationary lamps. The wood-fashioned kinnoroth, which David later would make out of berosh, were twanging, and the curious-shaped lyres also, punctuated by the percussion of the shalish, as the triangle was called. Stories of the victories were being put in the form of chants which later, no doubt, were set down in the chronicles of the lost Book of Jasher. When the *shophroth* sounded for evening prayers there was a triumphant note about them which had not been detected in their expectant tooting around the walls of Jericho.

It goes without saying that the camp buzzed with activity. There were so many things to be settled that the princes of the congregation were in constant session. And there were visitors now. The men of Gibeon, raised to the status of useful, if not equal, allies since they had proven the honesty of their intent, were there constantly, advising with the princes on the best steps to be taken to put the devastated lands back into production again, offering information as to the guarding of the new frontiers. The humility they had shown on their first visit was gone. Gibeon had played an inglorious part, but it had made the safe choice. The Hivites walked and talked with confidence in the widening confines of tented Gilgal.

There were other visitors as well. The violent eruption of Israel into Canaan had thrown the whole of the east-west traffic out of kilter, compelling the trade caravans to take other and more difficult routes across the Jordan. Now that the fighting seemed over, for a time at least, the traveling merchants were venturing again over the usual trails, sending emissaries ahead to ask questions and to plead for safe conduct. The sound of camel bells was often heard as the Egyptian and Babylonian caravans came gingerly down to make use of the Ford of the Partridges, pausing long enough to pay the new tolls (trust the Israelites to be alive to that possibility) and to wonder at the small number of the invaders. Where were the chariots and the horses, the siege mortars, the countless bands of armed men who had done these amazing things?

Joshua, we may assume, was taking little part in all such prosaic matters, being too wise a leader to arrogate to himself the control of all detail. Let little men decide the little things and so keep them satisfied and less likely to raise their voices when matters of real importance arose: a primary maxim of leadership, this. He had weightier matters on his mind, for he knew better than his people that this was no more than a prosperous beginning. If he sat in the council of the princes it was to end their deadlocks and to cut through their endless discussions with decisions they hastened to accept. He was tired. He took long walks, no longer encountering the man with drawn sword who came with comfort and Divine assurance; the need for that had passed.

Perhaps he went to the tent where Rahab lived in seclusion with her family. It is recorded that Rahab married a man named Salmon eventually, but of course there had not been time for a courtship to develop yet, and so the sole remaining Jerichite unit had little or no communion with the jealous people they had assisted. Perhaps he paused by the heap of stones where Achan was buried, thinking with regret of the necessity placed on his shoulders to rally the flagging morale of Israel at the expense of that unhappily acquisitive son of Judah.

The peace of Gilgal was of short duration, however. The word came to Joshua that the north was up!

II
THE JABIN OF HAZOR

INTO the record comes now a figure of considerable importance, the Jabin of Hazor.

News travels fast through the hills. The relief of Gibeon, the fate of the five kings, the sack of Gath, and the resounding defeat of Horam had spread alarm. News of that sort cuts two ways: it creates dread, but at the same time it drives those who fear the same fate into defensive activity. And so the north was up, with the Jabin leading it.

This north was unknown country to the tribes and to Joshua with his lack of maps. Old legends dating back to Abraham remained in their minds, but lacking all specific usefulness. Hints had been picked up from the caravans, and from them they learned something of the lyre-shaped lake which lay sixty and more long miles up the sunken Jordan. From its western edge, where the trail debouched, the long snowy crown of Hermon, the Lofty One, could actually be seen. They had heard of the furious storms which swept that water without warning and of the general belief that this was the work of devils, rushing through a narrow crack in the cliffs. Twenty miles it stretched northward, to where Jordan's upper course inflowed through treacherous marshes. Ten miles farther was another lake, shaped like the kinnor or harp of sweet singers, but far smaller, which impounded Jordan's parent streams off Hermon's flanks, where lay Laish, later to be called Dan. This was Lake Huleh, a few feet above sea level; Jordan's descent began there.

All around was fighting country. Today, as we have earlier remarked, we can trace the crusading story in the grim and monumental fortresses whose ruins punctuate for us that unlovely episode of Christendom; ruins whose names can still evoke graceful, stately ghosts of a vanished chivalry. Like a faint breath of ancient France, a soft wind out of old Provence across the sea, sound the un-Semitic names: Belvoir, Montfort, Belfort, Chastel Blanc, Château Pélerin, Rochetaille, Le Crac des Chevaliers, Blanche Garde. Some, like the vast, mysterious pile south of Aleppo, built presumably by knights from the Saône country, have been washed over by so many waves of history and language that no records whatever of them remain. Only their names, as in this case Arabized into Sahyun, still ring in men's ears and bear witness that they were once great places of war.

So, too, with the northern land—the names that have come down to us in Joshua's book. Two thousand years had already flowed over them when the first Crusaders began to straggle down through the Amanus passes. Yet their ancient meanings still glimmer up to our comprehension from those almost invisible deeps: Hazor, "fortified camp"; Madon, "place of contention"; Shimron, "the watchful"; Mizpeh, "watchtower."

Israel naturally had heard of the Jabin, for he was a very powerful ruler, much greater than any of the rash and impotent kings who had matched themselves against Israel so far. The title "Jabin" had something of the significance of Pharaoh, ranking the bearer above the comparatively humble kings of cities. Its meaning in Hebrew is "he whom God considered." Not a well-chosen title, however, for the one and only God was to give very little consideration to the great Jabin of Hazor.

Hazor itself was a mighty city. Its ruins indicate that it possessed a substantial degree of accumulated capital, and therefore great power. Its enormous earthen ramparts proved that it had unlimited labor to draw upon. The inhabitants numbered four thousand, according to the most authoritative reckoning, and the ramparts could accommodate thirty thousand men. This, then, was to be the real test.

To some scholars the known facts about Hazor sound like only one thing: the Hyksos. Whether it had been a Hyksos concentration point on the way south into Egypt, no man can say. Even three or four hundred years after its peak of power, when Joshua faced it, the place was still the chief city of Canaan. Doubtless, as so often in the case of other towns, its continued vitality was due to its key position. Jericho, for an opposite example, controlled nothing but its springs. With the river only a few miles away, geography held no seeds of resurrection for that sacked and burned town, whereby Joshua's curse lay unlifted for centuries —virtually, indeed, to the present day.

But Hazor was a different matter. Just west of Lake Huleh, and with ample springs close by, it controlled an immemorial crossroads. South ran the way to Lake Chinnereth (Gennesareth, Tiberias, Galilee), Hattin, the Plain of Esdraelon and its fortified passes through the Carmel ridge, then to Yehem, and so on down the ancient coast route to Gaza and Egypt. Northeasterly, going to Damascus, one crossed Upper Jordan just below Huleh (over the "Bridge of Jacob's Daughters," recite the guides) and climbed into the mountains, Hermon on the left hand always filling the north horizon. Still another road led due north up the Jordan headwaters until beyond the Huleh marshes, then branched west past Hermon's foot to ancient Laish, skirting Banias, the Roman Caesarea Philippi, and so inland, under the grim scrutiny of the Mizpeh, or "watchtower": a high conical hill at the valley's mouth, the ideal local sentinel, topped now by crusading ruins known as Kalat-el-Subeibeh. If one kept to the main road without branching off thus, but followed up the Litani (the Dog) River as it flowed south, one was on the direct road to Sidon, west of the mountains and on the sea.

But, more important yet than all these main avenues, Hazor commanded the only direct route joining Damascus and a seaport without crossing a mountain range: the straight road by Safad and Ramah to Acco (Roman Ptolemais, Crusaders' Acre); Acre, with its curving beach below the town, caressed by ranks of low, mild surf: room for all the little ships of the known world.

No wonder Hazor throve mightily and was, even as late as Joshua's day, a major political factor. No wonder it was still able to summon help from north, east, and west, to put down the upstart barbarians in the south. No wonder its defeat was to be Joshua's crowning victory.

The Jabin of Hazor was not to stand alone. Madon, Shimron, and Achsaph were among the cities throwing in with him in his mighty confederation. These cities lay far away on the coastal plain, only six or seven miles this side of Acre. The experts are not always sure of their exact locations. Long tradition includes among them the ancient fortress to the south, Hattin, only a few miles west of the lyre-shaped lake, Chinnereth. It controlled the main lakeside road, as well as other roads to the southwest, and is remembered today by its two ominous little peaks, the Horns of Hattin, where, anno Domini 1187, the Saracen was ultimately to break beyond repair the Christian power in Palestine.

The Jabin's writ seems to have run far. But it is interesting to observe that the chieftains summoned to his rendezvous mark out, with their towns, another rectangle, almost identical both in size and in shape, with the one Joshua had just circumambulated in South Canaan. And the reason for this was the same as obtained down south, a geographical one. Therefore, it must have been supremely important to Joshua.

The sharp ridge called Mount Carmel extends southeasterly from the sea, beginning south of Acre. This is the left-hand, or southwest, edge of the plain. The coast highway, running south, meets it and skirts its face until passes are found. There are four main ones, each guarded by a fort, before the Lebanon foothills are met at the bottom point. On the east, or left as you go south, the foothill scarp stretching north and northeast toward the Sea of Chinnereth encloses the plain, in the shape of a triangle. The defensive line thus formed, like a *V* right side up, has been an immemorial boundary between northern and southern Canaanites.

Acre was the main port for this region, in fact, for Damascus itself. The road inland ran through Hazor, where also centered the chief north-and-south ways, as well as smaller tracks, and this also we now know. For this reason, as well as others, Hazor was unique.

Although we have already considered its location: four miles west of Lake Huleh, opposite its southern tip, where the roads converged at a natural plateau, with wadies or water-courses protecting three sides, there are still details worth remembering. For instance, where the fourth side, to the south, was closed by the city proper, a huge mound lifted one hundred and sixty feet in the clear. North of this stretched the level camp floor, three quarters of a mile long by nearly half a mile wide, on all three sides of which rose the sloping rampart of solid earth which is still sixty feet from base to crest. Even after its greatest days, when the campground was given over to flimsy dwellings and the Jabin was no longer backed by the full power of Egypt, the mere look of the place must have been enormously impressive. How would it have seemed to the leader of a couple of thousand footsore infantrymen, armed only with swords, slings, and spears?

That question we can hardly answer. We are not Joshua. We know what he must have seen: not the vast low mounds of the present day, seamed by cattle tracks, empty and silent in their vaguely unnatural regularity of shape, but a bustling and bristling city, its eastern gate thronged with traffic, its royal stronghold perched solidly on the city's southern shoulder, and teeming with horses and war chariots.

Archaeologists agree that chariots were in general use in Egypt: powerful instruments, dreadful in war. When the tribes arrived in Canaan they were a commonplace. In battle, however, they were a new weapon to Hebrew fighters. And a new weapon must be met.

So again it was for the leader not only to decide what to do, but to evolve, out of his own head and in the lonely sweat of his own thinking, some effective defense. Strategy must wait on tactics.

III
A FORCED MARCH

HERE we must pause a moment to deny a baseless slur on the
memory of Joshua. Our old friend Josephus is at it again, but this
time we have him on the hip. A thousand years after the event,
with all the weight of his learning and prestige at his disposal,
he proceeds to question the leader's courage in the crisis he now
faces. After enumerating the Jabin's troops in his usual round
and breezy figures, he states flatly that "the multitude of the
enemies affrighted both Joshua himself and the Israelites; and
they . . . were superstitiously timorous, with the great terror
with which they were stricken. Whereupon," he continues
smugly, "God upbraided them with the fear they were in, and
asked them whether they desired a greater help than he could
afford them. . . . So Joshua became full of courage upon these
promises of God . . . and after five days' march he came upon
them . . ." and so on.

Joshua "affrighted" by mere numbers? Joshua "superstitiously
timorous" and stricken "with great terror"? Once, and once only,
have we seen him even "dismayed"—and that not at the prospect
of any confronting odds but at the unexpected weakness of his
own men. At that time the Lord had said unto Joshua what was
needful to remedy the situation, and the soldier had translated dismay into action.

It is possible, indeed probable, that the rank and file were
thrown into panic when the news circulated throughout the
camp. The name of the Jabin of Hazor was enough in itself to
inspire doubts. He and his strong allies and the army they could
lead to battle behind the shock of their chariots: here was something Israel had never faced before. It is easy to imagine the
kind of talk which spread from tent to tent. Chariots! The stout
Hebrew foot soldiers had never yet stood in the path of a chariot

charge, but they knew what it meant: maddened horses at full gallop, dragging forward those irresistible vehicles of war. Joshua found it no easy task to spread reassurance in the camp. We can be sure of that.

But was he himself dismayed? There has been too much evidence of his dauntless resolution for us to question his strength on this occasion. He had just emerged from a situation as trying as that which now faced him. With two enemy cities ahead, unknown country on one flank, known enemies in fenced cities on the other, a fresh army coming up behind him, he had shown no trace of being "superstitiously timorous." On the contrary, he had struck with such daring and such perfect strategic timing that the ring of adversaries had fallen one by one. There is nothing in the record to indicate a reversal in the man, a weakening of fiber.

The Book says simply enough: "And the Lord said unto Joshua, Be not afraid because of them: for tomorrow about this time will I deliver them up all slain before Israel. Thou shalt hough their horses, and burn their chariots with fire."

Josephus, we submit, has been guilty of a fault common to all fictionizing historians. He has strained himself to create additional dramatic suspense. He no doubt said to himself, how much more gripping the story of victory, if Joshua and his men went into battle with dread in their hearts and the whiplash of Jehovah goading them on!

The exact words of the biblical scribe cannot be used too literally. For instance, the phrase, "Tomorrow about this time." The tribes were still at Gilgal. They could not march to Hazor overnight. Josephus attempts to add verisimilitude to his otherwise bald and unconvincing narrative by the statement: "After five days' march he came upon them." The Book says nothing of the kind, yet for once Josephus may be right.

Again, what does the reassurance that the Lord conveyed to Joshua signify except that *he was reassured?* The words say just that and no more. No troop commander worth his salt is ever free from anxiety, for nothing is less predictable than warfare. Plainly, at some stage in the proceedings Joshua felt better about his chances. To build on that simple statement a picture of Joshua shaking in his shoes at the idea of the Jabin's numbers, as Josephus does, or to echo that libel, as do recent authorities by citing Joshua's "special encouragement" by Divinity, is both grossly unjust and entirely contrary to the evidence. The menace was both real and great. Joshua had good grounds for anxiety. The text merely records one more instance of his accurate estimate of the situation and his bold action thereupon.

The text records another item: namely, the solution of the chariot problem. Assuming that Joshua had found one (which events were to prove he had), surely no single circumstance would be more likely to bolster his confidence. The two were certainly cause and effect. How he met the chariot menace will be told in its proper time and place.

At the moment Joshua is more concerned with strategic problems. He knows that the four kings of the north have made the same initial mistake as the five kings at Gibeon. They have concentrated in one place, with no provision in advance for action upon his flanks or rear. They are planning, without a doubt, to roll in their great numbers down the caravan trail and overwhelm him and his exhausted forces. A good enough plan if Israel waits for the attack.

But Joshua has never been content with a defensive role, and there is the glaring weakness in their planning. They are badly disposed to meet attack.

The information he has received indicates that they are not concentrating at Hazor. The long-hallowed expression in the text, confirmed beyond questioning by the Masoretic Hebrew version, is that "all these kings . . . pitched together at the waters of Merom." This has led map makers until very recently to place the Jabin's meeting place at the edge of Lake Huleh, as being the nearest "waters" to Hazor, although scholars have racked their brains without result to construe a satisfactory "Merom" out of "Merrus," "Maron," and similar variants.

But modern research has located a far better place, nine or ten miles northwest of Hazor itself, around the base of a prominent mountain still called Jebel Marun. Here unusually plentiful water and the convenience of many crossroads draw to this day regular weekly markets at a village near the mountain's northern foot.

The landmark, the second highest peak in upper Galilee, and the great number of springs all around make it an obvious and excellent place to meet and camp. As for Hazor, there was no slightest reason for the Jabin and his subordinates to take shelter in that vast enclosure against Israelites who were, when last heard from, nearly a hundred miles away.

Joshua could see easily enough where his advantage lay. The enemy had concentrated in the space. The horses were in temporary quarters, and the chariots were still partially knocked down for trail transport from the outlying towns. An attack on the concentration itself might succeed. If so, and another rout took place, as after Gibeon, there would be ample time to deal with Hazor, or any other fortified but by then isolated city, at leisure and without interference. In spite of the overwhelming odds, the weak spot was just where those odds were most evident: the concentration.

For these reasons Joshua had confidence in the outcome of his battle. But the map still sets us wondering. Ninety miles on foot straight up the Jordan Valley, through hostile country, without allies or bases of supply, to attack superior forces—at least we are told they were "even as the sand that is upon the sea shore in multitude"—and with no relief or reinforcement to be looked for at the far end! A daring, not to say mad, plan!

Here is, indeed, a blurred passage in our palimpsest. Yet there are one or two highly suggestive features.

To begin with, it can be assumed that Joshua would not move any substantial body of men northward except by the regular caravan route. Here, no doubt, he began to draw dividends from his thrust south along it, from Hebron to Debir. There would be dividends, besides, from his initial raid up to Shechem, almost a third of the way to the enemy concentration. Beyond that known place the road shifts west through the pass into Samaria, turning Mount Ebal, and then winds north again soon to where the Great Plain of Esdraelon, overshadowed to this day by the black prophecies of Armageddon, runs out into a point in the hills guarding the Valley of Jezreel on the south.

So far so good. Reaching this point undetected because of the desolation he had already spread, he would be a third of the way

along the road. The steep sides of Mount Carmel and its train of
summits bear away northwest through Megiddo, "the place of
troops," to Haifa on the Great Sea; but Joshua's line of march
would continue due north, the plain on his left, and the foothills
on his right, until he passed through the station of Aphel. In the
steepening hills was Shunem and an ancient fountain called Dor,
said to be the haunt of witches. Beyond there it would be only
seven or eight miles to Nasra, later Nazareth, on its cupped
plateau, with the mass of Mount Tabor dominating the eastern
horizon. Here he would bear right, to the northeast, and wind
through the closing hills to the fertile shores of the Lyre Lake.

This would be two thirds of his way. Tall rocks like towers
now to be skirted; Migdal-el, one was named, "the tower of
God." Hereabouts we would have to watch carefully for devil
winds out of the Chasm of Doves before breaking away from
the shore line, becoming more difficult and marshy as we neared
the inflow of Upper Jordan and began to climb into the wild
uplands. Somewhere, twelve or fourteen miles ahead, lay Hazor,
chief fortress of all the people of Canaan: such a fortress as
Hebrew eyes never yet had seen. Somewhere, also, in this foreign
wilderness were the Jabin's allied forces, like unto the sands of
the sea in multitude. From here in he had best go warily.

From here he would meet the mountains. True, Lebanon does
not begin for some thirty miles yet, where the River of the
Dog (Litani) breaks its gorge westward to Tyre on the sea,
opposite the southern foot of Hermon's long white crest. But
the highest peak of all, short of that Great White One, lifted close
by (now Jebel Jarmuk), and ten miles north rose another peak,
Marun, which Joshua knew to be his objective.

The fields were wild, already green, with big patches of blue
and yellow flowers. Almond blossoms were out on their bare
branches, and the tiny green figs were swelling. Acacia, olive,
wild apple, juniper, and the tall locust, all showed refreshing
and new to hardened desert eyes.

> . . . *a mist of green,*
> *And nothing perfect.*

Perfect it might have been. Even the ever-present bramble
and thorn seemed milder, and the new green in the scrubby oaks

HAZOR CAMPAIGN

SCALE
20 MILES

N

and rare box trees made them glisten as if freshly washed and
anointed. Here it was at last, the land of milk and honey they
had been promised. Perfect it would have been save for one
thing: this was the very heart of enemy resistance; here was
set the scene for the final struggle. Perfect it would become if
Israel prevailed.

Joshua marched by night. No supposition, this; all the facts
made it clear that he shunned the obvious danger of daytime
marches. In no other way could he have covered the ninety-odd
miles through hostile territory to arrive unseen near the waters
of Merom. The record shows that he did not have to fight at any
point along the route. The Jabin seems to have been a poor
tactician, or completely overconfident, or both. Certainly he had
put out no advance detachments. But even the enemy's lack of
precaution would not have permitted the tribesmen to come upon
them suddenly if their advance had not been masked by darkness. The news of their approach would have reached the Jabin
in plenty of time for him to be ready.

For further proof we may fall back again on logistics. Along
the other immemorial corridor between Egypt and Syria, the
coastwise track, armies have for centuries conformed to a rough
march table of twenty miles a day—and not bad going for even
seasoned troops anywhere—an allowance dictated by the average
distance between good water holes. This consideration may have
ruled Josephus and given him his unsupported allowance of five
days for the march to Merom. Even at that, Joshua must have
driven his men hard.

IV
JOSHUA MAKES A RECONNAISSANCE

THE leader of Israel could not have made his battle dispositions
before arriving on the ground. He knew nothing of this mountain
country save the unconfirmed scraps of information his scouts

had brought back. He must see the camp of the enemy with his own eyes to determine how much was fact and how much hearsay. He must make his own reconnaissance.

This being so, as it obviously is, it becomes clear that the biblical scribe was not as vague or careless as he at first appeared. His phrase, which we were more than willing to discard, now falls into place and lights the whole scene for us.

The men of Israel had reached the end of the last night's march. They had made camp with the greatest care to the south of what is now called the Jebel Marun, where lay the famous "Village of a Hundred Wells."*

Hastily but noiselessly they had slaked their thirst and eaten the scraps of food still left in their shoulder bags. No fires had been lighted. Long before dawn they had carefully concealed themselves in the gullies and caves and in the thick brush and low trees clustering around the waters.

Joshua ventured out alone to look over the scene of the coming battle.

And now, for the last time in this study, we may well pause to enjoy our counterpart of the thrills which reward the decipherer of palimpsests and the uncoverer of great paintings. For we, too, piecing together bits here and there of fact, of recent discovery, of painful study by innumerable scholars, can see unrolling on the little hills and valleys of Palestine the outline of past deeds. Now the traces of ancient roads and forts, long believed lost, spring to our eyes. Hillocks and hollows, meaningless without their key, surrender their secrets.

For many centuries the key had lain sealed in the sacred vessels of ancient texts, so holy as to be immutable and untouchable, no matter how incomprehensible. Ours it had been not to question; ours only to accept and believe. Scholars might emend and correct translations, or sometimes even unearth new and more convincing versions. But since Joshua was accepted as a prophet, and since the Book reciting his doings stated thus and so, it was not for us to question the damming of Jordan, or the flattening

---

*The wells are there today, but there is no way of telling if villages stood then on the sites still to be seen at Tell-el-Khurbeh or Yarun.

of Jericho's walls, or the extra-long fighting time allowed him in the Vale of Ajalon. If these strange events should challenge our credulity we must reverently murmur: "A miracle!" and inquire no further.

But we believe we are no longer so constrained. Out of our study has come no atheistic or irreverent aspersions upon Divine power, but a perfectly credible and logical story of an entirely human and credible performance. Locked in the ancient texts, and now opened by the combined key work of modern research, we find these few but utterly convincing pictures of people—living, thinking, doing—three and a half thousand years ago. Untarnished, complete, vivid as when first recorded in their pristine stage of illiterate man's recollections, they have come down to us, and now we may see them in all their simplicity and freshness.

We know how and why Joshua moved his nomads, with all their animals and possessions, across the Jordan barrier in the face of seemingly impassable floods. We know that Rahab, the harlot, lived in an "upstairs" house, built on walls or beams joining the outer and inner walls. We know that her window faced west, to the abrupt and barren mountain that looms there today. We know its outline, the view that greeted her eyes every time she looked out. We know the strategy behind the weird daily circling of the city. And we know that it was somewhere near by, but not close enough for her house to be involved, that the dogged Hebrews dug and shored and mined away to the dramatic climax of storm and slaughter.

We have seen Joshua's mind at work: imaginative in conception, careful in preparation, swift and bold in execution, inflexible in completion. We have followed his reasoning in his first raids and campaigns. We have understood the fabled "long day," and that without help from the lost Book of Jasher. His lightning series of sieges and storms of the "fenced cities" and stronger walled towns is, we now realize, no mere traditional roll of conquest, slaughter, and rapine. Throughout we have caught glimpses of a leader taming, controlling, and ruling a group of fanatical, but strangely homogeneous, desert wanderers, irrupting from nowhere into the enfeebled heart of an outworn civilization.

We have followed him on a forced march which is rarely to be equaled in recorded warfare, in a most daring gamble against overwhelming odds. Failure, as he and we know, meant not only annihilation for him, but complete collapse of the entire invasion project between the Hazorite allies to the north and an aroused and implacable Pharaoh to the south. It is our last clear sight of him—this leader whose face will now be haggard with strain and fatigue, his wide-set eyes sunk deep in his head, but steady and clear as the brain behind them. He it is that has emerged most sharply from the so-long untouched records now yielding up their secrets. Let us look well before the centuries close their curtain.

Stopping only to fill his own waterskin and to eat a few mouthfuls, between instructions to his lieutenants about sentries, a message center, and such indispensable matters, he faced north in the lessening darkness. Presently he was gone, vanished toward the vague mass of rounded mountain blocking half the northern horizon only a mile or so away.

As the light grew this mountain showed its highest hump to the east. There, on some pile of scrub-grown boulders, Joshua found a safe lookout even before first fire-making, and there we ourselves may join him.

We are, in fact, on the highest point of the Upper Galilean plateau, but to us it all looks like a rolling sea of uneven earth waves. As the light broadens, the snowy crown of Hermon lifts clear, twenty miles or so to the northeast, and below the snow line the lesser summits take shape, their tops flat or rounded, like waves around a great rock. To our right, and only half as far away, a level strip of brightness betrays the little Lyre Lake, Huleh, soon to be hidden in haze. Farther south, and nearer yet —only eight miles, but hidden behind the eastern drop of the rolling hills—lies Hazor, the place of the camp. From behind us, around the hundred wells, where people are already astir, several dry valleys wind through the folding hills toward that fortress, and soon we shall see a stir of traffic up and down these natural pathways. Soldiers, slaves, village folk, even some horses and a chariot or two, will flow around our hill in the cool of the morning. And in the meantime, as we sweep the horizon around to the west and northwest and back to the north again, we begin to realize how truly desperate is the enterprise.

For there, at our feet, lies a depression or broad valley, shaped like a lopsided, three-pointed star.

There is no city in it—no proper place for one, anyway—but it is crowded, jammed, with life. Tents are everywhere; figures are on the move; hundreds of smokes rise, and there is an unusual, confused undertone of sound, strange to ears used to the distinctive noises of cattle, sheep, or goats. Horses!

Yes, there they are: long strings moving and milling about the water holes. In the brighter light we can take out the rough corrals of brush or thorn, the clusters of rough shelters that must protect their gathered fodder from dew and sun, and probably their chariots as well.

These are, of course, our main interest, but we see only a few men about them—early messengers, no doubt, or perhaps trainers. Shortly now the rising dust will blot out all details, radiating out in slow, wavering lines as the bands are herded into the hills to pasture before the noonday heat. But where are the chariots?

Joshua would not be in doubt on that score. Most of them have been brought to the concentration point, "knocked down," in modern phrase. The hill trails from Madon, Shimron, Achshaph, and many another unnamed vassal town of great Hazor "north of the mountains, and of the plains south of Chinneroth, and in the valley, and in the borders of Dor on the west," were little better than foot tracks, often worn deep into dry valleys and gullies. Chariots—even the wide-axled, springy Egyptian type— could not negotiate them. It was necessary to take them apart, a squad of porters or slaves to each chariot, and have the pieces carried one by one over the trails and assembled at the "waters," where at least there would be room to maneuver. But even if already set up, they would not be in motion: horses must be watered and fed first. And this fact again rules Joshua's decision.

With all this clearly before his eyes he makes his plans.

V
THE VICTORY AT MEROM

So THE next day, about this time, as at Gibeon, the tribesmen fell upon the allied host "suddenly": at dawn again, while that great mass of men and animals were still concentrated in tent and fenced corral. The Israelites emerged from their gullies and thickets without a sound, converging first on the horse lines and the space where the unoccupied chariots stood. The solution that Joshua had reached, already explained briefly in the biblical text, was a simple enough one: to burn the chariots and hamstring the horses while the army still slept. An easy enough plan to follow out if no resistance offered at once: a quick dash among the frightened horses, with swords slashing at their unprotected hocks, not hard for active desert fighters; then over to the chariots, with torches already lighted to apply to the wooden bodies.

The bloodcurdling screech of the maimed animals and the roar of the mounting flames wakened the men of the north to an accomplished fact. The great advantage the Jabin was to have had in battle with Israel had been wiped out.

The battle after that followed the pattern of the affairs at Ai and Gibeon and Hebron. It was a hurly-burly. No tactics, no deployment of the forces, no shifting of flanks or maneuvering; hand-to-hand fighting, from tent to tent, a mad and bloody clash at closest range. It was decided by the greater virility and determination of the tribesmen who smote lustily, as usual, with the sure knowledge that Jehovah approved and looked down on them. If the numbers of the enemy counted, it must have been the longest and sternest melee of all. The army of the north was a mighty one, much larger than the forces of the five kings and perhaps better equipped, and its power to resist that much more formidable. On the other hand, the northerners fought under more discouraging conditions. The surprise had been more complete, and their morale had been badly shattered by the catastrophe which preceded it. They were confused and frightened by the burning of the chariots and the disabling of the horses. Where had they sprung from, these desert devils, so confidently reported a hundred miles away? Was it another manifestation of the power of their warlike God that they could appear suddenly in the midst of an armed camp, with clouds of fire behind them, death in their gleaming eyes? Could mortal men stand against such a foe?

It developed into a rout, a shambles. The cohorts of the Jabin broke and fled, and once again the steel of Israel stayed not in its harvest of death. It is recorded that Joshua "chased them unto great Zidon" (Sidon on the far Mediterranean shore, forty miles away), "and unto Misrephoth-maim" (Zarephath, also on the coast), "and unto the valley of Mizpeh eastward." This last outpost, as already noted, guarded the Valley of Lebanon itself under Mount Hermon. The record adds, "And they smote them, until they left them none remaining."

Joshua had won his greatest victory. This was a major achievement, a smashing blow delivered after one of the greatest surprise marches in all the annals of warfare. It had been conceived with magnificent boldness, carried out with precision and a degree of daring to stagger the imagination. His reputation can rest on this.

The army of the north was in full flight, but the objective was not yet completely won.

The Jabin, seeing his army scattered and his prized chariots wrecked, retired into his castle at Hazor: a safer sanctuary, certainly, than the cave at Makkedah, but still not safe enough to escape the avenging arm of Joshua. The Hebrew leader was now to prove how well in hand he held his men. Seeming victories have been lost in the final stages by the inability of leaders to recall their scattered troops to meet new developments. Joshua had no difficulty. The sound of trumpets brought the pursuing tribesmen back to their rallying point, to be led at once against the city of the beaten king.

This speed in returning was an important factor. The resources of the Jabin were such that he could have gathered enough men, given the time, to hold the high walls of the city against attack. This time must not be allowed him. Joshua gathered his forces with sufficient celerity to strike before the men of Hazor could organize themselves for a successful defense. With the usual result: the city was taken, the people put to the sword, the king killed, the walls razed. Hazor, focal point of all resistance to Israel, had been wiped off the map. The northern confederacy was broken.

PART EIGHT

Settling the Promised Land

I

DAYS OF PEACE

Joshua had led his people into Canaan. Israel was now in possession of the Promised Land.

The conquest was not a complete one, however. Joshua had broken the back of the northern confederacy and thereby erased all active opposition to the taking over of the land, but the other cities which had thrown in with the Jabin were not reduced. The Book says: "As for the cities that stood still in their strength, Israel burned none of them, save Hazor only; that did Joshua burn." In the southwest the "Anakim" admittedly remained, "in Gaza, in Gath, and in Ashdod. . . ."

The reason can only be guessed at. Perhaps the bitter fighting had exhausted the tribes to the point where further aggression was no longer possible. Perhaps they had now acquired as much land as they needed, as much, at any rate, as they could hope to consolidate and hold. And Joshua was no longer young. He may have lacked the strength to lead them in more campaigns, and certainly there was no one to carry on with the vigor and foresight he had so consistently shown.

Whatever the reason, the tribes now settled down on the land they had taken. How it was divided between them is not neces-

sary to this record, although there will be references later to the
difficulties encountered in parceling it out; difficulties which
Joshua had to settle himself. As we are concerned with the man
Joshua, it is essential to speak of the share which fell to his own
tribe in order to visualize him in his closing years. The sons of
Ephraim did very well, inheriting a fine stretch of hill country
running north from Jericho as far as Shechem, that city of
abundant water and lush vineyards. It consisted of fertile upland
plains enclosed by mountains, well adapted for defense, reward-
ing to the labors of the husbandman. It became, naturally enough,
the center of administration for Israel. The Tabernacle was
located at Shiloh, where it was to remain with the ark mystically
housed behind its curtains for three hundred years. Shiloh, un-
inviting of outlook, with no advantages to make it the logical
choice for so high an honor, could have been selected for one
reason only: because it was there that the old leader had gone to
finish out his days. In Shiloh, therefore, dwelt the high priest and
the Levites. To Shiloh journeyed the people who had petitions to
present or complaints to make. Its greatness continued after
Joshua died, but when the ark was taken away the sun of Shiloh
went into eclipse.

The land of Ephraim was made memorable in other ways. It
was at Shechem that Joshua delivered his farewell speech, and it
was there under Abraham's oak that he set up the altar of witness. At Shechem, too, the bones of Joseph were finally laid down
in a tomb which stood alone on a gentle slope, enclosed with
white walls. It was natural that Joseph's resting place should be
on the dividing line between the inheritances of Ephraim and
Manasseh, they having been the two sons of the wise man who
once ruled Egypt under Pharaoh.

Of Joshua's life during the years which remained to him and
which he lived out in peace, we are given no glimpse, save for the
occasions when as elder statesman he came forward to assert his
authority. Did he occupy a house in Shiloh or did he take up
land in open country where he could have flocks and herds of
his own, and fig trees and vines? Most likely the first, for his
services seem to have been in pretty constant demand. The contentious people were no less aggressive now that they had a rich

inheritance to share, and so they stood in continuous need of a sagacious judge whose word was law.

It is pleasant to think of him as living with some ease in a house of cool stone walls with a door opening to the north for benefit of the breeze and from which he could catch some glimpse of the fat lands he had won for his own kin; his sword and his shield and his battered breastplate hanging on an inside wall, reminders of the miracles of generalship he had performed for his people; all the scant comforts about him which would seem like great luxuries to one who had marched the forty years in the wilderness.

Certainly he enjoyed the veneration of all the people of Israel in his declining years, sharing their obedience with the memory and the Law of Moses, his master.

II
THE LEADER STILL LEADS

Here the shades of a long-buried past settle down. In that uncertain dimness keen and persistent scholars have worked out a possible later history. It seems clear that the division of territory so confidently announced, according to the lottery set up and drawn by Joshua himself, was very largely a matter of "wishful thinking" by the Hebrews. The boundaries, later verified by careful priestly recorders and viewers of the land, served chiefly to settle intertribal disputes and to delimit jurisdictions. For modern research amply justifies the Book in its detailed catalogue of what cities and lands the Israelites did *not* take over.

Beneath all the lawyerlike enumeration of landmarks and boundaries we catch one or two flashes of what we must believe was the essential man—vigorous, wise, and outspoken, sometimes with more than a touch of weary scorn.

The textual experts assign to "later redactors" the whole passage wherein Caleb makes and Joshua grants a personal request for an allotment. But somehow one cannot doubt that, if it happened at all, it happened as set forth in the Book.

We remember Caleb: the only other one of Moses' spy-couriers who stood with Joshua in advising an attack on Canaan, in spite of its apparent strength and prosperity. He came to Joshua while the inheritances were being distributed. One cannot better the King's English: "Thou knowest the thing that the Lord said unto Moses the man of God concerning me and thee in Kadesh-barnea" (a lifetime ago) "and now, behold, the Lord hath kept me alive, as he said, these forty and five years. . . . As yet I am as strong this day as I was in the day that Moses sent me . . . for war, both to go out, and to come in." And he asked Joshua for, of all places, Hebron and its heights.

Was the old man boasting a tiny bit? Perhaps. He and Joshua were about of an age. Yet of Joshua it was shortly to be said that, like Moses, he was "old and stricken in age." It takes the truly great person to admit the ineluctable effects of time. There is something not quite ripe about the incurably young and untiringly athletic.

But Joshua, being Joshua, "blessed him, and gave unto Caleb . . . Hebron for an inheritance." And plenty of trouble did that rugged region and its rugged Anakim inhabitants make for Caleb and his family. We need not go into this here. But perhaps, in our historical reconstruction, we may catch a fleeting twitch of smile under Joshua's gray beard during the ritual blessing.

Another flash. The children of Manasseh (presumably the other half) had trouble with their inheritance. The best they could do with Beth-shean, Ibleam, Taanach, Megiddo, and other strong points along the lower and southwestern edge of Esdraelon Plain—the string of fortresses on the scarp of Carmel—was to put them "to tribute." They could not, the record states, "utterly drive them out."

We have noted that this was nothing unusual. Other tribes had their troubles too. But Manasseh was the younger branch of the House of Joseph; Ephraim, Joshua's own house, being the elder. There was pride in the children of Joseph. They complained that they had "but one portion and one lot to inherit, seeing I am a great people. . . ." It seems to have been the first substantial objection to Joshua's settlement.

To be expected, yes. But how does Joshua meet it?

Unanswerably. "If thou be a great people, then get thee up to the wood country, and cut down for thyself there in the land of the Perizzites and of the giants . . ." To this, of course, Manasseh had no reply, although they seem to have interjected the thought that the Canaanites had "chariots of iron." But the leader was not to be put off. The objectors were on record; they had asked and received their bonus; it was for them to take it up. "Thou art a great people, and hast great power . . . the mountain shall be thine . . . it is a wood, and thou shalt cut it down . . . for thou shalt drive out the Canaanites, though they have iron chariots. . . ." Chariots were no new thing. They should not deter a "great people." Let the "great power" be put to work, and the rest would follow. If Manasseh found any satisfactory retort it is not in the record.

Once again we find the old leader impatient. Even after the Tabernacle had been moved to Shiloh nothing had been done toward effecting the agreed partition of the land. Seven entire tribes were still, it seemed, waiting on their leader. He boiled over with contempt. "How long are ye slack to go to possess the land . . . ?" And he issued detailed instructions for representatives to view the ground and report to him. He alone, it seemed, could put things in motion, although so simple a preliminary could easily have been set on foot by the elders of the tribes themselves. After all, they were the parties most vitally interested.

But that appears to be, in this highly illogical and imperfect world, one of the inevitable burdens of leadership. Human nature always lies down, if possible, and surrenders initiative to the proven chief. He must, so long as he remains at the top, continue to push and pull. He can never eat of the fruit he has planted and cultivated. He can never expect to see the lessons he has so painfully taught applied by those for whom he has labored all his life. This is the tragic wisdom which Moses, as we know, repeated and re-repeated for Joshua's benefit.

Moses, indeed, came as close to realizing the dream of every leader as such men can, for he found and trained a successor. All chieftains try to do this; it is an essential part of their work, but it is seldom, indeed, that they are not, sooner or later, disappointed. For some reason we do not understand, genetic or psychological or otherwise a mystery, two brave, strong, and supple spirits, capable of being made wise by experience and free from the grosser frailties that flesh is heir to, almost never succeed each other in the same family. Moses and Joshua are this rarest of human combinations: a benevolent, affectionate senior, lavishing his experience and wisdom upon a keen, loyal, unselfish, and grateful junior. It does not recur in all the history of the Jews.

We are given one more glimpse of him in his role of mediator. He had not forgotten Reuben, Gad, and half-Manasseh, whose loyalty to their word had meant so much to him at the beginning of his own administration. Joshua, always in character, now kept his side of the bargain. The term of their enlistment was over. They had, he told them, not only "obeyed all that Moses . . . commanded you," but had also "obeyed my voice in all that I commanded you." The fighting advance guard, the personal police, the unencumbered spearhead of invasion, had well earned its quittance. "And now . . . therefore . . . return ye, and get you unto your tents . . . with much riches . . . and with very much cattle, with silver, and with gold, and with brass, and with iron, and with very much raiment . . ."

And so they did: departing out of Shiloh, "to go unto the country of Gilead, to the land of their possession." But the old soldier, as befitted their long-time commander, sounded even in discharging them the call which he and they had answered together throughout their joint service: the call of duty. "But take diligent heed to do the commandment and the law, which Moses the servant of the Lord charged you. . . ." Even after an honorable discharge the veterans were soldiers still.

The ex-drovers and herders were of course overjoyed at their final release. And so in their abounding gratitude to the Lord and entirely naïve disregard of Hebrew sensibilities they did just the wrong thing. Of all ways to express their joy, they chose the one most certain to make trouble for themselves. They built, if you please, *an altar!*—the one type of object which all Israel had been tearing down and trampling on wherever found, except their own, ever since leaving Sinai. Moreover, being solid, capable men, they made a good job of it, for the Book calls it "a great altar to see to."

One grows quite fond of Reuben, Gad, and half-Manasseh—at least of this generation. They were so honest, so straightforward, and they meant so well. Once before, it will be remembered, they found themselves, to their great surprise, completely misunderstood. Then they had been able to explain it all to Moses. Apparently it never occurred to them that their thin-skinned, intolerant, suspicious brethren, whose company they were so cheerfully leaving for their own matter-of-fact and simple relatives in Gilead and the comfortable care of sensible cows and uncomplicated sheep, would object to a thing like an altar. They meant no harm by it. Truth to tell, it cost no little time and labor, but they wanted to express, somehow, their gratitude. Had not the Lord commanded Moses, and Moses told Joshua, and Joshua carried it all out?

What they actually did was nearly to express themselves and their gratitude into a first-class civil war. The children of Israel went wild with indignation. An abomination of heathenry, an altar, probably with idols too (did anybody remember a small golden calf?)—right on the edge of Jordan! Unspeakable! And "the whole congregation . . . gathered themselves together at Shiloh, to go up to war against them."

But it did not come quite to that; and, reading behind the lines, we can believe we understand why. For Phineas, the priest, son of the High Priest Eleazar, went on an embassy. He took ten "princes," one for each tribe, with him, and he made speech with the cattlemen.

The gist of the Israelite complaint was that the altar builders had, *ipso facto*, not only trespassed against the Lord, but risked calling down Divine vengeance on all the other tribes. They were willing, Phineas avers, to share their inheritances on this side Jordan if the rebels against tradition had found Gilead "unclean," but they implore: "Rebel not against the Lord, nor rebel against us, in building you an altar beside the altar of the Lord our God." And Phineas, like all good envoys and advocates, could cite precedent. He called to mind the case of Achan, the looter, who did also "commit a trespass . . . and wrath fell on all the congregation . . . and that man perished not alone in his iniquity."

Another point of guesswork: the rumor in the congregation at
Shiloh was that the offending altar had been built "in the borders
of Jordan, at the passage of the children of Israel." Phineas complained that it was "beside the altar of the Lord our God." One
may suspect that the good Reubenites and their friends had followed the natural back trail down to Gilgal and halted there for
the pious work before recrossing the familiar Ford of the Partridges. Of course their altar would be right beside the twelve
stones of commemoration which Joshua had set up, and dead in
the center of the holy tradition he had founded. They had blun-
dered into the midst of a sacred circle, indeed, and nobody was
more surprised than they at the sudden appearance of their hostile
and most unexpected fellow tribesmen.

So Reuben, Gad, and half-Manasseh must explain again. They
had no idea of trespass or rebellion or of making sacrifices or burnt
offerings. Theirs was not that kind of altar. They merely meant
it for a memorial to future generations, to mark the fact that they,
too, were of the Israelite nation, although across Jordan in Gilead.
Indeed, that was all there was to it.

And Phineas, and the princes, and the tribes to whom he reported were "pleased" and abandoned their intention "to go up
against them in battle." Useless bloodshed, caused by a misunder-
standing, had been prevented.

Prevented by whom? Obviously, by Joshua. Who else would
have sent Phineas? Moses and Joshua, first together, then Joshua
alone, had always worked with Aaron and Eleazar, his son, in all
matters wherein the priests could be useful. Who but Joshua could
command Phineas? Who else could have restrained the rabid
tribesmen bursting with pious indignation against their bucolic
cousins? Josephus, for one, has no doubts whatever: Joshua
"restrained them," and to Joshua Phineas reported, which is one
of the pious chronicler's ipse dixits in which we can readily believe.

III
THE ELDER STATESMAN

W<small>E CATCH</small> one definite glimpse of Joshua in the role of elder
statesman when he set about the selection of cities of sanctuary. It
is recorded in the Book that he made Kedesh, Shechem, Hebron,
Bezer, Ramoth, and Golam the designated spots where men could
flee when in danger of their lives. Perhaps the names selected for
them grew out of this designation. At any rate, Kedesh means
"holiness"; Ramoth, "rest in high places"; Golam, "joy."

The step that the old leader took was a very necessary one. It
has often been pointed out that the children of Israel were a contentious people. They quarreled frequently and in the heat of
dispute were prone to come to blows. Further, when a man killed
another it became the duty of the dead man's kin to exact vengeance. It was, therefore, to stop the spreading of these family feuds
that Joshua set up his chain of sanctuary cities where a man would
be safe from summary punishment until the courts could try his
case.

Josephus has endeavored to identify the Sanhedrim, the great
court which later governed the internal affairs of all Judah, with
the court of seventy elders which Moses established. If his conclusion were correct we could assume that the Sanhedrim in its
earliest form was functioning in the days of Joshua. There is
nothing to support the theory, however, save the undoubted fact
that the germ of all subsequent development in Hebraic law and
government is to be found in the principles laid down by Moses.

Certain it is that the care Joshua showed in thus safeguarding
human life resulted in many curious regulations of the Sanhedrim.
We know that it functioned along lines which gave the defend-
ant the benefit of every doubt. When the court decided unani-
mously for conviction the prisoner was acquitted because *such
unanimity was proof of a general prejudice*. Sitting in a solemn

semicircle, they pronounced their decisions in turn, the younger men speaking first so that they would not be influenced by the wisdom of their elders. Sentences could not be pronounced until the day after the vote had been taken, presumably to allow due consideration of new evidence. Even when the convicted man was being led away to the place of execution he could gain a stay and a rehearing by bringing up some point which had not been previously discussed. When this happened one of the guards would raise a flag and the court would reassemble at once. Five times this was allowed before it was assumed that the guilt of the prisoner had been established beyond any possibility of mistake.

From a beginning where families took the law into their own hands and bloody feuds could develop out of accidental encounters, it was a long step to the establishment of such extraordinary precautions for the prevention of miscarriages of justice. The first incentive came, we believe, from the wise decision made by Joshua to stop feuding within the ranks. Out of the establishment of this line of sanctuary cities grew the feeling that justice was something sacred, that every man had the right to a fair hearing before his life could be taken away.

There were many curious methods practiced by Jewish courts, such as the rule that local judges (three sitting together even there) could not try cases of more importance than robbery and assault, the refusal of a man to marry the wife of a deceased brother, the redemption of the produce of fruit trees during the first four years of growth. There was a soundness to the general conception of Hebraic law, however, which has set a stamp on all code making since and which can be traced back to the clear thinking of Moses. ·

In this one instance we see Joshua emerge as a contributing factor in the conception of a fundamental truth.

IV
THE CURTAIN FALLS

THE darkness comes down rapidly now. In holy Shechem, again, the tribes gathered. They seem to have been at peace and in possession of this inheritance, at least. The last words attributed to Joshua were not remarkable in themselves: a succinct summary of past history, a stern warning against backsliding, and the posing of a definite choice. But, as almost always, inspection reveals persuasively authentic traits, such as we have long learned to expect.

To begin with, Joshua made no bones about his approaching death. There was no drama of ultimate frustration, no yearning Pisgah sight. "I am old and stricken in age. . . . Behold, this day I am going the way of all the earth." (Neither Joshua nor Moses appears to have looked forward to any form of life after death; nor have the scholars found any such dogma among Hebrew root beliefs. They assign its earliest mention, in the Book of Daniel, to about 150 B.C.) His valedictory was simple, solid, four-square. He repeated Moses' warnings against compounding with the Canaanites. He related all the Israelite success and good fortune solely to the Lord's efforts. Certainly, we can sense, he held no high opinion of the tribes in this regard: "the hornet" (probably a cryptic reference to the collapse of Egyptian control) "drove them" (Amorites, Perizzites, et al.) "from before you . . . but not with *thy* sword, nor with *thy* bow." And one hears the measured voice, detached and biting, charged with memories of a hundred near-lost fights, underlining *thy*.

Significantly, not once did Joshua invoke the authority of Moses. His was the Law, of course, and the people were strongly impressed that the Law of Moses must be obeyed. But it was Joshua himself who set up the simple choice between his God, the Lord, and any other gods "which are among you." It was to

Joshua alone that the people made covenant, witnessed by the "great stone . . . under an oak," which Joshua raised up. For, said he, that stone "hath heard all the words of the Lord which he spake unto us: it shall be therefore a witness unto you, lest ye deny your God."

The final clear note sounds through the routine exhortations we have been listening to. It is a part of the man, and, with complete unity of dramatic feeling, it rises—as it should—together with the name of his former chief. "All that is written in the book of the law of Moses" (turning), "not aside therefrom to the right hand or to the left," must the people keep and do. Simple enough to prescribe it, but in the admonition rings Joshua's own personal and private device, whereby he has lived and whereby he is now dying. "Be ye therefore very courageous. . . ."

The centuries close their curtain.

PART NINE

A Study in Leadership

W HAT is leadership?

The question appears superfluous—almost flippant. Surely everybody knows what leadership is. Or at least everybody can recognize it when he sees it. Or at least everybody thinks he can.

Yet there are probably only two other questions in mankind's vast armory of curiosity more often debated: What is life? And: What is truth?

Bigots alone claim answers to these last. All three questions are interrelated in their fundamental importance to human living. Yet life goes on, regardless of our ignorance of it. And truth must, it seems, regrettably remain "this to me, and that to thee."

Yet when we come, as we must, to making some answer to the first question we have asked we find ourselves in a logical contradiction from which there is no escape. For the only leadership worthy of the name is *true* leadership. But where is the dividing line? What kind of leadership is false, and what is true?

We are dealing with human affairs, not metaphysics. Consequently we must frankly abandon, for this purpose, any philosophic detachment about "truth" and assert that there is such a thing as "true" leadership. Furthermore, we must frankly maintain that we can tell the difference between it and the "false" variety. We have a criterion, a touchstone, a measuring rod. We have already mentioned it during our survey of Joshua, in connection with some of his doings and sayings. It is this: *true leadership is that which most contributes to the welfare of the led.*

History is gorged, replete, surfeited with leaders. The very breadth of the term makes it hard to grasp and hold: anything— a ditching gang, an army, a religious movement, a band of criminals, a selling campaign—has a leader. But this study can consider leadership only in its widest manifestations: the guiding and controlling of entire groups or nations of men, primarily and more obviously in war, secondarily and more significantly in their thinking.

Similarities exist between Joshua's working conditions and those governing heads of states since his day. There is another which did not arise until the second quarter of our twentieth century: the ability to communicate instantly with all his people. Joshua could do this; so could England's fighting Prime Minister, Churchill. Leaders before him could not—Abraham Lincoln, or George Washington, or the first Napoleon, or even Julius Caesar.

The far-reaching political effects of modern radio are a study in themselves and outside our present field, but the parallelism which their existence forces upon our attention is quite important. In Joshua's day, and wherever else the individual chief could reach those he led with the sound of his voice and the impact of his personality, leadership was under a continual acid test. Orators may inflame and sway, but they cannot control. For that something more is needed than a silver tongue. As expanding communications widened the campfire circle to continental limits men were compelled to accept substitutes for their own firsthand judgment. They were forced to act not on what they heard or saw of the chief, but on what others reported of him, which, by devious and still much-disputed processes, brought about the so-called "representative" system of government.

Radio brought back the era of personal address from the council rock or stump. With the voice it brought back also personality; and moving pictures, even before television, did the rest. The shame of so many so-called leaders into whose keeping was thus

returned the priceless advantage of personal speech, not with a few
hundreds, but with many millions, was that they so often pros-
tituted it for partisan or selfish purposes. Thus radio, so often made
a tool of the "ins" against the "outs," soon sank in totalitarian
countries to the level of a government-controlled press. When
nobly and honestly used, as by England's Churchill and by Presi-
dent Roosevelt, it brought these rulers of masses unimaginable by
Joshua up to his own level of political efficiency.

Freedom is a highly relative term, as well as a most elastic and
protean concept: "this to me, and that to thee," with a vengeance.
But the average man and woman, of whatever nationality and
walk in life, needs no word splitting to decide whether there is
more or less food, shelter, and clothing; more or less ability to
work as and where convenient or desirable to the worker; more
or less capacity to circulate, to earn and save, to speak, read, and
write uncensored, to worship and vote and protest according
to conscience; more or less safety from oppression and injus-
tice; more or less equality before the law, under one form of government or another. By these rough standards has freedom been
measured since man recorded himself. By them is freedom to be
measured today.

Therefore, we need not draw any fine distinctions between
those who so confidently assume the titles and arrogate to themselves the powers of leadership. The question is a simple one: Do
they, or did they, help or hurt their people in the long run?

Those who helped are very, very few; those who did not are
legion. Joshua is one of the few in the first category.

War leadership, by its essence the more spectacular type, is
something apart. Often the truly great national leader is also, due
to the force of circumstances, a great military commander. There
are exceptions: Lincoln, for instance. But especially in earlier and
simpler times, many of the same qualities that make a commander
successful served him equally well on his statesman side. And once
more we must grant Joshua place in this category as in the other.

Yet it does not by any means follow that a military victor will,
ipso facto, be, or become, a true leader. Indeed, many of the
world's most tragic and ruinous holocausts have stemmed from
nothing more than sheer inability to grasp this fact. Worst of

these (in the sense of involving more people and destroying more property over wider territory) than any previous was the World War of 1914–18, prepared and precipitated by a warrior caste whose mentality had not developed beyond the warring stage. Its revival by the same caste—or rather by outcaste imitators holding even more barbarous and unenlightened views of world economy —was on a far grander scale. But this increased scope was a function, not of a wider outlook on the brute savage's part, but of great strides in scientific knowledge which the savage turned to destruction's use. The airplane and the radio, in their many manifestations, were made weapons of barbarous aggression, but they could not transform their users into leaders of men.

Those who can read history are fortunate. The labors of countless self-sacrificing, even heroic, scholars and other workers have preserved to our use records of our own past. These records may, through the misdirected and mischievous destructiveness of irresponsible human brutes armed with knowledge exceeding their moral stature, be damaged or even blotted out completely, as has happened before. But while they are available we commit an unforgivable crime if we do not use them for our own guidance. Joshua, it may be said, had no history to read. Instead he made it.

Would you know a true leader? Strong, and of good courage; careful; bold after decision, regardless of fresh obstacles; definite in his aims; clear in his instructions; unshaken by rumor or failure; utterly honest with his people; a keeper of treaties; an upholder of the law; farsighted; straight-thinking; without jealousy, vainglory, or vengefulness; tolerant in religion; sparing neither himself nor others; not to be turned aside by trivialities; without thought of personal gain or dynastic ambition; a man who sees visions and keeps them to himself; the sympathetic insight of a poet, and a great poet's power to uplift the minds of men.

Such a leader they buried, says the tale, in "Timnath-serah, which is in Mount Ephraim, on the north side of the hill of Gaash"—twenty miles or so northward from that Gibeon where he so nobly fought, and within the limits of the lands allotted to his own house.

His grave, like that of Moses, no man has found.

Bibliography

The Holy Bible, S. S. teachers' ed. (King James or Authorized Version), with additional matter, "Helps to the Study of the Bible," maps, etc.; Oxford University Press, London and New York.

The Outline of History, by H. G. Wells, 3rd ed.; The Macmillan Co., New York, 1922.

The Works of Flavius Josephus, comprising the "Antiquities of the Jews," etc. (transl. William Whiston), 2 vols.; Jas. B. Smith & Co., Philadelphia, 1858.

Oriental Assembly, by T. E. Lawrence (ed. A. W. Lawrence), with photographs; Williams & Norgate, Ltd., London, 1939.

The Times Survey Atlas of the World, London, 1920.

Map of Bible Lands, The National Geographic Society, Washington, 1938.

Lawrence and the Arabian Adventure, by Robert Graves; Doubleday, Doran & Co., Inc., New York, 1928.

The Old Testament: one of "Manuals of Religious Instruction" (ed. Rev. J. P. Norris, D.D.), by Edmund I. Gregory, M.A., new ed.; Rivingtons, London, 1883.

The National Geographic Magazine, The National Geographic Society, Washington, as listed:

Vol. L, No. 6, December 1926, "In the Birthplace of Christianity," by three authors.

Vol. LII, No. 6, December 1927, "East of Suez to the Mount of the Decalogue," by M. O. Williams; "The Pageant of Jerusalem," by Major E. Keith-Roach.

Vol. LIX, No. 3, March 1931, "Crusader Castles in the Near East," by W. H. Hall.

Vol. LXIV, No. 6, December 1933, "The Road of the Crusaders," by Harold Lamb.

Vol. LXXIV, No. 6, December 1938, "Change Comes to Bible Lands," by Frederick Simpich.

Vol. LXXVIII, No. 6, December 1940, "Canoeing down the River Jordan," by John D. Whiting.

Vol. LXXX, No. 4, October 1941, "Daily Life in Ancient Egypt," by William C. Hayes, painting by H. M. Herget, p. 493.

The Constitutional History of England, by William Stubbs, 2nd ed.; Clarendon Press, Oxford, 1875.

The Economics of Force, by Frank Munk, 1st ed.; George W. Stewart, New York, 1940.

"What Hitler Told Me about Peace," by Dr. Otto Strasser, article in *Liberty Magazine,* issue of April 26, 1941, pp. 10–11. *Time Magazine,* issue of April 28, 1941 (Vol. XXVII, No. 17), p. 59: Report of proceedings of American Oriental Society, meeting at University of Chicago, week of April 21–26, 1941.

The Encyclopedia Americana, The Americana Corporation, New York and Chicago, 1924.

Plutarch's Lives: transl. called Dryden's (ed. A. H. Clough); Little, Brown and Co., Boston, 1859.

The Works of Philo Judaeus (transl. C. D. Yonge), Henry G. Bohn, London, 1855.

Studies of Religious History and Criticism, by Ernest Renan, collected essays (transl. O. B. Frothingham); Carleton, New York, 1864.

The Strategy of Terror, by Edmond Taylor; Houghton Mifflin Co., Boston, 1940.

Sartor Resartus, by Thomas Carlyle; Thomas Y. Crowell & Co., New York and Boston (no date).

History of the Crusades, by J. F. Michaud (transl. anon.), with illustrations by Gustave Doré; George Barrie, Philadelphia (no date).

Napoleon, by Emil Ludwig; Boni and Liveright, New York, 1926.

Histoire de la Nation Française, Gabriel Hanotaux, editor in chief, Librairie Plon, Paris, 1920 *et seq.,* Vol. VIII (copyright 1927), "Histoire Militaire et Navale," 2me vol., 1ere partie, par le général Mangin.

Caesar's Gallic War (ed. Allen & Greenough, re-ed. James B. Greenough and others), Ginn & Co., Boston, 1898.

Julius Caesar, by W. Warde Fowler; G. P. Putnam's Sons, New York, 1891.

The Roman Republic, by T. Rice Holmes; Clarendon Press, Oxford, 1923.

The Cambridge Ancient History (esp. Vol. IX), University Press, Cambridge, 1932.

The Battle Ground, by Hilaire Belloc; Cassell & Co., Ltd., London, 1936.

Hitler's Twelve Apostles, by Oswald Dutch; Robert M. McBride & Co., New York, 1940.

Ambassador Dodd's Diary (ed. William E. Dodd, Jr., and Martha Dodd), Harcourt, Brace & Co., New York, 1941.

The Foundations of Bible History: Joshua, Judges, by John Garstang; Constable & Co., Ltd., London, 1931.

Dead Towns and Living Men, by C. Leonard Woolley; Oxford University Press, London and New York, 1929.

Egypt and Israel, by Willis Brewer, The Torch Press, Cedar Rapids, Iowa, 1910.

The Book of a Thousand Nights and a Night (transl. Richard F. Burton, Luristan limited ed.; The Burton Club (for private subscribers only).

Saint Paul, by Ernest Renan (transl. Ingersoll Lockwood), Carleton, New York, 1869.

A New Commentary on Holy Scripture (ed. Gore, Goudge, and Guillaume), The Macmillan Co., New York, 1928; article on Joshua by L. E. P. Erith, pp. 189 ff.

Personalities of the Old Testament, by Fleming James; Charles Scribner's Sons, Ltd., London, 1939.

Through Lands of the Bible, by H. V. Morton; Dodd, Mead & Co., New York, 1938.

The Music of the Most Ancient Nations, by Carl Engel; William Reeves, London, 1864 (issue of 1909); Chapter VI, p. 314, merely quotes Joshua VI: 4, 5. Text apparently confuses "trumpet" with rams' horns; otherwise a compilation of learning, uncritical.

Encyclopédie de la Musique et Dictionnaire du Conservatoire, by A. Lavignac; Iere partie, "Histoire de la Musique—Antiquité—Moyen Age"; Librairie Delagrave, Paris, 1913; article "Hébreux," by Grand Rabbi Abraham Cahen, refers to the *Schofar,* "fait de cornes de belier," rams' horns, whose sounds were "saccadés et comme brisés"; Fig. 124, p. 69, picture of *Schofar*—"en usage encore aujourd'hui dans les synagogues." Recognizes difference between *haçoceroth*—silver or brass trumpets.

Alexander the Great, by Arthur Weigall; Keystone Library, Thornton Butterworth, Ltd., London, 1933.

Instructions Militaires du Roi de Prusse pour ses Généraux, pub. M. Faesch; nouvelle édition augmentée avec les Instructions pour la Petite Guerre, etc.; London, 1777 (being the handbook prepared by Frederick the Great, including instructions for how and when to massacre prisoners).

A Treatise of Military Discipline, by Humphrey Bland, 4th ed.; Sam Buckley, London, 1740.

Essai Général de Tactique, by Jacques Antoine Hippolyte Guibert; C. Plomteux, Liège, 1775.

The Encyclopaedia Britannica, 14th ed., Vol. XII, article "Infantry," signed: "F. I. M.; B. H. L. H." (Capt. B. H. Liddell Hart?).

War in the Desert: the Battle for Africa, by Raoul Aglion; Henry Holt & Co., New York, 1941.

Memoirs of a Napoleonic Officer, Jean-Baptiste Barrès (ed. Maurice Barrès, transl. Bernard Miall), Lincoln MacVeagh, The Dial Press, New York, 1925.

Generals and Generalship: The Lees Knowles Lectures, Trinity College, Cambridge, 1939, by General Sir Archibald Wavell; The Macmillan Co., New York, 1941.

The Bible and Archaeology, by Sir Frederic Kenyon; George G. Harrap & Co., Ltd., London, 1940.

Talleyrand, by Duff Cooper; Jonathan Cape, London, 1932.

Talleyrand: The Training of a Statesman, by Anna Bowman Dodd; G. P. Putnam's Sons, New York and London, 1927.

Marlborough: His Life and Times, by Winston S. Churchill; Charles Scribner's Sons, New York, 1933; Vol. V. (pub. 1937).

Hebrewisms of West Africa, by Joseph J. Williams, S.J.; Lincoln MacVeagh, The Dial Press, New York, 1931.

The Nile: Notes for Travellers, by E. A. Wallis Budge, 12th ed.; Thos. Cook & Son (Egypt), Ltd., London, 1912.

The Dawn of Civilization: Egypt and Chaldea, by Gaston Maspero (ed. A. H. Sayce, transl. M. L. McClure); Society for Promoting Christian Knowledge, The Macmillan Company, London and Toronto, 1922 (2nd reprint of 4th ed.).

Defense Will Not Win the War, by Lt. Col. W. F. Kernan, U.S.A.; Little, Brown & Co., Boston, 1942.

Roots of Strategy (ed. Maj. Thomas R. Phillips, U.S.A.), Military Service Pub. Co., Harrisburg, Pa. (no date).

A Short History of the Jews—Down to the Roman Period, by E. E. Kellett; Lincoln MacVeagh, The Dial Press, New York, 1929.

The Book of Joshua

CHAPTER 1

1 Now after the death of Moses the servant of the LORD it came to pass, that the LORD spake unto Joshua the son of Nun, Moses' minister, saying,

2 Moses my servant is dead; now therefore arise, go over this Jordan, thou, and all this people, unto the land which I do give to them, *even* to the children of Israel.

3 Every place that the sole of your foot shall tread upon, that have I given unto you, as I said unto Moses.

4 From the wilderness and this Lebanon even unto the great river, the river Euphrates, all the land of the Hittites, and unto the great sea toward the going down of the sun, shall be your coast.

5 There shall not any man be able to stand before thee all the days of thy life: as I was with Moses, *so* I will be with thee: I will not fail thee, nor forsake thee.

6 Be strong and of a good courage: for unto this people shalt thou divide for an inheritance the land, which I sware unto their fathers to give them.

7 Only be thou strong and very courageous, that thou mayest observe to do according to all the law, which Moses my servant commanded thee: turn not from it *to* the right hand or *to* the left, that thou mayest prosper whithersoever thou goest.

8 This book of the law shall not depart out of thy mouth; but thou shalt meditate therein day and night, that thou mayest observe to do according to all that is written therein: for then thou shalt make thy way prosperous, and then thou shalt have good success.

9 Have not I commanded thee? Be strong and of a good courage; be not afraid, neither be thou dismayed: for the LORD thy God *is* with thee whithersoever thou goest.

10 Then Joshua commanded the officers of the people, saying,

11 Pass through the host, and command the people, saying, Prepare you victuals; for within three days ye shall pass over this Jordan, to go in to possess the land, which the LORD your God giveth you to possess it.

12 And to the Reubenites, and to the Gadites, and to half the tribe of Manasseh, spake Joshua, saying,

13 Remember the word which Moses the servant of the LORD commanded you, saying, The LORD your God hath given you rest, and hath given you this land.

14 Your wives, your little ones, and your cattle, shall remain in the land which Moses gave you on this side Jordan; but ye shall pass before your brethren armed, all the mighty men of valour, and help them;

15 Until the LORD have given your brethren rest, as *he hath given* you, and they also have possessed the land which the LORD your God giveth them: then ye shall return unto the land of your possession, and enjoy it, which Moses the LORD's servant gave you on this side Jordan toward the sunrising.

16 And they answered Joshua,

saying, All that thou commandest us we will do, and whithersoever thou sendest us, we will go.

17 According as we hearkened unto Moses in all things, so will we hearken unto thee: only the LORD thy God be with thee, as he was with Moses.

18 Whosoever *he be* that doth rebel against thy commandment, and will not hearken unto thy words in all that thou commandest him, he shall be put to death: only be strong and of a good courage.

CHAPTER 2

1 And Joshua the son of Nun sent out of Shittim two men to spy secretly, saying, Go view the land, even Jericho. And they went, and came into an harlot's house, named Rahab, and lodged there.

2 And it was told the king of Jericho, saying, Behold, there came men in hither to night of the children of Israel to search out the country.

3 And the king of Jericho sent unto Rahab, saying, Bring forth the men that are come to thee, which are entered into thine house: for they be come to search out all the country.

4 And the woman took the two men, and hid them, and said thus, There came men unto me, but I wist not whence they *were:*

5 And it came to pass *about the time* of shutting of the gate, when it was dark, that the men went out: whither the men went I wot not: pursue after them quickly; for ye shall overtake them.

6 But she had brought them up to the roof of the house, and hid them with the stalks of flax, which she had laid in order upon the roof.

7 And the men pursued after them the way to Jordan unto the fords: and as soon as they which pursued

after them were gone out, they shut the gate.

8 And before they were laid down, she came up unto them upon the roof;

9 And she said unto the men, I know that the LORD hath given you the land, and that your terror is fallen upon us, and that all the inhabitants of the land faint because of you.

10 For we have heard how the LORD dried up the water of the Red sea for you, when ye came out of Egypt; and what ye did unto the two kings of the Amorites, that *were* on the other side Jordan, Sihon and Og, whom ye utterly destroyed.

11 And as soon as we had heard *these things,* our hearts did melt, neither did there remain any more courage in any man, because of you: for the LORD your God, he *is* God in heaven above, and in earth beneath.

12 Now therefore, I pray you, swear unto me by the LORD, since I have shewed you kindness, that ye will also shew kindness unto my father's house, and give me a true token:

13 And *that* ye will save alive my father, and my mother, and my brethren, and my sisters, and all that they have, and deliver our lives from death.

14 And the men answered her, Our life for yours, if ye utter not this our business. And it shall be, when the LORD hath given us the land, that we will deal kindly and truly with thee.

15 Then she let them down by a cord through the window: for her house *was* upon the town wall, and she dwelt upon the wall.

16 And she said unto them, Get you to the mountain, lest the pursuers meet you; and hide yourselves there three days, until the pursuers be returned: and afterward may ye go your way.

17 And the men said unto her, We *will be* blameless of this thine oath which thou hast made us swear.

18 Behold, *when* we come into the land, thou shalt bind this line of scarlet thread in the window which thou didst let us down by: and thou shalt bring thy father, and thy mother, and thy brethren, and all thy father's household, home unto thee.

19 And it shall be, *that* whosoever shall go out of the doors of thy house into the street, his blood *shall be* upon his head, and we *will be* guiltless: and whosoever shall be with thee in the house, his blood *shall be* on our head, if *any* hand be upon him.

20 And if thou utter this our business, then we will be quit of thine oath which thou hast made us to swear.

21 And she said, According unto your words, so *be* it. And she sent them away, and they departed: and she bound the scarlet line in the window.

22 And they went, and came unto the mountain, and abode there three days, until the pursuers were returned: and the pursuers sought *them* throughout all the way, but found *them* not.

23 So the two men returned, and descended from the mountain, and passed over, and came to Joshua the son of Nun, and told him all *things* that befell them:

24 And they said unto Joshua, Truly the LORD hath delivered into our hands all the land; for even all the inhabitants of the country do faint because of us.

CHAPTER 3

1 And Joshua rose early in the morning; and they removed from Shittim, and came to Jordan, he and all the children of Israel, and lodged there before they passed over.

2 And it came to pass after three days, that the officers went through the host;

3 And they commanded the people, saying, When ye see the ark of the covenant of the LORD your God, and the priests the Levites bearing it, then ye shall remove from your place, and go after it.

4 Yet there shall be a space between you and it, about two thousand cubits by measure: come not near unto it, that ye may know the way by which ye must go: for ye have not passed *this* way heretofore.

5 And Joshua said unto the people, Sanctify yourselves: for to morrow the LORD will do wonders among you.

6 And Joshua spake unto the priests, saying, Take up the ark of the covenant, and pass over before the people. And they took up the ark of the covenant, and went before the people.

7 And the LORD said unto Joshua, This day will I begin to magnify thee in the sight of all Israel, that they may know that, as I was with Moses, *so* I will be with thee.

8 And thou shalt command the priests that bear the ark of the covenant, saying, When ye are come to the brink of the water of Jordan, ye shall stand still in Jordan.

9 And Joshua said unto the children of Israel, Come hither, and hear the words of the LORD your God.

10 And Joshua said, Hereby ye shall know that the living God *is* among you, and *that* he will without fail drive out from before you the Canaanites, and the Hittites, and the Hivites, and the Perizzites, and the Girgashites, and the Amorites, and the Jebusites.

11 Behold, the ark of the covenant of the Lord of all the earth passeth over before you into Jordan.

12 Now therefore take you twelve men out of the tribes of Israel, out of every tribe a man.

13 And it shall come to pass, as soon as the soles of the feet of the priests that bear the ark of the LORD, the Lord of all the earth, shall rest in the waters of Jordan, *that* the waters of Jordan shall be cut off *from* the waters that come down from above; and they shall stand upon an heap.

14 And it came to pass, when the people removed from their tents, to pass over Jordan, and the priests bearing the ark of the covenant before the people;

15 And as they that bare the ark were come unto Jordan, and the feet of the priests that bare the ark were dipped in the brim of the water, (for Jordan overfloweth all his banks all the time of harvest,)

16 That the waters which came down from above stood *and* rose up upon an heap very far from the city Adam, that *is* beside Zaretan: and those that came down toward the sea of the plain, *even* the salt sea, failed, *and* were cut off: and the people passed over right against Jericho.

17 And the priests that bare the ark of the covenant of the LORD stood firm on dry ground in the midst of Jordan, and all the Israelites passed over on dry ground, until all the people were passed clean over Jordan.

CHAPTER 4

1 And it came to pass, when all the people were clean passed over Jordan, that the LORD spake unto Joshua, saying,

2 Take you twelve men out of the people, out of every tribe a man,

3 And command ye them, saying, Take you hence out of the midst of Jordan, out of the place where the priests' feet stood firm, twelve stones, and ye shall carry them over with you, and leave them in the lodging place, where ye shall lodge this night.

4 Then Joshua called the twelve men, whom he had prepared of the children of Israel, out of every tribe a man:

5 And Joshua said unto them, Pass over before the ark of the LORD your God into the midst of Jordan, and take you up every man of you a stone upon his shoulder, according unto the number of the tribes of the children of Israel:

6 That this may be a sign among you, *that* when your children ask *their fathers* in time to come, saying, What *mean* ye by these stones?

7 Then ye shall answer them, That the waters of Jordan were cut off before the ark of the covenant of the LORD; when it passed over Jordan, the waters of Jordan were cut off: and these stones shall be for a memorial unto the children of Israel for ever.

8 And the children of Israel did so as Joshua commanded, and took up twelve stones out of the midst of Jordan, as the LORD spake unto Joshua, according to the number of the tribes of the children of Israel, and carried them over with them unto the place where they lodged, and laid them down there.

9 And Joshua set up twelve stones in the midst of Jordan, in the place where the feet of the priests which bare the ark of the covenant stood: and they are there unto this day.

10 For the priests which bare the ark stood in the midst of Jordan, until every thing was finished that the LORD commanded Joshua to speak unto the people, according to all that Moses commanded Joshua: and the people hasted and passed over.

11 And it came to pass, when all the people were clean passed over,

that the ark of the Lord passed over, and the priests, in the presence of the people.

12 And the children of Reuben, and the children of Gad, and half the tribe of Manasseh, passed over armed before the children of Israel, as Moses spake unto them:

13 About forty thousand prepared for war passed over before the Lord unto battle, to the plains of Jericho.

14 On that day the Lord magnified Joshua in the sight of all Israel; and they feared him, as they feared Moses, all the days of his life.

15 And the Lord spake unto Joshua, saying,

16 Command the priests that bear the ark of the testimony, that they come up out of Jordan.

17 Joshua therefore commanded the priests, saying, Come ye up out of Jordan.

18 And it came to pass, when the priests that bare the ark of the covenant of the Lord were come up out of the midst of Jordan, *and* the soles of the priests' feet were lifted up unto the dry land, that the waters of Jordan returned unto their place, and flowed over all his banks, as *they did* before.

19 And the people came up out of Jordan on the tenth *day* of the first month, and encamped in Gilgal, in the east border of Jericho.

20 And those twelve stones, which they took out of Jordan, did Joshua pitch in Gilgal.

21 And he spake unto the children of Israel, saying, When your children shall ask their fathers in time to come, saying, What *mean* these stones?

22 Then ye shall let your children know, saying, Israel came over this Jordan on dry land.

23 For the Lord your God dried up the waters of Jordan from before you, until ye were passed over, as the Lord your God did to the Red sea, which he dried up from before us, until we were gone over:

24 That all the people of the earth might know the hand of the Lord, that it *is* mighty: that ye might fear the Lord your God for ever.

CHAPTER 5

1 And it came to pass, when all the kings of the Amorites, which *were* on the side of Jordan westward, and all the kings of the Canaanites, which *were* by the sea, heard that the Lord had dried up the waters of Jordan from before the children of Israel, until we were passed over, that their heart melted, neither was there spirit in them any more, because of the children of Israel.

2 At that time the Lord said unto Joshua, Make thee sharp knives, and circumcise again the children of Israel the second time.

3 And Joshua made him sharp knives, and circumcised the children of Israel at the hill of the foreskins.

4 And this *is* the cause why Joshua did circumcise: All the people that came out of Egypt, *that were* males, *even* all the men of war, died in the wilderness by the way, after they came out of Egypt.

5 Now all the people that came out were circumcised: but all the people *that were* born in the wilderness by the way as they came forth out of Egypt, *them* they had not circumcised.

6 For the children of Israel walked forty years in the wilderness, till all the people *that were* men of war, which came out of Egypt, were consumed, because they obeyed not the voice of the Lord: unto whom the Lord sware that he would not shew them the land, which the Lord sware unto their fathers that he would give

us, a land that floweth with milk and honey.

7 And their children, *whom* he raised up in their stead, them Joshua circumcised: for they were uncircumcised, because they had not circumcised them by the way.

8 And it came to pass, when they had done circumcising all the people, that they abode in their places in the camp, till they were whole.

9 And the Lord said unto Joshua, This day have I rolled away the reproach of Egypt from off you. Wherefore the name of the place is called Gilgal unto this day.

10 And the children of Israel encamped in Gilgal, and kept the passover on the fourteenth day of the month at even in the plains of Jericho.

11 And they did eat of the old corn of the land on the morrow after the passover, unleavened cakes, and parched *corn* in the selfsame day.

12 And the manna ceased on the morrow after they had eaten of the old corn of the land; neither had the children of Israel manna any more; but they did eat of the fruit of the land of Canaan that year.

13 And it came to pass, when Joshua was by Jericho, that he lifted up his eyes and looked, and, behold, there stood a man over against him with his sword drawn in his hand: and Joshua went unto him, and said unto him, *Art* thou for us, or for our adversaries?

14 And he said, Nay; but *as* captain of the host of the Lord am I now come. And Joshua fell on his face to the earth, and did worship, and said unto him, What saith my lord unto his servant?

15 And the captain of the Lord's host said unto Joshua, Loose thy shoe from off thy foot; for the place whereon thou standest *is* holy. And Joshua did so.

CHAPTER 6

1 Now Jericho was straitly shut up because of the children of Israel: none went out, and none came in.

2 And the Lord said unto Joshua, See, I have given into thine hand Jericho, and the king thereof, *and* the mighty men of valour.

3 And ye shall compass the city, all *ye* men of war, *and* go round about the city once. Thus shalt thou do six days.

4 And seven priests shall bear before the ark seven trumpets of rams' horns: and the seventh day ye shall compass the city seven times, and the priests shall blow with the trumpets.

5 And it shall come to pass, that when they make a long *blast* with the ram's horn, *and* when ye hear the sound of the trumpet, all the people shall shout with a great shout; and the wall of the city shall fall down flat, and the people shall ascend up every man straight before him.

6 And Joshua the son of Nun called the priests, and said unto them, Take up the ark of the covenant, and let seven priests bear seven trumpets of rams' horns before the ark of the Lord.

7 And he said unto the people, Pass on, and compass the city, and let him that is armed pass on before the ark of the Lord.

8 And it came to pass, when Joshua had spoken unto the people, that the seven priests bearing the seven trumpets of rams' horns passed on before the Lord, and blew with the trumpets: and the ark of the covenant of the Lord followed them.

9 And the armed men went before the priests that blew with the trumpets, and the rereward came after the ark, *the priests* going on, and blowing with the trumpets.

10 And Joshua had commanded

the people, saying, Ye shall not shout, nor make any noise with your voice, neither shall *any* word proceed out of your mouth, until the day I bid you shout; then shall ye shout.

11 So the ark of the LORD compassed the city, going about *it* once and they came into the camp, and lodged in the camp.

12 And Joshua rose early in the morning, and the priests took up the ark of the LORD.

13 And seven priests bearing seven trumpets of rams' horns before the ark of the LORD went on continually, and blew with the trumpets: and the armed men went before them; but the rereward came after the ark of the LORD, *the priests* going on, and blowing with the trumpets.

14 And the second day they compassed the city once, and returned into the camp: so they did six days.

15 And it came to pass on the seventh day, that they rose early about the dawning of the day, and compassed the city after the same manner seven times: only on that day they compassed the city seven times.

16 And it came to pass at the seventh time, when the priests blew with the trumpets, Joshua said unto the people, Shout; for the LORD hath given you the city.

17 And the city shall be accursed, *even* it, and all that *are* therein, to the LORD: only Rahab the harlot shall live, she and all that *are* with her in the house, because she hid the messengers that we sent.

18 And ye, in any wise keep *yourselves* from the accursed thing, lest ye make *yourselves* accursed, when ye take of the accursed thing, and make the camp of Israel a curse, and trouble it.

19 But all the silver, and gold, and vessels of brass and iron, *are* consecrated unto the LORD: they shall come into the treasury of the LORD.

20 So the people shouted when *the priests* blew with the trumpets: and it came to pass, when the people heard the sound of the trumpet, and the people shouted with a great shout, that the wall fell down flat, so that the people went up into the city, every man straight before him, and they took the city.

21 And they utterly destroyed all that *was* in the city, both man and woman, young and old, and ox, and sheep, and ass, with the edge of the sword.

22 But Joshua had said unto the two men that had spied out the country, Go into the harlot's house, and bring out thence the woman, and all that she hath, as ye sware unto her.

23 And the young men that were spies went in, and brought out Rahab, and her father, and her mother, and her brethren, and all that she had; and they brought out all her kindred, and left them without the camp of Israel.

24 And they burnt the city with fire, and all that *was* therein: only the silver, and the gold, and the vessels of brass and of iron, they put into the treasury of the house of the LORD.

25 And Joshua saved Rahab the harlot alive, and her father's household, and all that she had; and she dwelleth in Israel *even* unto this day; because she hid the messengers, which Joshua sent to spy out Jericho.

26 And Joshua adjured *them* at that time, saying, Cursed *be* the man before the LORD, that riseth up and buildeth this city Jericho: he shall lay the foundation thereof in his first-born, and in his youngest *son* shall he set up the gates of it.

27 So the LORD was with Joshua; and his fame was *noised* throughout all the country.

CHAPTER 7

1 But the children of Israel committed a trespass in the accursed thing: for Achan, the son of Carmi, the son of Zabdi, the son of Zerah, of the tribe of Judah, took of the accursed thing: and the anger of the LORD was kindled against the children of Israel.

2 And Joshua sent men from Jericho to Ai, which is beside Bethaven, on the east side of Beth-el, and spake unto them, saying, Go up and view the country. And the men went up and viewed Ai.

3 And they returned to Joshua, and said unto him, Let not all the people go up; but let about two or three thousand men go up and smite Ai; and make not all the people to labour thither; for they are but few.

4 So there went up thither of the people about three thousand men: and they flew before the men of Ai.

5 And the men of Ai smote of them about thirty and six men: for they chased them from before the gate even unto Shebarim, and smote them in the going down: wherefore the hearts of the people melted, and became as water.

6 And Joshua rent his clothes, and fell to the earth upon his face before the ark of the LORD until the eventide, he and the elders of Israel, and put dust upon their heads.

7 And Joshua said, Alas, O Lord GOD, wherefore hast thou at all brought this people over Jordan, to deliver us into the hand of the Amorites, to destroy us? would to God we had been content, and dwelt on the other side Jordan!

8 O Lord, what shall I say, when Israel turneth their backs before their enemies!

9 For the Canaanites and all the inhabitants of the land shall hear of it, and shall environ us round, and cut off our name from the earth: and what wilt thou do unto thy great name?

10 And the LORD said unto Joshua, Get thee up; wherefore liest thou thus upon thy face?

11 Israel hath sinned, and they have also transgressed my covenant which I commanded them: for they have even taken of the accursed thing, and have also stolen, and dissembled also, and they have put it even among their own stuff.

12 Therefore the children of Israel could not stand before their enemies, but turned their backs before their enemies, because they were accursed: neither will I be with you any more, except ye destroy the accursed from among you.

13 Up, sanctify the people, and say, Sanctify yourselves against to morrow: for thus saith the LORD God of Israel, There is an accursed thing in the midst of thee. O Israel: thou canst not stand before thine enemies, until ye take away the accursed thing from among you.

14 In the morning therefore ye shall be brought according to your tribes: and it shall be, that the tribe which the LORD taketh shall come according to the families thereof; and the family which the LORD shall take shall come by households; and the household which the LORD shall take shall come man by man.

15 And it shall be, that he that is taken with the accursed thing shall be burnt with fire, he and all that he hath: because he hath transgressed the covenant of the LORD, and because he hath wrought folly in Israel.

16 So Joshua rose up early in the morning, and brought Israel by their tribes; and the tribe of Judah was taken:

17 And he brought the family of Judah; and he took the family of the Zarhites: and he brought the family

of the Zarhites man by man; and
Zabdi was taken:

18 And he brought his household
man by man; and Achan, the son of
Carmi, the son of Zabdi, the son of
Zerah, of the tribe of Judah, was
taken.

19 And Joshua said unto Achan,
My son, give, I pray thee, glory to
the LORD God of Israel, and make
confession unto him; and tell me
now what thou hast done; hide it
not from me.

20 And Achan answered Joshua,
and said, Indeed I have sinned against
the LORD God of Israel, and thus
and thus have I done:

21 When I saw among the spoils a
goodly Babylonish garment, and two
hundred shekels of silver, and a
wedge of gold of fifty shekels
weight, then I coveted them, and
took them; and, behold, they are hid
in the earth in the midst of my tent,
and the silver under it.

22 So Joshua sent messengers, and
they ran unto the tent; and, behold,
it was hid in his tent, and the silver
under it.

23 And they took them out of the
midst of the tent, and brought them
unto Joshua, and unto all the children of Israel, and laid them out before the LORD.

24 And Joshua, and all Israel with
him, took Achan the son of Zerah,
and the silver, and the garment, and
the wedge of gold, and his sons, and
his daughters, and his oxen, and his
asses, and his sheep, and his tent, and
all that he had: and they brought
them unto the valley of Achor.

25 And Joshua said, Why hast
thou troubled us? the LORD shall
trouble thee this day. And all Israel
stoned him with stones, and burned
them with fire, after they had stoned
them with stones.

26 And they raised over him a
great heap of stones unto this day.
So the LORD turned from the fierceness of his anger. Wherefore the
name of that place was called, The
valley of Achor, unto this day.

CHAPTER 8

1 And the LORD said unto Joshua,
Fear not, neither be thou dismayed:
take all the people of war with thee,
and arise, go up to Ai: see, I have
given into thy hand the king of Ai,
and his people, and his city, and his
land:

2 And thou shalt do to Ai and her
king as thou didst unto Jericho and
her king: only the spoil thereof, and
the cattle thereof, shall ye take for
a prey unto yourselves: lay thee an
ambush for the city behind it.

3 So Joshua arose, and all the people of war, to go up against Ai: and
Joshua chose out thirty thousand
mighty men of valour, and sent
them away by night.

4 And he commanded them, saying, Behold, ye shall lie in wait
against the city, even behind the
city: go not very far from the city,
but be ye all ready:

5 And I, and all the people that
are with me, will approach unto the
city: and it shall come to pass, when
they come out against us, as at the
first, that we will flee before them,

6 (For they will come out after us)
till we have drawn them from the
city; for they will say, They flee
before us, as at the first: therefore
we will flee before them.

7 Then ye shall rise up from the
ambush, and seize upon the city: for
the LORD your God will deliver it
into your hand.

8 And it shall be, when ye have
taken the city, that ye shall set the
city on fire: according to the commandment of the LORD shall ye do.
See, I have commanded you.

9 Joshua therefore sent them
forth: and they went to lie in ambush, and abode between Bethel and

Ai, on the west side of Ai: but Joshua lodged that night among the people.

10 And Joshua rose up early in the morning, and numbered the people, and went up, he and the elders of Israel, before the people to Ai.

11 And all the people, *even the people* of war that *were* with him, went up, and drew nigh, and came before the city, and pitched on the north side of Ai: now *there was* a valley between them and Ai.

12 And he took about five thousand men, and set them to lie in ambush between Bethel and Ai, on the west side of the city.

13 And when they had set the people, *even* all the host that *was* on the north of the city, and their liers in wait on the west of the city, Joshua went that night into the midst of the valley.

14 And it came to pass, when the king of Ai saw *it*, that they hasted and rose up early, and the men of the city went out against Israel to battle, he and all his people, at a time appointed, before the plain; but he wist not that *there were* liers in ambush against him behind the city.

15 And Joshua and all Israel made as if they were beaten before them, and fled by the way of the wilderness.

16 And all the people that *were* in Ai were called together to pursue after them: and they pursued after Joshua, and were drawn away from the city.

17 And there was not a man left in Ai or Bethel, that went not out after Israel: and they left the city open, and pursued after Israel.

18 And the LORD said unto Joshua, Stretch out the spear that *is* in thy hand toward Ai; for I will give it into thine hand. And Joshua stretched out the spear that *he had* in his hand toward the city.

19 And the ambush arose quickly out of their place, and they ran as soon as he had stretched out his hand: and they entered into the city, and took it, and hasted and set the city on fire.

20 And when the men of Ai looked behind them, they saw, and, behold, the smoke of the city ascended up to heaven, and they had no power to flee this way or that way: and the people that fled to the wilderness turned back upon the pursuers.

21 And when Joshua and all Israel saw that the ambush had taken the city, and that the smoke of the city ascended, then they turned again, and slew the men of Ai.

22 And the other issued out of the city against them; so they were in the midst of Israel, some on this side, and some on that side: and they smote them, so that they let none of them remain or escape.

23 And the king of Ai they took alive, and brought him to Joshua.

24 And it came to pass, when Israel had made an end of slaying all the inhabitants of Ai in the field, in the wilderness wherein they chased them, and when they were all fallen on the edge of the sword, until they were consumed, that all the Israelites returned unto Ai, and smote it with the edge of the sword.

25 And *so* it was, *that* all that fell that day, both of men and women, *were* twelve thousand, *even* all the men of Ai.

26 For Joshua drew not his hand back, wherewith he stretched out the spear, until he had utterly destroyed all the inhabitants of Ai.

27 Only the cattle and the spoil of that city Israel took for a prey unto themselves, according unto the word of the LORD which he commanded Joshua.

28 And Joshua burnt Ai, and made it an heap for ever, *even* a desolation unto this day.

29 And the king of Ai he hanged on a tree until eventide: and as soon as the sun was down, Joshua commanded that they should take his carcase down from the tree, and cast it at the entering of the gate of the city, and raise thereon a great heap of stones, *that remaineth* unto this day.

30 Then Joshua built an altar unto the LORD God of Israel in mount Ebal,

31 As Moses the servant of the LORD commanded the children of Israel, as it is written in the book of the law of Moses, an altar of whole stones, over which no man hath lift up *any* iron; and they offered thereon burnt offerings unto the LORD, and sacrificed peace offerings.

32 And he wrote there upon the stones a copy of the law of Moses, which he wrote in the presence of the children of Israel.

33 And all Israel, and their elders, and officers, and their judges, stood on this side the ark and on that side before the priests the Levites, which bare the ark of the covenant of the LORD, as well the stranger, as he that was born among them; half of them over against mount Gerizim, and half of them over against mount Ebal; as Moses the servant of the LORD had commanded before, that they should bless the people of Israel.

34 And afterward he read all the words of the law, the blessings and cursings, according to all that is written in the book of the law.

35 There was not a word of all that Moses commanded, which Joshua read not before all the congregation of Israel, with the women, and the little ones, and the strangers that were conversant among them.

CHAPTER 9

1 And it came to pass, when all the kings which *were* on this side Jordan, in the hills, and in the valleys, and in all the coasts of the great sea over against Lebanon, the Hittite, and the Amorite, the Canaanite, the Perizzite, the Hivite, and the Jebusite, heard *thereof;*

2 That they gathered themselves together, to fight with Joshua and with Israel, with one accord.

3 And when the inhabitants of Gibeon heard what Joshua had done unto Jericho and to Ai,

4 They did work wilily, and went and made as if they had been ambassadors, and took old sacks upon their asses, and wine bottles, old, and rent, and bound up;

5 And old shoes and clouted upon their feet, and old garments upon them; and all the bread of their provision was dry *and* mouldy.

6 And they went to Joshua unto the camp at Gilgal, and said unto him, and to the men of Israel, We be come from a far country: now therefore make ye a league with us.

7 And the men of Israel said unto the Hivites, Peradventure ye dwell among us; and how shall we make a league with you?

8 And they said unto Joshua, We *are* thy servants. And Joshua said unto them, Who *are* ye? and from whence come ye?

9 And they said unto him, From a very far country thy servants are come because of the name of the LORD thy God: for we have heard the fame of him, and all that he did in Egypt,

10 And all that he did to the two kings of the Amorites, that *were* beyond Jordan, to Sihon king of Heshbon, and to Og king of Bashan, which *was* at Ashtaroth.

11 Wherefore our elders and all the inhabitants of our country spake to us, saying, Take victuals with you for the journey, and go to meet them, and say unto them, We *are*

your servants: therefore now make ye a league with us.

12 This our bread we took hot *for* our provision out of our houses on the day we came forth to go unto you; but now, behold, it is dry, and it is mouldy:

13 And these bottles of wine, which we filled, *were* new; and, behold, they be rent: and these our garments and our shoes are become old by reason of the very long journey.

14 And the men took of their victuals, and asked not *counsel* at the mouth of the LORD.

15 And Joshua made peace with them, and made a league with them, to let them live: and the princes of the congregation sware unto them.

16 And it came to pass at the end of three days after they had made a league with them, that they heard that they *were* their neighbours, and *that* they dwelt among them.

17 And the children of Israel journeyed, and came unto their cities on the third day. Now their cities *were* Gibeon, and Chephirah, and Beeroth, and Kirjath-jearim.

18 And the children of Israel smote them not, because the princes of the congregation had sworn unto them by the LORD God of Israel. And all the congregation murmured against the princes.

19 But all the princes said unto all the congregation, We have sworn unto them by the LORD God of Israel: now therefore we may not touch them.

20 This we will do to them; we will even let them live, lest wrath be upon us, because of the oath which we sware unto them.

21 And the princes said unto them, Let them live; but let them be hewers of wood and drawers of water unto all the congregation; as the princes had promised them.

22 And Joshua called for them, and he spake unto them, saying, Wherefore have ye beguiled us, saying, We *are* very far from you; when ye dwell among us?

23 Now therefore ye *are* cursed, and there shall none of you be freed from being bondmen, and hewers of wood and drawers of water for the house of my God.

24 And they answered Joshua, and said, Because it was certainly told thy servants, how that the LORD thy God commanded his servant Moses to give you all the land, and to destroy all the inhabitants of the land from before you, therefore we were sore afraid of our lives because of you, and have done this thing.

25 And now, behold, we *are* in thine hand: as it seemeth good and right unto thee to do unto us, do.

26 And so did he unto them, and delivered them out of the hand of the children of Israel, that they slew them not.

27 And Joshua made them that day hewers of wood and drawers of water for the congregation, and for the altar of the LORD, even unto this day, in the place which he should choose.

CHAPTER 10

1 Now it came to pass, when Adonizedec king of Jerusalem had heard how Joshua had taken Ai, and had utterly destroyed it; as he had done to Jericho and her king, so he had done to Ai and her king; and how the inhabitants of Gibeon had made peace with Israel, and were among them;

2 That they feared greatly, because Gibeon *was* a great city, as one of the royal cities, and because it *was* greater than Ai, and all the men thereof *were* mighty.

3 Wherefore Adonizedec king of Jerusalem sent unto Hoham king of Hebron, and unto Piram king of Jar-

muth, and unto Japhia king of Lachish, and unto Debir king of Eglon, saying,

4 Come up unto me, and help me, that we may smite Gibeon: for it hath made peace with Joshua and with the children of Israel.

5 Therefore the five kings of the Amorites, the king of Jerusalem, the king of Hebron, the king of Jarmuth, the king of Lachish, the king of Eglon, gathered themselves together, and went up, they and all their hosts, and encamped before Gibeon, and made war against it.

6 And the men of Gibeon sent unto Joshua to the camp to Gilgal, saying, Slack not thy hand from thy servants; come up to us quickly, and save us, and help us: for all the kings of the Amorites that dwell in the mountains are gathered together against us.

7 So Joshua ascended from Gilgal, he, and all the people of war with him, and all the mighty men of valour.

8 And the LORD said unto Joshua, Fear them not: for I have delivered them into thine hand; there shall not a man of them stand before thee.

9 Joshua therefore came unto them suddenly, *and* went up from Gilgal all night.

10 And the LORD discomfited them before Israel, and slew them with a great slaughter at Gibeon, and chased them along the way that goeth up to Bethhoron, and smote them to Azekah, and unto Makkedah.

11 And it came to pass, as they fled from before Israel, *and* were in the going down to Bethhoron, that the LORD cast down great stones from heaven upon them unto Azekah, and they died: *they were* more which died with hailstones than *they* whom the children of Israel slew with the sword.

12 Then spake Joshua to the LORD in the day when the LORD delivered up the Amorites before the children of Israel, and he said in the sight of Israel, Sun, stand thou still upon Gibeon; and thou, Moon, in the valley of Ajalon.

13 And the sun stood still, and the moon stayed, until the people had avenged themselves upon their enemies. *Is* not this written in the book of Jasher? So the sun stood still in the midst of heaven, and hasted not to go down about a whole day.

14 And there was no day like that before it or after it, that the LORD hearkened unto the voice of a man: for the LORD fought for Israel.

15 And Joshua returned, and all Israel with him, unto the camp to Gilgal.

16 But these five kings fled, and hid themselves in a cave at Makkedah.

17 And it was told Joshua, saying, The five kings are found hid in a cave at Makkedah.

18 And Joshua said, Roll great stones upon the mouth of the cave, and set men by it for to keep them:

19 And stay ye not, *but* pursue after your enemies, and smite the hind-most of them; suffer them not to enter into their cities: for the LORD your God hath delivered them into your hand.

20 And it came to pass, when Joshua and the children of Israel had made an end of slaying them with a very great slaughter, till they were consumed, that the rest *which* remained of them entered into fenced cities.

21 And all the people returned to the camp to Joshua at Makkedah in peace: none moved his tongue against any of the children of Israel.

22 Then said Joshua, Open the mouth of the cave, and bring out those five kings unto me out of the cave.

23 And they did so, and brought

forth those five kings unto him out of the cave, the king of Jerusalem, the king of Hebron, the king of Jarmuth, the king of Lachish, *and* the king of Eglon.

24 And it came to pass, when they brought out those kings unto Joshua, that Joshua called for all the men of Israel, and said unto the captains of the men of war which went with him, Come near, put your feet upon the necks of these kings. And they came near, and put their feet upon the necks of them.

25 And Joshua said unto them, Fear not, nor be dismayed, be strong and of good courage: for thus shall the LORD do to all your enemies against whom ye fight.

26 And afterward Joshua smote them, and slew them, and hanged them on five trees: and they were hanging upon the trees until the evening.

27 And it came to pass at the time of the going down of the sun, *that* Joshua commanded, and they took them down off the trees, and cast them into the cave wherein they had been hid, and laid great stones in the cave's mouth, *which remain* until this very day.

28 And that day Joshua took Makkedah, and smote it with the edge of the sword, and the king thereof he utterly destroyed, them, and all the souls that *were* therein; he let none remain: and he did to the king of Makkedah as he did unto the king of Jericho.

29 Then Joshua passed from Makkedah, and all Irael with him, unto Libnah, and fought against Libnah:

30 And the LORD delivered it also and the king thereof, into the hand of Israel; and he smote it with the edge of the sword, and all the souls that *were* therein; he let none remain in it; but did unto the king thereof as he did unto the king of Jericho.

31 And Joshua passed from Libnah, and all Israel with him, unto Lachish, and encamped against it, and fought against it:

32 And the LORD delivered Lachish into the hand of Israel, which took it on the second day, and smote it with the edge of the sword, and all the souls that *were* therein, according to all that he had done to Libnah.

33 Then Horam king of Gezer came up to help Lachish; and Joshua smote him and his people, until he had left him none remaining.

34 And from Lachish Joshua passed unto Eglon, and all Israel with him; and they encamped against it, and fought against it:

35 And they took it on that day, and smote it with the edge of the sword, and all the souls that *were* therein he utterly destroyed that day, according to all that he had done to Lachish.

36 And Joshua went up from Eglon, and all Israel with him, unto Hebron; and they fought against it:

37 And they took it, and smote it with the edge of the sword, and the king thereof, and all the cities thereof, and all the souls that *were* therein; he left none remaining, according to all that he had done to Eglon; but destroyed it utterly, and all the souls that *were* therein.

38 And Joshua returned, and all Israel with him, to Debir; and fought against it:

39 And he took it, and the king thereof, and all the cities thereof; and they smote them with the edge of the sword, and utterly destroyed all the souls that *were* therein; he left none remaining: as he had done to Hebron, so he did to Debir, and to the king thereof; as he had done also to Libnah, and to her king.

40 So Joshua smote all the country of the hills, and of the south, and of the vale, and of the springs, and all

their kings: he left none remaining, but utterly destroyed all that breathed, as the LORD God of Israel commanded.

41 And Joshua smote them from Kadesh-barnea even unto Gaza, and all the country of Goshen, even unto Gibeon.

42 And all these kings and their land did Joshua take at one time, because the LORD God of Israel fought for Israel.

43 And Joshua returned, and all Israel with him, unto the camp to Gilgal.

CHAPTER 11

1 And it came to pass, when Jabin king of Hazor had heard *those things,* that he sent to Jobab king of Madon, and to the king of Shimron, and to the king of Achshaph,

2 And to the kings that *were* on the north of the mountains, and of the plains south of Chinneroth, and in the valley, and in the borders of Dor on the west,

3 *And to* the Canaanite on the east and on the west, and *to* the Amorite, and the Hittite, and the Perizzite, and the Jebusite in the mountains, and *to* the Hivite under Hermon in the land of Mizpeh.

4 And they went out, they and all their hosts with them, much people, even as the sand that *is* upon the sea shore in multitude, with horses and chariots very many.

5 And when all these kings were met together, they came and pitched together at the waters of Merom, to fight against Israel.

6 And the LORD said unto Joshua, Be not afraid because of them: for to morrow about this time will I deliver them up all slain before Israel: thou shalt hough their horses, and burn their chariots with fire.

7 So Joshua came, and all the people of war with him, against them by the waters of Merom suddenly; and they fell upon them.

8 And the LORD delivered them into the hand of Israel, who smote them, and chased them unto great Zidon, and unto Misrephoth-maim, and unto the valley of Mizpeh eastward; and they smote them, until they left them none remaining.

9 And Joshua did unto them as the LORD bade him: he houghed their horses, and burnt their chariots with fire.

10 And Joshua at that time turned back, and took Hazor, and smote the king thereof with the sword: for Hazor beforetime was the head of all those kingdoms.

11 And they smote all the souls that *were* therein with the edge of the sword, utterly destroying *them:* there was not any left to breathe: and he burnt Hazor with fire.

12 And all the cities of those kings, and all the kings of them, did Joshua take, and smote them with the edge of the sword, *and* he utterly destroyed them, as Moses the servant of the LORD commanded.

13 But *as for* the cities that stood still in their strength, Israel burned none of them, save Hazor only; *that* did Joshua burn.

14 And all the spoil of these cities, and the cattle, the children of Israel took for a prey unto themselves; but every man they smote with the edge of the sword, until they had destroyed them, neither left they any to breathe.

15 As the LORD commanded Moses his servant, so did Moses command Joshua, and so did Joshua; he left nothing undone of all that the LORD commanded Moses.

16 So Joshua took all that land, the hills, and all the south country, and all the land of Goshen, and the valley, and the plain, and the mountain of Israel, and the valley of the same;

17 *Even* from the mount Halak, that goeth up to Seir, even unto Baal-gad in the valley of Lebanon under mount Hermon: and all their kings he took, and smote them, and slew them.

18 Joshua made war a long time with all those kings.

19 There was not a city that made peace with the children of Israel, save the Hivites the inhabitants of Gibeon: all *other* they took in battle.

20 For it was of the LORD to harden their hearts, that they should come against Israel in battle, that he might destroy them utterly, *and* that they might have no favour, but that he might destroy them, as the LORD commanded Moses.

21 And at that time came Joshua, and cut off the Anakims from the mountains, from Hebron, from Debir, from Anab, and from all the mountains of Judah, and from all the mountains of Israel: Joshua destroyed them utterly with their cities.

22 There was none of the Anakims left in the land of the children of Israel: only in Gaza, in Gath, and in Ashdod, there remained.

23 So Joshua took the whole land, according to all that the LORD said unto Moses; and Joshua gave it for an inheritance unto Israel according to their divisions by their tribes. And the land rested from war.

CHAPTER 12

1 Now these *are* the kings of the land, which the children of Israel smote, and possessed their land on the other side Jordan toward the rising of the sun, from the river Arnon unto mount Hermon, and all the plain on the east:

2 Sihon king of the Amorites, who dwelt in Heshbon, *and* ruled from Aroer, which *is* upon the bank of the river Arnon, and from the middle of the river, and from half Gilead, even unto the river Jabbok, *which is* the border of the children of Ammon;

3 And from the plain to the sea of Chinneroth on the east, and unto the sea of the plain, *even* the salt sea on the east, the way to Beth-jeshimoth; and from the south, under Ashdoth-pisgah:

4 And the coast of Og king of Bashan, *which was* of the remnant of the giants, that dwelt at Ashtaroth and at Edrei,

5 And reigned in mount Hermon, and in Salcah, and in all Bashan, unto the border of the Geshurites and the Maachathites, and half Gilead, the border of Sihon king of Heshbon.

6 Them did Moses the servant of the LORD and the children of Israel smite: and Moses the servant of the LORD gave it *for* a possession unto the Reubenites, and the Gadites, and the half tribe of Manasseh.

7 And these *are* the kings of the country which Joshua and the children of Israel smote on this side Jordan on the west, from Baal-gad in the valley of Lebanon even unto the mount Halak, that goeth up to Seir; which Joshua gave unto the tribes of Israel *for* a possession according to their divisions;

8 In the mountains, and in the valleys, and in the plains, and in the springs, and in the wilderness, and in the south country; the Hittites, the Amorites, and the Canaanites, the Perizzites, the Hivites, and the Jebusites:

9 The king of Jericho, one; the king of Ai, which *is* beside Beth-el, one;

10 The king of Jerusalem, one; the king of Hebron, one;

11 The king of Jarmuth, one; the king of Lachish, one;

12 The king of Eglon, one; the king of Gezer, one;

13 The king of Debir, one; the king of Geder, one;

14 The king of Hormah, one; the king of Arad, one;

15 The king of Libnah, one; the king of Adullam, one;

16 The king of Makkedah, one; the king of Beth-el, one;

17 The king of Tappuah, one; the king of Hepher, one;

18 The king of Aphek, one; the king of Lasharon, one;

19 The king of Madon, one; the king of Hazor, one;

20 The king of Shimron-meron, one; the king of Achshaph, one;

21 The king of Taanach, one; the king of Megiddo, one;

22 The king of Kedesh, one; the king of Jokneam of Carmel, one;

23 The king of Dor in the coast of Dor, one; the king of the nations of Gilgal, one;

24 The king of Tirzah, one: all the kings thirty and one.

CHAPTER 13

1 Now Joshua was old *and* stricken in years; and the LORD said unto him, Thou art old *and* stricken in years, and there remaineth yet very much land to be possessed.

2 This *is* the land that yet remaineth: all the borders of the Philistines, and all Geshuri,

3 From Sihor, which *is* before Egypt, even unto the borders of Ekron northward, *which* is counted to the Canaanite: five lords of the Philistines; the Gazathites, and the Ashdothites, the Eshkalonites, the Gittites, and the Ekronites; also the Avites:

4 From the south, all the land of the Canaanites, and Mearah that *is* beside the Sidonians, unto Aphek, to the borders of the Amorites:

5 And the land of the Giblites, and all Lebanon, toward the sunrising, from Baal-gad under mount Hermon unto the entering into Hamath.

6 All the inhabitants of the hill country from Lebanon unto Misrephoth-maim, *and* all the Sidonians, them will I drive out from before the children of Israel: only divide thou it by lot unto the Israelites for an inheritance, as I have commanded thee.

7 Now therefore divide this land for an inheritance unto the nine tribes, and the half tribe of Manasseh,

8 With whom the Reubenites and the Gadites have received their inheritance, which Moses gave them, beyond Jordan eastward, *even* as Moses the servant of the LORD gave them;

9 From Aroer, that *is* upon the bank of the river Arnon, and the city that *is* in the midst of the river, and all the plain of Medeba unto Dibon;

10 And all the cities of Sihon king of the Amorites, which reigned in Heshbon, unto the border of the children of Ammon;

11 And Gilead, and the border of the Geshurites and Maachathites, and all mount Hermon, and all Bashan unto Salcah;

12 All the kingdom of Og in Bashan, which reigned in Ashtaroth and in Edrei, who remained of the remnant of the giants: for these did Moses smite, and cast them out.

13 Nevertheless the children of Israel expelled not the Geshurites, nor the Maachathites: but the Geshurites and the Maachathites dwell among the Israelites until this day.

14 Only unto the tribe of Levi he gave none inheritance; the sacrifices of the LORD God of Israel made by fire *are* their inheritance, as he said unto them.

15 And Moses gave unto the tribe of the children of Reuben *inheritance* according to their families.

16 And their coast was from Aroer, that *is* on the bank of the river Arnon, and the city that *is* in the midst of the river, and all the plain by Medeba;

17 Heshbon, and all her cities that *are* in the plain; Dibon, and Bamothbaal, and Beth-baal-meon,

18 And Jahaza, and Kedemoth, and Mephaath,

19 And Kirjathaim, and Sibmah, and Zareth-shahar in the mount of the valley,

20 And Beth-peor, and Ashdoth-pisgah, and Beth-jeshimoth,

21 And all the cities of the plain, and all the kingdom of Sihon king of the Amorites, which reigned in Heshbon, whom Moses smote with the princes of Midian, Evi, and Rekem, and Zur, and Hur, and Reba, *which were* dukes of Sihon, dwelling in the country.

22 Balaam also the son of Beor, the soothsayer, did the children of Israel slay with the sword among them that were slain by them.

23 And the border of the children of Reuben was Jordan, and the border *thereof.* This *was* the inheritance of the children of Reuben after their families, the cities and the villages thereof.

24 And Moses gave *inheritance* unto the tribe of Gad, *even* unto the children of Gad according to their families.

25 And their coast was Jazer, and all the cities of Gilead, and half the land of the children of Ammon, unto Aroer that *is* before Rabbah;

26 And from Heshbon unto Ramath-mizpeh, and Betonim; and from Mahanaim unto the border of Debir;

27 And in the valley, Beth-aram, and Beth-nimrah, and Succoth, and Zaphon, the rest of the kingdom of Sihon king of Heshbon, Jordan and *his* border, *even* unto the edge of the sea of Chinnereth on the other side Jordan eastward.

28 This *is* the inheritance of the children of Gad after their families, the cities, and their villages.

29 And Moses gave *inheritance* unto the half tribe of Manasseh: and *this* was *the possession* of the half tribe of the children of Manasseh by their families.

30 And their coast was from Mahanaim, all Bashan, all the kingdom of Og king of Bashan, and all the towns of Jair, which *are* in Bashan, threescore cities:

31 And half Gilead, and Ashtaroth, and Edrei, cities of the kingdom of Og in Bashan, *were pertaining* unto the children of Machir the son of Manasseh, *even* to the one half of the children of Machir by their families.

32 These *are the countries* which Moses did distribute for inheritance in the plains of Moab, on the other side Jordan, by Jericho, eastward.

33 But unto the tribe of Levi Moses gave not *any* inheritance: the LORD God of Israel *was* their inheritance, as he said unto them.

CHAPTER 14

1 And these *are the countries* which the children of Israel inherited in the land of Canaan, which Eleazar the priest, and Joshua the son of Nun, and the heads of the fathers of the tribes of the children of Israel, distributed for inheritance to them.

2 By lot *was* their inheritance, as the LORD commanded by the hand of Moses, for the nine tribes, and *for* the half tribe.

3 For Moses had given the inheritance of two tribes and an half tribe on the other side Jordan: but unto the Levites he gave none inheritance among them.

4 For the children of Joseph were

two tribes, Manasseh and Ephraim: therefore they gave no part unto the Levites in the land, save cities to dwell *in*, with their suburbs for their cattle and for their substance.

5 As the LORD commanded Moses, so the children of Israel did, and they divided the land.

6 Then the children of Judah came unto Joshua in Gilgal: and Caleb the son of Jephunneh the Kenezite said unto him, Thou knowest the thing that the LORD said unto Moses the man of God concerning me and thee in Kadesh-barnea.

7 Forty years old *was* I when Moses the servant of the LORD sent me from Kadesh-barnea to espy out the land; and I brought him word again as *it was* in mine heart.

8 Nevertheless my brethren that went up with me made the heart of the people melt: but I wholly followed the LORD my God.

9 And Moses sware on that day, saying, Surely the land whereon thy feet have trodden shall be thine inheritance, and thy children's for ever, because thou hast wholly followed the LORD my God.

10 And now, behold, the LORD hath kept me alive, as he said, these forty and five years, even since the LORD spake this word unto Moses, while *the children of* Israel wandered in the wilderness: and now, lo, I *am* this day fourscore and five years old.

11 As yet I *am* as strong this day as *I was* in the day that Moses sent me: as my strength *was* then, even so *is* my strength now, for war, both to go out, and to come in.

12 Now therefore give me this mountain, whereof the LORD spake in that day; for thou heardest in that day how the Anakims *were* there, and *that* the cities *were* great *and* fenced: if so be the LORD *will be* with me, then I shall be able to drive them out, as the LORD said.

13 And Joshua blessed him, and gave unto Caleb the son of Jephunneh Hebron for an inheritance.

14 Hebron therefore became the inheritance of Caleb the son of Jephunneh the Kenezite unto this day, because that he wholly followed the LORD God of Israel.

15 And the name of Hebron before *was* Kirjath-arba; *which Arba was* a great man among the Anakims. And the land had rest from war.

CHAPTER 15

1 *This* then was the lot of the tribe of the children of Judah by their families; *even* to the border of Edom the wilderness of Zin southward *was* the uttermost part of the south coast.

2 And their south border was from the shore of the salt sea, from the bay that looketh southward:

3 And it went out to the south side to Maaleh-acrabbim, and passed along to Zin, and ascended up on the south side unto Kadesh-barnea, and passed along to Hezron, and went up to Adar, and fetched a compass to Karkaa:

4 *From thence* it passed toward Azmon, and went out unto the river of Egypt; and the goings out of that coast were at the sea: this shall be your south coast.

5 And the east border *was* the salt sea, *even* unto the end of Jordan. And *their* border in the north quarter *was* from the bay of the sea at the uttermost part of Jordan:

6 And the border went up to Beth-hogla, and passed along by the north of Beth-arabah; and the border went up to the stone of Bohan the son of Reuben:

7 And the border went up toward Debir from the valley of Achor, and so northward, looking

toward Gilgal, that *is* before the going up to Adummim, which *is* on the south side of the river: and the border passed toward the waters of Enshemesh, and the goings out thereof were at Enrogel:

8 And the border went up by the valley of the son of Hinnom unto the south side of the Jebusite; the same *is* Jerusalem: and the border went up to the top of the mountain that *lieth* before the valley of Hinnom westward, which *is* at the end of the valley of the giants northward:

9 And the border was drawn from the top of the hill unto the fountain of the water of Nephtoah, and went out to the cities of mount Ephron; and the border was drawn to Baalah, which *is* Kirjath-jearim:

10 And the border compassed from Baalah westward unto mount Seir, and passed along unto the side of mount Jearim, which *is* Chesalon, on the north side, and went down to Beth-shemesh, and passed on to Timnah:

11 And the border went out unto the side of Ekron northward: and the border was drawn to Shicron, and passed along to mount Baalah, and went out unto Jabneel; and the goings out of the border were at the sea.

12 And the west border *was* to the great sea, and the coast *thereof.* This *is* the coast of the children of Judah round about according to their families.

13 And unto Caleb the son of Jephunneh he gave a part among the children of Judah, according to the commandment of the LORD to Joshua, *even* the city of Arba the father of Anak, which *city is* Hebron.

14 And Caleb drove thence the three sons of Anak, Sheshai, and Ahiman, and Talmai, the children of Anak.

15 And he went up thence to the inhabitants of Debir: and the name of Debir before *was* Kirjath-sepher.

16 And Caleb said, He that smiteth Kirjath-sepher, and taketh it, to him will I give Achsah my daughter to wife.

17 And Othniel the son of Kenaz, the brother of Caleb, took it: and he gave him Achsah his daughter to wife.

18 And it came to pass, as she came *unto him,* that she moved him to ask of her father a field: and she lighted off *her* ass; and Caleb said unto her, What wouldest thou?

19 Who answered, Give me a blessing; for thou hast given me a south land; give me also springs of water. And he gave her the upper springs, and the nether springs.

20 This *is* the inheritance of the tribe of the children of Judah according to their families.

21 And the uttermost cities of the tribe of the children of Judah toward the coast of Edom southward were Kabzeel, and Eder, and Jagur,

22 And Kinah, and Dimonah, and Adadah,

23 And Kedesh, and Hazor, and Ithnan,

24 Ziph, and Telem, and Bealoth,

25 And Hazor, Hadattah, and Kerioth, *and* Hezron, which *is* Hazor,

26 Amam, and Shema, and Moladah,

27 And Hazar-gaddah, and Heshmon, and Beth-palet,

28 And Hazar-shual, and Beersheba, and Bizjothjah,

29 Baalah, and Iim, and Azem,

30 And Eltolad, and Chesil, and Hormah,

31 And Ziklag, and Madmannah, and Sansannah,

32 And Lebaoth, and Shilhim, and Ain, and Rimmon: all the cities *are* twenty and nine, with their villages:

33 *And* in the valley, Eshtaol, and Zoreah, and Ashnah,

34 And Zanoah, and En-gannim, Tappuah, and Enam,

35 Jarmuth, and Adullam, Socoh, and Azekah,

36 And Sharaim, and Adithaim, and Gederah, and Gederothaim; fourteen cities with their villages:

37 Zenan, and Hadashah, and Mig-dal-gad,

38 And Dilean, and Mizpeh, and Joktheel,

39 Lachish, and Bozkath, and Eglon,

40 And Cabbon, and Lahmam, and Kithlish,

41 And Gederoth, Beth-dagon, and Naamah, and Makkedah; sixteen cities with their villages:

42 Libnah, and Ether, and Ashan,

43 And Jiphtah, and Ashnah, and Nezib,

44 And Keilah, and Achzib, and Mareshah; nine cities with their villages:

45 Ekron, with her towns and her villages:

46 From Ekron even unto the sea, all that *lay* near Ashdod, with their villages:

47 Ashdod with her towns and her villages, Gaza with her towns and her villages, unto the river of Egypt, and the great sea, and the border *thereof:*

48 And in the mountains, Shamir, and Jattir, and Socoh,

49 And Dannah, and Kirjath-san-nah, which *is* Debir,

50 And Anab, and Eshtemoh, and Anim,

51 And Goshen, and Holon, and Giloh; eleven cities with their villages:

52 Arab, and Dumah, and Eshean,

53 And Janum, and Beth-tappuah, and Aphekah,

54 And Humtah, and Kirjath-arba, which *is* Hebron, and Zior; nine cities with their villages:

55 Maon, Carmel, and Ziph, and Juttah,

56 And Jezreel, and Jokdeam, and Zanoah,

57 Cain, Gibeah, and Timnah; ten cities with their villages:

58 Halhul, Beth-zur, and Gedor,

59 And Maarath, and Beth-anoth, and Eltekon; six cities with their villages:

60 Kirjath-baal, which *is* Kirjath-jearim, and Rabbah; two cities with their villages:

61 In the wilderness, Beth-arabah, Middin, and Secacah,

62 And Nibshan, and the city of Salt, and En-gedi; six cities with their villages.

63 As for the Jebusites the inhabitants of Jerusalem, the children of Judah could not drive them out: but the Jebusites dwell with the children of Judah at Jerusalem unto this day.

CHAPTER 16

1 And the lot of the children of Joseph fell from Jordan by Jericho, unto the water of Jericho on the east, to the wilderness that goeth up from Jericho throughout mount Beth-el,

2 And goeth out from Beth-el to Luz, and passeth along unto the borders of Archi to Ataroth,

3 And goeth down westward to the coast of Japhleti, unto the coast of Beth-horon the nether, and to Gezer: and the goings out thereof are at the sea.

4 So the children of Joseph, Manasseh and Ephraim, took their inheritance.

5 And the border of the children of Ephraim according to their families was *thus:* even the border of their inheritance on the east side was Ataroth-addar, unto Beth-horon the upper;

6 And the border went out toward the sea to Michmethah on the north side; and the border went about east-

ward unto Taanath-shiloh, and passed by it on the east to Janohah;

7 And it went down from Janohah to Ataroth, and to Naarath, and came to Jericho, and went out at Jordan.

8 The border went out from Tappuah westward unto the river Kanah; and the goings out thereof were at the sea. This *is* the inheritance of the tribe of the children of Ephraim by their families.

9 And the separate cities for the children of Ephraim *were* among the inheritance of the children of Manasseh, all the cities with their villages.

10 And they drave not out the Canaanites that dwelt in Gezer: but the Canaanites dwell among the Ephraimites unto this day, and serve under tribute.

CHAPTER 17

1 There was also a lot for the tribe of Manasseh; for he *was* the firstborn of Joseph; *to wit*, for Machir the firstborn of Manasseh, the father of Gilead: because he was a man of war, therefore he had Gilead and Bashan.

2 There was also *a lot* for the rest of the children of Manasseh by their families; for the children of Abiezer, and for the children of Helek, and for the children of Asriel, and for the children of Shechem, and for the children of Hepher, and for the children of Shemida: these *were* the male children of Manasseh the son of Joseph by their families.

3 But Zelophehad, the son of Hepher, the son of Gilead, the son of Machir, the son of Manasseh, had no sons, but daughters: and these *are* the names of his daughters, Mahlah, and Noah, Hoglah, Milcah, and Tirzah.

4 And they came near before Eleazar the priest, and before Joshua the son of Nun, and before the princes, saying, The LORD commanded Moses to give us an inheritance among our brethren. Therefore according to the commandment of the LORD he gave them an inheritance among the brethren of their father.

5 And there fell ten portions to Manasseh, beside the land of Gilead and Bashan, which *were* on the other side Jordan;

6 Because the daughters of Manasseh had an inheritance among his sons: and the rest of Manasseh's sons had the land of Gilead.

7 And the coast of Manasseh was from Asher to Michmethah, that *lieth* before Shechem; and the border went along on the right hand unto the inhabitants of En-tappuah.

8 *Now* Manasseh had the land of Tappuah: but Tappuah on the border of Manasseh *belonged* to the children of Ephraim;

9 And the coast descended unto the river Kanah, southward of the river: these cities of Ephraim *are* among the cities of Manasseh: the coast of Manasseh also *was* on the north side of the river, and the outgoings of it were at the sea:

10 Southward *it was* Ephraim's, and northward *it was* Manasseh's, and the sea is his border; and they met together in Asher on the north, and in Issachar on the east.

11 And Manasseh had in Issachar and in Asher Beth-shean and her towns, and Ibleam and her towns, and the inhabitants of Dor and her towns, and the inhabitants of En-dor and her towns, and the inhabitants of Taanach and her towns, and the inhabitants of Megiddo and her towns, *even* three countries.

12 Yet the children of Manasseh could not drive out *the inhabitants of* those cities; but the Canaanites would dwell in that land.

13 Yet it came to pass, when the

children of Israel were waxen strong, that they put the Canaanites to tribute; but did not utterly drive them out.

14 And the children of Joseph spake unto Joshua, saying, Why hast thou given me *but* one lot and one portion to inherit, seeing I *am* a great people, forasmuch as the LORD hath blessed me hitherto?

15 And Joshua answered them, If thou *be* a great people, *then* get thee up to the wood *country*, and cut down for thyself there in the land of the Perizzites and of the giants, if mount Ephraim be too narrow for thee.

16 And the children of Joseph said, The hill is not enough for us: and all the Canaanites that dwell in the land of the valley have chariots of iron, *both they* who *are* of Bethshean and her towns, and *they* who *are* of the valley of Jezreel.

17 And Joshua spake unto the house of Joseph, *even* to Ephraim and to Manasseh, saying, Thou *art* a great people, and hast great power: thou shalt not have one lot *only*:

18 But the mountain shall be thine; for it *is* a wood, and thou shalt cut it down: and the outgoings of it shall be thine: for thou shalt drive out the Canaanites, though they have iron chariots, *and* though they *be* strong.

CHAPTER 18

1 And the whole congregation of the children of Israel assembled together at Shiloh, and set up the tabernacle of the congregation there. And the land was subdued before them.

2 And there remained among the children of Israel seven tribes, which had not yet received their inheritance.

3 And Joshua said unto the children of Israel, How long *are* ye slack to go to possess the land, which the LORD God of your fathers hath given you?

4 Give out from among you three men for *each* tribe: and I will send them, and they shall rise, and go through the land, and describe it according to the inheritance of them; and they shall come *again* to me.

5 And they shall divide it into seven parts: Judah shall abide in their coast on the south, and the house of Joseph shall abide in their coasts on the north.

6 Ye shall therefore describe the land *into* seven parts, and bring *the description* hither to me, that I may cast lots for you here before the LORD our God.

7 But the Levites have no part among you; for the priesthood of the LORD *is* their inheritance: and Gad, and Reuben, and half the tribe of Manasseh, have received their inheritance beyond Jordan on the east, which Moses the servant of the LORD gave them.

8 And the men arose, and went away: and Joshua charged them that went to describe the land, saying, Go and walk through the land, and describe it, and come again to me, that I may here cast lots for you before the LORD in Shiloh.

9 And the men went and passed through the land, and described it by cities into seven parts in a book, and came *again* to Joshua to the host at Shiloh.

10 And Joshua cast lots for them in Shiloh before the LORD: and there Joshua divided the land unto the children of Israel according to their divisions.

11 And the lot of the tribe of the children of Benjamin came up according to their families: and the coast of their lot came forth between the children of Judah and the children of Joseph.

12 And their border on the north side was from Jordan; and the border went up to the side of Jericho on the north side, and went up through the mountains westward; and the goings out thereof were at the wilderness of Beth-aven.

13 And the border went over from thence toward Luz, to the side of Luz, which *is* Beth-el, southward; and the border descended to Ataroth-adar, near the hill that *lieth* on the south side of the nether Beth-horon.

14 And the border was drawn *thence*, and compassed the corner of the sea southward, from the hill that *lieth* before Beth-horon southward; and the goings out thereof were at Kirjath-baal, which *is* Kirjath-jearim, a city of the children of Judah: this *was* the west quarter.

15 And the south quarter *was* from the end of Kirjath-jearim, and the border went out on the west, and went out to the well of waters of Nephtoah:

16 And the border came down to the end of the mountain that *lieth* before the valley of the son of Hinnom, *and* which *is* in the valley of the giants on the north, and descended to the valley of Hinnom, to the side of Jebusi on the south, and descended to En-rogel,

17 And was drawn from the north, and went forth to En-shemesh, and went forth toward Geliloth, which *is* over against the going up of Adummim, and descended to the stone of Bohan the son of Reuben,

18 And passed along toward the side over against Arabah northward, and went down unto Arabah:

19 And the border passed along to the side of Beth-hoglah northward: and the outgoings of the border were at the north bay of the salt sea at the south end of Jordan: this *was* the south coast.

20 And Jordan was the border of it on the east side. This *was* the inheritance of the children of Benjamin, by the coasts thereof round about, according to their families.

21 Now the cities of the tribe of the children of Benjamin according to their families were Jericho, and Beth-hoglah, and the valley of Keziz,

22 And Beth-arabah, and Zemaraim, and Beth-el,

23 And Avim, and Parah, and Ophrah,

24 And Chephar-haammonai, and Ophni, and Gaba; twelve cities with their villages:

25 Gibeon, and Ramah, and Beeroth,

26 And Mizpeh, and Chephirah, and Mozah,

27 And Rekem, and Irpeel, and Taralah,

28 And Zelah, Eleph, and Jebusi, which *is* Jerusalem, Gibeath, *and* Kirjath; fourteen cities with their villages. This *is* the inheritance of the children of Benjamin according to their families.

CHAPTER 19

1 And the second lot came forth to Simeon, *even* for the tribe of the children of Simeon according to their families: and their inheritance was within the inheritance of the children of Judah.

2 And they had in their inheritance Beer-sheba, and Sheba, and Moladah,

3 And Hazar-shual, and Balah, and Azem,

4 And Eltolad, and Bethul, and Hormah,

5 And Ziklag, and Beth-marcaboth, and Hazar-susah,

6 And Beth-lebaoth, and Sharuhen; thirteen cities and their villages:

7 Ain, Remmon, and Ether, and Ashan; four cities and their villages:

8 And all the villages that *were* round about these cities to Baalath-beer, Ramath of the south. This *is* the inheritance of the tribe of the children of Simeon according to their families.

9 Out of the portion of the children of Judah *was* the inheritance of the children of Simeon: for the part of the children of Judah was too much for them: therefore the children of Simeon had their inheritance within the inheritance of them.

10 And the third lot came up for the children of Zebulun according to their families: and the border of their inheritance was unto Sarid:

11 And their border went up toward the sea, and Maralah, and reached to Dabbasheth, and reached to the river that *is* before Jokneam;

12 And turned from Sarid eastward toward the sunrising unto the border of Chisloth-tabor, and then goeth out to Daberath, and goeth up to Japhia,

13 And from thence passeth on along on the east to Gittah-hepher, to Ittah-kazin, and goeth out to Remmon-methoar to Neah;

14 And the border compasseth it on the north side to Hannathon: and the outgoings thereof are in the valley of Jiphthah-el:

15 And Kattath, and Nahallal, and Shimron, and Idalah, and Beth-lehem: twelve cities with their villages.

16 This *is* the inheritance of the children of Zebulun according to their families, these cities with their villages.

17 *And* the fourth lot came out to Issachar, for the children of Issachar according to their families.

18 And their border was toward Jezreel, and Chesulloth, and Shunem,

19 And Haphraim, and Shihon, and Anaharath,

20 And Rabbith, and Kishion, and Abez,

21 And Remeth, and En-gannim, and En-haddah, and Beth-pazzez;

22 And the coast reacheth to Tabor, and Shahazimah, and Beth-shemesh; and the outgoings of their border were at Jordan: sixteen cities with their villages.

23 This *is* the inheritance of the tribe of the children of Issachar according to their families, the cities and their villages.

24 And the fifth lot came out for the tribe of the children of Asher according to their families.

25 And their border was Helkath, and Hali, and Beten, and Achshaph,

26 And Alammelech, and Amad, and Misheal; and reacheth to Carmel westward, and to Shihor-libnath;

27 And turneth toward the sunrising to Beth-dagon, and reacheth to Zebulun, and to the valley of Jiphthah-el toward the north side of Beth-emek, and Neiel, and goeth out to Cabul on the left hand,

28 And Hebron, and Rehob, and Hammon, and Kanah, *even* unto great Zidon;

29 And *then* the coast turneth to Ramah, and to the strong city Tyre; and the coast turneth to Hosah; and the outgoings thereof are at the sea from the coast to Achzib:

30 Ummah also, and Aphek, and Rehob: twenty and two cities with their villages.

31 This *is* the inheritance of the tribe of the children of Asher according to their families, these cities with their villages.

32 The sixth lot came out to the children of Naphtali *even* for the children of Naphtali according to their families.

33 And their coast was from Heleph, from Allon to Zaanannim, and Adami, Nekeb, and Jabneel, unto Lakum; and the outgoings thereof were at Jordan:

34 And *then* the coast turneth westward to Aznoth-tabor, and

goeth out from thence to Hukkok, and reacheth to Zebulun on the south side, and reacheth to Asher on the west side, and to Judah upon Jordan toward the sunrising.

35 And the fenced cities *are* Ziddim, Zer, and Hammath, Rakkath, and Chinnereth,

36 And Adamah, and Ramah, and Hazor,

37 And Kedesh, and Edrei, and En-hazor,

38 And Iron, and Migdal-el, Horem, and Beth-anath, and Beth-shemesh; nineteen cities with their villages.

39 This *is* the inheritance of the tribe of the children of Naphtali according to their families, the cities and their villages.

40 *And* the seventh lot came out for the tribe of the children of Dan according to their families.

41 And the coast of their inheritance was Zorah, and Eshtaol, and Ir-shemesh,

42 And Shaalabbin, and Ajalon, and Jethlah,

43 And Elon, and Thimnathah, and Ekron,

44 And Eltekeh, and Gibbethon, and Baalath,

45 And Jehud, and Bene-berak, and Gath-rimmon,

46 And Me-jarkon, and Rakkon, with the border before Japho.

47 And the coast of the children of Dan went out *too little* for them: therefore the children of Dan went up to fight against Leshem, and took it, and smote it with the edge of the sword, and possessed it, and dwelt therein, and called Leshem, Dan, after the name of Dan their father.

48 This *is* the inheritance of the tribe of the children of Dan according to their families, these cities with their villages.

49 When they had made an end of dividing the land for inheritance by their coasts, the children of Israel gave an inheritance to Joshua the son of Nun among them:

50 According to the word of the LORD they gave him the city which he asked, *even* Timnath-serah in mount Ephraim: and he built the city, and dwelt therein.

51 There *are* the inheritances, which Eleazar the priest, and Joshua the son of Nun, and the heads of the fathers of the tribes of the children of Israel, divided for an inheritance by lot in Shiloh before the LORD, at the door of the tabernacle of the congregation. So they made an end of dividing the country.

CHAPTER 20

1 The LORD also spake unto Joshua, saying,

2 Speak to the children of Israel, saying, Appoint out for you cities of refuge, whereof I spake unto you by the hand of Moses:

3 That the slayer that killeth *any* person unawares *and* unwittingly may flee thither: and they shall be your refuge from the avenger of blood.

4 And when he that doth flee unto one of those cities shall stand at the entering of the gate of the city, and shall declare his cause in the ears of the elders of that city, they shall take him into the city unto them, and give him a place that he may dwell among them.

5 And if the avenger of blood pursue after him, then they shall not deliver the slayer up into his hand; because he smote his neighbour unwittingly, and hated him not beforetime.

6 And he shall dwell in that city, until he stand before the congregation for judgment, *and* until the death of the high priest that shall be in those days: then shall the slayer

return, and come unto his own city, and unto his own house, unto the city from whence he fled.

7 And they appointed Kedesh in Galilee in mount Naphtali, and Shechem in mount Ephraim, and Kirjath-arba, which *is* Hebron, in the mountain of Judah.

8 And on the other side Jordan by Jericho eastward, they assigned Bezer in the wilderness upon the plain out of the tribe of Reuben, and Ramoth in Gilead out of the tribe of Gad, and Golan in Bashan out of the tribe of Manasseh.

9 These were the cities appointed for all the children of Israel, and for the stranger that sojourneth among them, that whosoever killeth *any* person at unawares might flee thither, and not die by the hand of the avenger of blood, until he stood before the congregation.

CHAPTER 21

1 Then came near the heads of the fathers of the Levites unto Eleazar the priest, and unto Joshua the son of Nun, and unto the heads of the fathers of the tribes of the children of Israel;

2 And they spake unto them at Shiloh in the land of Canaan, saying, The LORD commanded by the hand of Moses to give us cities to dwell in, with the suburbs thereof for our cattle.

3 And the children of Israel gave unto the Levites out of their inheritance, at the commandment of the LORD, these cities and their suburbs.

4 And the lot came out for the families of the Kohathites: and the children of Aaron the priest, *which were* of the Levites, had by lot out of the tribe of Judah, and out of the tribe of Simeon, and out of the tribe of Benjamin, thirteen cities.

5 And the rest of the children of Kohath *had* by lot out of the fami-

lies of the tribe of Ephraim, and out of the tribe of Dan, and out of the half tribe of Manasseh, ten cities.

6 And the children of Gershon *had* by lot out of the families of the tribe of Issachar, and out of the tribe of Asker, and out of the tribe of Naphtali, and out of the half tribe of Manasseh in Bashan, thirteen cities.

7 The children of Merari by their families *had* out of the tribe of Reuben, and out of the tribe of Gad, and out of the tribe of Zebulun, twelve cities.

8 And the children of Israel gave by lot unto the Levites these cities with their suburbs, as the LORD commanded by the hand of Moses.

9 And they gave out of the tribe of the children of Judah, and out of the tribe of the children of Simeon, these cities which are *here* mentioned by name.

10 Which the children of Aaron, *being* of the families of the Kohathites, *who were* of the children of Levi, had: for theirs was the first lot.

11 And they gave them the city of Arba the father of Anak, which *city is* Hebron, in the hill *country* of Judah, with the suburbs thereof round about it.

12 But the fields of the city, and the villages thereof, gave they to Caleb the son of Jephunneh for his possession.

13 Thus they gave to the children of Aaron the priest Hebron with her suburbs, *to be* a city of refuge for the slayer; and Libnah with her suburbs,

14 And Jattir with her suburbs, and Eshtemoa with her suburbs,

15 And Holon with her suburbs, and Debir with her suburbs,

16 And Ain with her suburbs, and Juttah with her suburbs, *and* Beth-shemesh with her suburbs; nine cities out of those two tribes.

17 And out of the tribe of Benja-

min, Gibeon with her suburbs, Geba with her suburbs,

18 Anathoth with her suburbs, and Almon with her suburbs; four cities.

19 All the cities of the children of Aaron, the priests, *were* thirteen cities with their suburbs.

20 And the families of the children of Kohath, the Levites which remained of the children of Kohath, even they had the cities of their lot out of the tribe of Ephraim.

21 For they gave them Shechem with her suburbs in mount Ephraim, *to be* a city of refuge for the slayer; and Gezer with her suburbs,

22 And Kibzaim with her suburbs, and Beth-horon with her suburbs; four cities.

23 And out of the tribe of Dan, Eltekeh with her suburbs, Gibbethon with her suburbs,

24 Aijalon with her suburbs, Gathrimmon with her suburbs; four cities.

25 And out of the half tribe of Manasseh, Tanach with her suburbs, and Gath-rimmon with her suburbs; two cities.

26 All the cities *were* ten with their suburbs for the families of the children of Kohath that remained.

27 And unto the children of Gershon, of the families of the Levites, out of the *other* half tribe of Manasseh *they gave* Golan in Bashan with her suburbs, *to be* a city of refuge for the slayer; and Beesh-terah with her suburbs; two cities.

28 And out of the tribe of Issachar, Kishon with her suburbs, Dabareh with her suburbs,

29 Jarmuth with her suburbs, Engannim with her suburbs; four cities.

30 And out of the tribe of Asher, Mishal with her suburbs, Abdon with her suburbs,

31 Helkath with her suburbs, and Rehob with her suburbs; four cities.

32 And out of the tribe of Naphtali, Kedesh in Galilee with her sub-

urbs, *to be* a city of refuge for the slayer; and Hammoth-dor with her suburbs, and Kartan with her suburbs; three cities.

33 All the cities of the Gershonites according to their families *were* thirteen cities with their suburbs.

34 And unto the families of the children of Merari, the rest of the Levites, out of the tribe of Zebulun, Jokneam with her suburbs, and Kartah with her suburbs,

35 Dimnah with her suburbs, Nahalal with her suburbs; four cities.

36 And out of the tribe of Reuben, Bezer with her suburbs, and Jahazah with her suburbs,

37 Kedemoth with her suburbs, and Mephaath with her suburbs; four cities.

38 And out of the tribe of Gad, Ramoth in Gilead with her suburbs, *to be* a city of refuge for the slayer; and Mahanaim with her suburbs,

39 Heshbon with her suburbs, Jazer with her suburbs; four cities in all.

40 So all the cities for the children of Merari by their families, which were remaining of the families of the Levites, were *by* their lot twelve cities.

41 All the cities of the Levites within the possession of the children of Israel *were* forty and eight cities with their suburbs.

42 These cities were every one with their suburbs round about them: thus *were* all these cities.

43 And the LORD gave unto Israel all the land which he sware to give unto their fathers; and they possessed it, and dwelt therein.

44 And the LORD gave them rest round about, according to all that he sware unto their fathers: and there stood not a man of all their enemies before them; the LORD delivered all their enemies into their hand.

45 There failed not ought of any

good thing which the LORD had spoken unto the house of Israel; all came to pass.

CHAPTER 22

1 Then Joshua called the Reubenites, and the Gadites, and the half tribe of Manasseh,

2 And said unto them, Ye have kept all that Moses the servant of the LORD commanded you, and have obeyed my voice in all that I commanded you:

3 Ye have not left your brethren these many days unto this day, but have kept the charge of the commandment of the LORD your God.

4 And now the LORD your God hath given rest unto your brethren, as he promised them: therefore now return ye, and get you unto your tents, *and* unto the land of your possession, which Moses the servant of the LORD gave you on the other side Jordan.

5 But take diligent heed to do the commandment and the law, which Moses the servant of the LORD charged you, to love the LORD your God, and to walk in all his ways, and to keep his commandments, and to cleave unto him, and to serve him with all your heart and with all your soul.

6 So Joshua blessed them, and sent them away: and they went unto their tents.

7 Now to the *one* half of the tribe of Manasseh Moses had given *possession* in Bashan: but unto the *other* half thereof gave Joshua among their brethren on this side Jordan westward. And when Joshua sent them away also unto their tents, then he blessed them,

8 And he spake unto them, saying, Return with much riches unto your tents, and with very much cattle, with silver, and with gold, and with brass, and with iron, and with very much raiment: divide the spoil of your enemies with your brethren.

9 And the children of Reuben and the children of Gad and the half tribe of Manasseh returned, and departed from the children of Israel out of Shiloh, which *is* in the land of Canaan, to go unto the country of Gilead, to the land of their possession, whereof they were possessed, according to the word of the LORD by the hand of Moses.

10 And when they came unto the borders of Jordan, that *are* in the land of Canaan, the children of Reuben and the children of Gad and the half tribe of Manasseh built there an altar by Jordan, a great altar to see to.

11 And the children of Israel heard say, Behold, the children of Reuben and the children of Gad and the half tribe of Manasseh have built an altar over against the land of Canaan, in the borders of Jordan, at the passage of the children of Israel.

12 And when the children of Israel heard *of* it, the whole congregation of the children of Israel gathered themselves together at Shiloh, to go up to war against them.

13 And the children of Israel sent unto the children of Reuben, and to the children of Gad, and to the half tribe of Manasseh, into the land of Gilead, Phinehas the son of Eleazar the priest.

14 And with him ten princes, of each chief house a prince throughout all the tribes of Israel; and each one *was* an head of the house of their fathers among the thousands of Israel.

15 And they came unto the children of Reuben, and to the children of Gad, and to the half tribe of Manasseh, unto the land of Gilead, and they spake with them, saying,

16 Thus saith the whole congregation of the LORD, What trespass *is*

this that ye have committed against the God of Israel, to turn away this day from following the LORD, in that ye have builded you an altar, that ye might rebel this day against the LORD?

17 *Is* the iniquity of Peor too little for us, from which we are not cleansed until this day, although there was a plague in the congregation of the LORD,

18 But that ye must turn away this day from following the LORD? and it will be, *seeing* ye rebel to day against the LORD, that to morrow he will be wroth with the whole congregation of Israel.

19 Notwithstanding, if the land of your possession *be* unclean, *then* pass ye over unto the land of the possession of the LORD, wherein the LORD's tabernacle dwelleth, and take possession among us: but rebel not against the LORD, nor rebel against us, in building you an altar beside the altar of the LORD our God.

20 Did not Achan the son of Zerah commit a trespass in the accursed thing, and wrath fell on all the congregation of Israel? and that man perished not alone in his iniquity.

21 Then the children of Reuben and the children of Gad and the half tribe of Manasseh answered, and said unto the heads of the thousands of Israel,

22 The LORD God of gods, the LORD God of gods, he knoweth, and Israel he shall know; if *it be* in rebellion, or if in transgression against the LORD, (save us not this day,)

23 That we have built us an altar to turn from following the LORD, or if to offer thereon burnt offering or meat offering, or if to offer peace offerings thereon, let the LORD himself require *it;*

24 And if we have not *rather* done it for fear of *this* thing, saying, In time to come your children might speak unto our children, saying,

What have ye to do with the LORD God of Israel?

25 For the LORD hath made Jordan a border between us and you, ye children of Reuben and children of Gad; ye have no part in the LORD: so shall your children make our children cease from fearing the LORD.

26 Therefore we said, Let us now prepare to build us an altar, not for burnt offering, nor for sacrifice:

27 But *that* it *may be* a witness between us, and you, and our generations after us, that we might do the service of the LORD before him with our burnt offerings, and with our sacrifices, and with our peace offerings; that your children may not say to our children in time to come, Ye have no part in the LORD.

28 Therefore said we, that it shall be, when they should *so* say to us or to our generations in time to come, that we may say *again,* Behold the pattern of the altar of the LORD, which our fathers made, not for burnt offerings, nor for sacrifices; but it *is* a witness between us and you.

29 God forbid that we should rebel against the LORD, and turn this day from following the LORD, to build an altar for burnt offerings, for meat offerings, or for sacrifices, beside the altar of the LORD our God that *is* before his tabernacle.

30 And when Phinehas the priest, and the princes of the congregation and heads of the thousands of Israel which *were* with him, heard the words that the children of Reuben and the children of Gad and the children of Manasseh spake, it pleased them.

31 And Phinehas the son of Eleazar the priest said unto the children of Reuben, and to the children of Gad, and to the children of Manasseh, This day we perceive that the LORD *is* among us, because ye have not committed this trepass against

the LORD: now ye have delivered the children of Israel out of the hand of the LORD.

32 And Phinehas the son of Eleazar the priest, and the princes, returned from the children of Reuben, and from the children of Gad, out of the land of Gilead, unto the land of Canaan, to the children of Israel, and brought them word again.

33 And the thing pleased the children of Israel; and the children of Israel blessed God, and did not intend to go up against them in battle, to destroy the land wherein the children of Reuben and Gad dwelt.

34 And the children of Reuben and the children of Gad called the altar *Ed:* for it *shall be* a witness between us that the LORD *is* God.

CHAPTER 23

1 And it came to pass a long time after that the LORD had given rest unto Israel from all their enemies round about, that Joshua waxed old *and* stricken in age.

2 And Joshua called for all Israel, *and* for their elders, and for their heads, and for their judges, and for their officers, and said unto them, I am old *and* stricken in age:

3 And ye have seen all that the LORD your God hath done unto all these nations because of you; for the LORD your God *is* he that hath fought for you.

4 Behold, I have divided unto you by lot these nations that remain, to be an inheritance for your tribes, from Jordan, with all the nations that I have cut off, even unto the great sea westward.

5 And the LORD your God, he shall expel them from before you, and drive them from out of your sight; and ye shall possess their land, as the LORD your God hath promised unto you.

6 Be ye therefore very courageous to keep and to do all that is written in the book of the law of Moses, that ye turn not aside therefrom *to* the right hand or *to* the left;

7 That ye come not among these nations, these that remain among you; neither make mention of the name of their gods, nor cause to swear *by them,* neither serve them, nor bow yourselves unto them:

8 But cleave unto the LORD your God, as ye have done unto this day.

9 For the LORD hath driven out from before you great nations and strong: but *as for* you, no man hath been able to stand before you unto this day.

10 One man of you shall chase a thousand: for the LORD your God, he *it is* that fighteth for you, as he hath promised you.

11 Take good heed therefore unto yourselves, that ye love the LORD your God.

12 Else if ye do in any wise go back, and cleave unto the remnant of these nations, *even* these that remain among you, and shall make marriages with them, and go in unto them, and they to you:

13 Know for a certainty that the LORD your God will no more drive out *any of* these nations from before you; but they shall be snares and traps unto you, and sourges in your sides, and thorns in your eyes, until ye perish from off this good land which the LORD your God hath given you.

14 And, behold, this day I *am* going the way of all the earth: and ye know in all your hearts and in all your souls, that not one thing hath failed of all the good things which the LORD your God spake concerning you; all are come to pass unto you, *and* not one thing hath failed thereof.

15 Therefore it shall come to pass, *that* as all good things are come upon you, which the LORD your God

promised you; so shall the LORD bring upon you all evil things, until he have destroyed you from off this good land which the LORD your God hath given you.

16 When ye have transgressed the covenant of the LORD your God, which he commanded you, and have gone and served other gods, and bowed yourselves to them; then shall the anger of the LORD be kindled against you, and ye shall perish quickly from off the good land which he hath given unto you.

CHAPTER 24

1 And Joshua gathered all the tribes of Israel to Shechem, and called for the elders of Israel, and for their heads, and for their judges, and for their officers; and they presented themselves before God.

2 And Joshua said unto all the people, Thus saith the LORD God of Israel, Your fathers dwelt on the other side of the flood in old time, *even* Terah, the father of Abraham, and the father of Nachor: and they served other gods.

3 And I took your father Abraham from the other side of the flood, and led him throughout all the land of Canaan, and multiplied his seed, and gave him Isaac.

4 And I gave unto Isaac Jacob and Esau: and I gave unto Esau mount Seir, to possess it; but Jacob and his children went down into Egypt.

5 I sent Moses also and Aaron, and I plagued Egypt, according to that which I did among them: and afterward I brought you out.

6 And I brought your fathers out of Egypt: and ye came unto the sea; and the Egyptians pursued after your fathers with chariots and horsemen unto the Red sea.

7 And when they cried unto the LORD, he put darkness between you and the Egyptians, and brought the sea upon them, and covered them; and your eyes have seen what I have done in Egypt: and ye dwelt in the wilderness a long season.

8 And I brought you into the land of the Amorites, which dwelt on the other side Jordan; and they fought with you: and I gave them into your hand, that ye might possess their land; and I destroyed them from before you.

9 Then Balak the son of Zippor, king of Moab, arose and warred against Israel, and sent and called Balaam the son of Beor to curse you:

10 But I would not hearken unto Balaam; therefore he blessed you still: so I delivered you out of his hand.

11 And ye went over Jordan, and came unto Jericho: and the men of Jericho fought against you, the Amorites, and the Perizzites, and the Canaanites, and the Hittites, and the Girgashites, the Hivites, and the Jebusites; and I delivered them into your hand.

12 And I sent the hornet before you, which drave them out from before you, *even* the two kings of the Amorites; *but* not with thy sword, nor with thy bow.

13 And I have given you a land for which ye did not labour, and cities which ye built not, and ye dwell in them; of the vineyards and olive-yards which ye planted not do ye eat.

14 Now therefore fear the LORD, and serve him in sincerity and in truth: and put away the gods which your fathers served on the other side of the flood, and in Egypt; and serve ye the LORD.

15 And if it seem evil unto you to serve the LORD, choose you this day whom ye will serve; whether the gods which your fathers served that *were* on the other side of the flood, or the gods of the Amorites, in

whose land ye dwell: but as for me and my house, we will serve the LORD.

16 And the people answered and said, God forbid that we should forsake the LORD, to serve other gods;

17 For the LORD our God, he *it is* that brought us up and our fathers out of the land of Egypt, from the house of bondage, and which did those great signs in our sight, and preserved us in all the way wherein we went, and among all the people through whom we passed:

18 And the LORD drave out from before us all the people, even the Amorites which dwelt in the land: *therefore* will we also serve the LORD; for he *is* our God.

19 And Joshua said unto the people, Ye cannot serve the LORD: for he *is* an holy God; he *is* a jealous God; he will not forgive your transgressions nor your sins.

20 If ye forsake the LORD, and serve strange gods, then he will turn and do you hurt, and consume you, after that he hath done you good.

21 And the people said unto Joshua, Nay; but we will serve the LORD.

22 And Joshua said unto the people, Ye *are* witnesses against yourselves that ye have chosen you the LORD, to serve him. And they said, *We are* witnesses.

23 Now therefore put away, *said he*, the strange gods which *are* among you, and incline your heart unto the LORD God of Israel.

24 And the people said unto Joshua, The LORD our God will we serve, and his voice will we obey.

25 So Joshua made a covenant with the people that day, and set them a statute and an ordinance in Shechem.

26 And Joshua wrote these words in the book of the law of God, and took a great stone, and set it up there under an oak, that *was* by the sanctuary of the LORD.

27 And Joshua said unto all the people, Behold, this stone shall be a witness unto us; for it hath heard all the words of the LORD which he spake unto us: it shall be therefore a witness unto you, lest ye deny your God.

28 So Joshua let the people depart, every man unto his inheritance.

29 And it came to pass after these things, that Joshua the son of Nun, the servant of the LORD, died, *being* an hundred and ten years old.

30 And they buried him in the border of his inheritance in Timnath-serah, which *is* in mount Ephraim, on the north side of the hill of Gaash.

31 And Israel served the LORD all the days of Joshua, and all the days of the elders that overlived Joshua, and which had known all the works of the LORD, that he had done for Israel.

32 And the bones of Joseph, which the children of Israel brought up out of Egypt, buried they in Shechem, in a parcel of ground which Jacob bought of the sons of Hamor the father of Shechem for an hundred pieces of silver: and it became the inheritance of the children of Joseph.

33 And Eleazar the son of Aaron died; and they buried him in a hill *that pertained to* Phinehas his son, which was given him in mount Ephraim.